Greenberg's
GUIDES 8.

AMERICAN FLYER®

POCKET PRICE GUIDE

Edited by Roger Carp

Kalmbach
Media

Kalmbach Media
21027 Crossroads Circle
Waukesha, Wisconsin 53186
www.KalmbachHobbyStore.com

Published in 2018
Thirty-first Edition

Manufactured in the United States of America

ISBN: 978-1-62700-531-9

Front cover photo: American Flyer no. 21139 UP 4-8-4 Northern
Locomotive, model courtesy John Heck

Back cover photo: American Flyer no. 787 Log Loader

Library of Congress Control Number: 2018931234

CONTENTS

INTRODUCTION

The latest and greatest guide

Welcome to the latest edition of what hobbyists regard as the most
authoritative and trusted price guide to the trains and accessories
produced by the leading S gauge firms of the past 71 years.
Whether you're a longtime S gauge enthusiast or a newcomer to
the toy train hobby, in this guide, you'll find the information you
need to identify and evaluate the thousands of items made by
various S gauge manufacturers between 1946 and 2019. Most of
all, you will have at your fingertips the most up-to-date prices for
locomotives, freight cars, passenger cars, stations, tunnels, signals,
track sections, transformers, and catalogs.

Over the years, hundreds of enthusiasts have contributed
extensive research to each edition of the *American Flyer Pocket
Price Guide*. This 2019 edition represents the culmination of
tremendous effort by many contributors. As a result, this 31st
edition contains information on just about every toy train product
marketed by the A.C. Gilbert Co. for its American Flyer line
between 1946 and 1966. Also collected between the two covers of
this guide are complete listings of all the S gauge trains put out by
Lionel (using Gilbert tooling as well as its own), American Models,
S-Helper Service, and MTH.

What is listed and what isn't

When the first editions of this pocket price guide were published,
the only S gauge products included were the classic trains and
accessories developed by the A.C. Gilbert Co. for its American
Flyer line. You'll still find those terrific models listed in **Section 1**,
which includes locomotives, freight cars, and passenger cars
cataloged between 1946 and 1966. Also included are American
Flyer accessories, track sections, and transformers.

Gilbert released its final, abbreviated line of American Flyer
trains in 1966 and declared bankruptcy a year later. In one of
those "who'd-a-thunk-it?" scenarios, Lionel, which dominated the
toy train industry in the postwar era, acquired the tools and dies
that Gilbert had used to mass-produce American Flyer trains and
related items.

Finally, in 1979, Lionel brought out a selection of Flyer trains
and accessories. Ever since, thanks to old and new tooling, Lionel
has been cataloging train sets, locomotives, cars, and accessories
for its revamped American Flyer line.

Section 2 covers items that Lionel has produced or sponsored
for that line since 1979. The vast majority of these items
represent postwar models that Lionel has updated with different
paint and lettering schemes and improved motors. Popular
operating accessories have been revived, much to the delight of
S gauge hobbyists as well as O gauge operators, who agree that
particular freight loaders, light towers, and other accessories

work equally well on their layouts. Other Lionel-produced models appear as uncataloged items offered by toy train collecting associations, museums, and other organizations for promotional purposes.

Section 3 covers every set, locomotive, and car made and marketed by American Models since the company entered the toy train field in 1981. Over the past 38 years, this firm has offered S gauge collectors and operators a wide range of popular electric-profile and diesel locomotives and, more recently, steam locomotives and tenders. The types of freight and passenger cars American Models has developed are impressive in terms of their variety and decoration. Also part of the company's S gauge line are sections of track and remote control switches.

Section 4 features the S gauge trains of MTH Electric Trains. MTH purchased the tooling of S-Helper Service's Showcase Line. MTH used this tooling to reintroduce and add to the freight cars and locomotives of S-Helper Service. Its locomotives include Proto-Sound, MTH's sound and control system.

Section 5 covers locomotives and cars made by S-Helper Service from 1994, when production began, through 2012, when its owners retired. The number of items this manufacturer put out is breathtaking—more than 1,500 train sets, diesel and steam locomotives, freight and passenger cars, switches, trucks, and couplers. Its locomotives and rolling stock feature an incredible array of railroad names.

Section 6 features a listing of the catalogs and other paperwork that A.C. Gilbert put out for consumers and dealers.

About the only notable American Flyer items not included in Section 1 are the boxed train sets that Gilbert cataloged. These S gauge sets are omitted from this guide because, to be considered complete, they must have all the items, including ancillary ones, that Gilbert packed with them. In addition, they should be in their original boxes. The level of completeness demanded for American Flyer sets puts them beyond the scope of this guide.

Also left out of the *American Flyer Pocket Price Guide* are rare items that have surfaced. These unique pieces include mock-ups of products that were assembled by members of Gilbert's Engineering Department. They also include models created for company executives to evaluate different paint and lettering schemes. These items, some of which are one of a kind, are so scarce that values cannot be assigned to them.

The guide's focus on S gauge trains of the post-World War II years explains other omissions. You won't find mention of the O gauge trains that Gilbert cataloged between 1939 and 1942 or the HO scale trains that it offered after the war. For the same reason, information on the Wide and O gauge trains produced by American Flyer Manufacturing is also absent.

How values are determined

Every user of the *American Flyer Pocket Price Guide* wants to know how the values are ascertained. There's nothing mysterious or arbitrary about the process. Over the years, we at Kalmbach Media have gained the cooperation of many dealers and hobbyists, some of whom serve on our national review panel. These knowledgeable individuals share information about the trains and accessories they have bought and sold. They report on transactions conducted at meets across the United States, in retail outlets, and at live and online auctions. The editors of this guide study the information and supplement it with data from the publications of hobby groups that relates to buying and selling S gauge trains.

The values presented here are an averaged reflection of prices for items bought and sold across the country over the year prior to the publication of this edition. These values are offered as guidelines and should be viewed as starting points that buyers and sellers can use to begin informed and reasonable negotiations.

Values for individual items may differ from what is listed in this price guide due to a few key factors. Where collectible trains are scarce and demand outruns supply, actual values may exceed what is shown. Values may also rise where certain items are especially popular, often because of their road names. And as with all collectibles, national and local economic conditions will impact values, which tend to drop when times are tough and demand falls.

Another factor influencing what a toy train is worth relates to the venue in which it is being sold. Antiques dealers generally ask more for an item than do folks putting it out at a garage sale. Mail-order and retail outlets tend to charge more for trains than do individuals at shows because they need to be compensated for the additional costs generated by operating a store, compiling and distributing price lists, and packing and shipping trains. Of course, the cost of any item can balloon far beyond its listed value when two or more people compete for it at a live or online auction.

HOW TO READ THIS GUIDE

Number	Description	Condition——Good	Exc	
24067	Keystone Line Boxcar, *60* u	1350	2425	___
24076	Union Pacific Stock Car, *57–60*			
	(A) Knuckle couplers	32	85	___
	(B) Pike Master couplers	28	71	___

Reading an entry

Each section is arranged in numerical order by catalog numbers. Every item is listed by the product's catalog number or other number assigned by its manufacturer. A catalog number often appears on the product as its road number.

A basic description of the model follows the number. It gives the type of product, lists the name of any railroad identified with it, and includes identifying characteristics, such as color or lettering. If the item has a road number that differs from its catalog number, that number is shown in quotation marks. Abbreviations used in the descriptions, including those of railroad names, are found at the back of the price guide.

Next, you'll find the year or years during which that item was cataloged. The years are shown in italics. If one is followed by a *u*, then this item was uncataloged, most likely a promotional item and not part of the manufacturer's cataloged line.

In the American Models section, items are continually manufactured, so no years are listed. MTH and S-Helper Service products are also undated. Some entries show an asterisk (*) after the year. This mark indicates that a reproduction of the item has been made.

Some entries feature variations, each indicated by a separate letter (A, B, and so forth). Variations amount to slight yet noteworthy differences in appearance that distinguish models that otherwise seem identical. These differences can relate to color, lettering, and details that were added or deleted. For items having many variations, an entry may not include every variation.

An entry concludes with an indication of the item's value for several common conditions.

Condition

American Flyer and S gauge enthusiasts should be familiar with the condition and grading standards established by the Train Collectors Association, which are used as the basis for evaluating the condition of toy trains and accessories:

C-10   **Mint:** brand new—all original, unused, and unblemished.

C-9   **Factory New:** same condition as Mint but with evidence of factory rubs or slight signs of handling, shipping, and being test run at the factory.

C-8   **Like New:** complete and all original with no rust or no missing parts; may show effects of being displayed or signs of age and may have been run.

C-7   **Excellent:** all original and may have minute scratches and paint nicks; no rust, no missing parts, and no distortion of component parts.

C-6   **Very Good:** has minor scratches, paint nicks, or minor spots of surface rust; is free of dents and may have minor parts replaced.

C-5   **Good:** shows evidence of heavy use and signs of play wear—small dents, scratches, minor paint loss, and minor surface rust.

C-4   **Fair:** shows evidence of heavy use—scratches and dents, moderate paint loss, missing parts, and surface rust.

C-3   **Poor:** requires major body repair and is a candidate for restoration; major rust, missing parts, and heavily scratched.

C-2   **Restoration:** needs to be restored.

C-1   **Junk:** parts value only.

In this guide, Gilbert American Flyer trains are evaluated in Good (C-5) and Excellent (C-7) conditions. Lionel-produced trains are assessed in Mint (C-10) condition. American Models, MTH, and S-Helper items are listed with their last suggested retail price.

You may also see NRS listed as a value in the guide. NRS (No Reported Sales) refers to an item for which no adequate pricing data is available. Typically, these items are so scarce that only a handful have been reported.

Gilbert catalogs and paper items are evaluated in Good (P-5) and Excellent (P-7) conditions according to the following paper grading standards established by the Train Collectors Association:

P-10 **Mint:** Brand new, complete, all original as manufactured, and unused. Free of all flaws. Original folds are crisp with no signs of damage, and individual pages appear to have never been opened. No rusty staples, creases, tears, fading, or wear marks.

P-9 **Store New:** Complete, all original, and unused. Item may have merchant additions such as store stamps and price tags. May have been handled since leaving the original factory, but original folds are crisp without signs of wear.

P-8 **Like New:** Complete and all original. There is evidence of light use and aging. Item may have notations (discrete) added since leaving the manufacturer.

P-7 **Excellent:** Complete and all original. Item can show signs of moderate use, but it is completely intact. Original paper folds can show minute signs of damage including evidence of bending and folding. Item may have rusty staples that have not affected the paper.

P-6 **Very Good:** Complete and all original. Item shows signs of usage such as minor abrasions and creases. It is completely intact, but original paper folds show signs of damage. All printing is legible; however, there may be weathering, slight fading, pencil or ink marks, and soiling from rust, grease, or oil. Pages may have tears.

P-5 **Good:** Item shows substantial wear which can include moderate abrasions, creases, and folds. All existing printing is legible; however, the item is severely worn. Colors may be extensively faded, and original folds and edges may be damaged, Rusty staples may have stained pages. (Any paper having been repaired cannot be graded above P-5.)

P-4 **Fair:** Shows heavy damage but printing is generally legible. Paper may be brittle or have been repaired. Could have grease, oil, or water damage.

S GAUGE MARKETPLACE

When to consult this guide

Many readers of the *American Flyer Pocket Price Guide* use it after the fact. They already have some trains and accessories and now want to identify and evaluate those items. The *American Flyer Pocket Price Guide* can also help you think about what to acquire in the future. That's really when the fun begins! Once you have a general idea of how to enjoy this hobby, you can make informed decisions about which trains you want.

Postwar trains and accessories

This is an interesting time to be concentrating on postwar American Flyer. On the one hand, serious collectors are paying record prices for Like New and Mint items, boxes are escalating in value, and demand for original and complete sets, top-of-the-line locomotives, and scarce variations continues to rise.

On the other hand, the need that operators once felt to acquire postwar pieces to run on their S gauge layouts has all but vanished. The selection of realistic steam and diesel locomotives and colorful freight and passenger cars becomes greater each year.

As a result, folks who want to run trains can choose from models that promise superior performance and outstanding detail. Few S gauge enthusiasts can say that the postwar line from Gilbert surpassed what is available today, which is why operators are devouring new catalogs and paying less attention to what was offered 50 years ago.

Anyone who wants Good and even Excellent trains to display or operate will find that all but the most deluxe and exotic models are available in abundant supply and at affordable prices. Collectors with deep pockets and high standards may turn up their noses at common pieces as well as notable ones because those items are graded below Like New or do not come with all their original packaging.

So collectors willing to forgo a box and accept a scratch or paint chip may find items available that they once thought were beyond their aspirations. They may also benefit from the shift of operators away from postwar trains to contemporary ones. Operating cars, especially those models and road names that are considered fairly common, deserve more attention. In contrast, passenger cars continue to dazzle serious collectors, and so their prices have stayed at the same level or even climbed.

Demand for certain items in the higher grades seems stronger, which means that those same trains in Good or possibly Excellent condition may be overlooked. For example, the big steam locomotives, sleek PA diesels, realistic boxcars, and impressive tank cars that Gilbert cataloged in the 1950s continue to gain strength on the collector market. The same can be said of different freight loaders, figures, and stations. Originals draw more attention, probably because reproductions have flooded the market.

Modern trains and accessories

Flip through Sections 2 through 5 and you'll come across S gauge models of many of the best-known diesel locomotives and any kind of freight or passenger car imaginable. Railroads, large and small, prominent and forgotten, are represented.

Increasing numbers of S gauge enthusiasts are jumping on the contemporary bandwagon and buying trains of recent vintage to operate. They have found dozens of locomotives to run, including the EMD diesels and GG1 electrics that Gilbert never made as well as a variety of steamers.

When it comes to cars for any of these powerful, detailed locomotives, hobbyists have a selection of rolling stock that overshadows what was available in the 1950s and 1960s. Lionel and other current manufacturers have brought out superb models of vintage and contemporary boxcars, tankers, refrigerator cars, and covered hoppers. The array of loads carried on flatcars is amazing, and the range of caboose styles and road names continues to grow.

Kleer-Pak

In 1960, the following items came packaged in a Kleer-Pak, which significantly increases its value if found in the Kleer-Pak.

23743	Track Maintenance Car
24029	BAR State of Maine Boxcar
24055	Gold Belt Line Boxcar
24065	NYC Boxcar
24067	Keystone Line Boxcar
24125	Bethlehem Steel Gondola
24216	Union Pacific Hopper
24221	C&EI Hopper
24225	Santa Fe Hopper
24323	Baker's Chocolate Tank Car (white ends)
24425	BAR Reefer
24426	Rath Packing Reefer
24533	AFL Track Cleaning Car
24549	Erie Floodlight Car
24557	U.S. Navy Flatcar with jeeps
24565	FY&PRR Flatcar with cannon
24574	U.S. Air Force Flatcar with rocket fuel tanks
24575	National Car Co. Flatcar
24577	Illinois Central Flatcar with jet engine
24579	Illinois Central Flatcar
25046	Rocket Launcher Car
25057	TNT Exploding Boxcar
25515	U.S. Air Force Flatcar with rocket sled

		Good	Exc
_____ 1	Transformer, 25 watts, *49-52*	2	4
_____ 1	Transformer, 35 watt, *56*	4	9
_____ 1A	Transformer, 40 watts, *57 u*	3	10
_____ 1B	Transformer, 50 watts, *56*	1	5
_____ 1 1/2	Transformer, 45 watts, *53*	1	5
_____ 1 1/2	Transformer, 50 watts, *54-55*	1	5
_____ 1 1/2 B	Transformer, 50 watts, *56*	1	5
_____ 2	Transformer, 75 watts, *47-53*	3	13
_____ 2B	Transformer, 75 watts, *47-48*	3	29
_____ 3	Transformer, 50 watts, *46 u*	1	6
_____ 4B	Transformer, 100 watts, *49-56*	10	19
_____ 4B-EX	Transformer, 100 watts, made for export 49-56	20	95
_____ 5	Transformer, 50 watts, *46*	1	6
_____ 5A	Transformer, 50 watts, *46*	1	6
_____ 5B	Transformer, 50 watts, *46*	3	6
_____ 6	Transformer, 75 watts, *46*	1	8
_____ 6A	Transformer, 75 watts, *46*	1	7
_____ 7	Transformer, 75 watts, *46 u*	2	9
_____ 7B	Transformer, 75 watts, *46*	2	9
_____ 8B	Transformer, 100 watts, *46-52*	11	43
_____ 8B-EX	Transformer, 100 watts, made for export, *46-52*	20	95
_____ 9B	Transformer, 150 watts, *46*	18	25
_____ 10	DC Inverter, 46	6	17
_____ 11	Circuit Breaker, 46	3	23
_____ 12B	Transformer, 250 watts, *46-52*	35	93
_____ 13	Circuit Breaker, 52-55	4	10
_____ 14	Rectiformer, 47-49	9	105
_____ 15	Rectifier-48-52	5	26
_____ 15B	Transformer, 110 watts, *53*	13	56
_____ 16	Rectiformer, 50	10	41
_____ 16B	Transformer, 175 watts, *54-56*	23	99
_____ 16B	Transformer, 190 watts, *53*	30	80
_____ 16C	Transformer, 35 watts, *58*	6	17
_____ 17B	Transformer, 190 watts, *52*	33	69
_____ 18	Filter, *50 u*		NRS
_____ 18B	Transformer, 175 watts, *54-56*	27	115
_____ 18B	Transformer, 190 watts, *53*	33	120
_____ 18B-EX	Transformer, 175 watts, made for export, *54-56*	35	140
_____ 19B	Transformer, 300 watts, *52-55*	60	160
_____ 21	Imitation Grass, *49-50*	15	35
_____ 21A	Imitation Grass, *51-56*	15	35
_____ 22	Scenery Gravel, *49-56*	13	21
_____ 23	Artificial Coal, *49-56*	14	34

		Good	Exc
24	Rainbow Wire, *49-56*	3	11 ____
25	Smoke Cartridge, *47-56*	5	25 ____
26	Service Kit, *52-56*	8	36 ____
27	Track Cleaning Fluid, *52-56*	2	11 ____
28	Track Ballast, *50*	5	16 ____
28A	Track Ballast, *51-53*	5	24 ____
29	Imitation Snow, *50*	45	247 ____
29A	Imitation Snow, *51-53*	50	294 ____
30	Highway Signs, *49*	81	115 ____
30A	Street Signs, *51-52*	70	140 ____
30B	Transformer, 300 watts, *53-56*	70	171 ____
31	Railroad Signs, *49-50*	100	181 ____
31A	Railroad Signs, *51-52*	75	252 ____
32	City Street Equipment, *49-50*	55	206 ____
32A	Park Set, *51*	55	229 ____
33	Passenger and Train Figure Set, *51-52*	75	404 ____
34	Railway Figure Set, *53*	145	826 ____
35	Brakeman with lantern, *50-52*	71	171 ____
40	Smoke Set, *53-56*	2	4 ____
50	District School, *53-54*	90	171 ____
91 1/2 B	Transformer, 50 watts, made for export, *56*	20	95 ____
160	Station Platform, *53*	219	590 ____
161	Bungalow, *53*	115	249 ____
162	Factory, *53*	80	166 ____
163	Flyerville Station, *53*	154	311 ____
164	Red Barn, *53*	105	513 ____
165	Grain Elevator, *53*	105	169 ____
166	Church, *53*	95	427 ____
167	Town Hall, *53*	108	284 ____
168	Hotel, *53*	120	276 ____
247	Tunnel, *46-48*	20	42 ____
248	Tunnel, *46-48*	20	45 ____
249	Tunnel, *47-56*	14	43 ____
270	News and Frank Stand, light or dark blue, *52-53*	55	124 ____
271	Whistle Stop Set, 3 pieces, *52-53*	65	234 ____
271-1	Waiting Station, brown, *52-53*	21	60 ____
271-2	Refreshment Booth, white, *52-53*	21	60 ____
271-3	Newsstand, green, *52-53*	21	60 ____
272	Glendale Station and Newsstand, *52-53*	64	148 ____
273	Suburban Railroad Station, *52-53*	65	231 ____
274	Harbor Junction Freight Station, *52-53*	55	240 ____
275	Eureka Diner, *52-53*	49	257 ____
282	C&NW 4-6-2 Pacific Locomotive, *52-53*		
	(A) AF tender, plastic or metal, *52*	34	61 ____
	(B) AF or AFL tender with coal pusher, *53*	44	92 ____
283	C&NW 4-6-2 Pacific Locomotive, *54-57*	32	68 ____
285	C&NW 4-6-2 Pacific Locomotive, *52*	52	111 ____
287	C&NW 4-6-2 Pacific Locomotive, *54*	21	67 ____

			Good	Exc
_____	**289**	C&NW 4-6-2 Pacific Locomotive, *56 u*	332	401
_____	**290**	American Flyer 4-6-2 Pacific Locomotive, *49-51*	38	76
	293	NYNH&H 4-6-2 Pacific Locomotive, *53-58*		
_____		(A) Reverse in tender, *53-57*	77	115
_____		(B) Reverse in cab, *58 u*	150	390
_____	**295**	American Flyer 4-6-2 Pacific Locomotive, *51*	95	142
_____	**296**	NYNH&H 4-6-2 Pacific Locomotive, *55 u*	105	396
_____	**299**	Reading 4-4-2 Atlantic Locomotive, *54 u*	79	201
	300	Reading 4-4-2 Atlantic Locomotive, *46 47-52*		
_____		(A) Reading, *46-47*	19	52
_____		(B) Other variations, *47-52*	15	33
	300AC	Reading 4-4-2 Atlantic Locomotive, *48-51*		
_____		(A) 4-piece boiler, *48*	20	63
_____		(B) Other variations, *49-51*	15	34
	301	Reading 4-4-2 Atlantic Locomotive		
_____		(A) Metal tender, *46*	15	43
_____		(B) Plastic tender, *53*	15	32
	302	Reading 4-4-2 Atlantic Locomotive, *48, 51-53*		
_____		(A) Smoke in boiler	18	46
_____		(B) Plastic boiler	17	35
	302AC	Reading 4-4-2 Atlantic Locomotive, *48, 50-52*		
_____		(A) 4-piece boiler	17	48
_____		(B) Other variations	18	32
_____	**303**	Reading 4-4-2 Atlantic Locomotive, *54-56*	17	41
_____	**307**	Reading 4-4-2 Atlantic Locomotive, *54-57*	18	52
_____	**308**	Reading 4-4-2 Atlantic Locomotive, *56*	24	72
	310	PRR 4-6-2 Pacific Locomotive		
_____		(A) Pennsylvania, *46 u*	92	156
_____		(B) PRR-AFL, *47 u*	40	84
	312	PRR 4-6-2 Pacific Locomotive, *46-48, 51-52*		
_____		(A) Pennsylvania, s-i-t, *46*	55	125
_____		(B) Other variations	65	111
_____	**312AC**	PRR 4-6-2 Pacific Locomotive, *49-51*	55	84
	313	PRR 4-6-2 Pacific Locomotive, *55-57*		
_____		(A) Small motor, *55*	75	145
_____		(B) Large motor, *56-57*	95	208
	314AW	PRR 4-6-2 Pacific Locomotive, *49-50*		
_____		(A) Die-cast trailing truck, *49*		356
_____		(B) One-piece trailing truck and drawbar assembly, *50*		223
_____	**315**	PRR 4-6-2 Pacific Locomotive, *52*	75	220
_____	**316**	PRR 4-6-2 Pacific Locomotive, *53-54*	77	213
	320	NYC 4-6-4 Hudson Locomotive, *46-47*		
_____		(A) New York Central, *46*	50	245
_____		(B) NYC-AFL, *47*	45	137

		Good	Exc
321	NYC 4-6-4 Hudson Locomotive		
	(A) New York Central-s-i-t, *46*	75	303____
	(B) NYC-AFL, *47*	50	185____
322	NYC 4-6-4 Hudson Locomotive, *46-49*		
	(A) New York Central-s-i-t, *46*	90	134____
	(B) American Flyer Lines, s-i-t or s-i-b, *47-49*	38	132 ____
322AC	NYC 4-6-4 Hudson Locomotive, *49-51*	44	155____
324AC	NYC 4-6-4 Hudson Locomotive, *50*	70	145____
325AC	NYC 4-6-4 Hudson Locomotive, *51*	60	145____
K325	NYC 4-6-4 Hudson Locomotive, *52*		
	(A) Early coupler riveted to truck	155	483____
	(B) Other variations	55	181____
326	NYC 4-6-4 Hudson Locomotive, *53-57*		
	(A) Small motor, *53-54*	60	144____
	(B) Large motor, *54-57*	138	246____
332	UP 4-8-4 Northern Locomotive, *46-49*		
	(A) AC, Union Pacific, s-i-t, *46*		NRS____
	(B) AC, American Flyer Lines, s-i-t, *47*	1050	2800____
	(C) DC-American Flyer Lines, s-i-t, *47*	1300	3000____
	(D) AC, American Flyer Lines, *47-48*	170	382____
	(E) DC-American Flyer Lines, *48-49*	170	542____
332AC	UP 4-8-4 Northern Locomotive. 51	170	402____
332DC	UP 4-8-4 Northern Locomotive, *49*	155	416____
334DC	UP 4-8-4 Northern Locomotive, *50*	170	415____
K335	UP 4-8-4 Northern Locomotive, *52*	210	364____
336	UP 4-8-4 Northern Locomotive, *53-56*		
	(A) Small motor, *53*	170	386____
	(B) Large motor	248	465____
342	NKP 0-8-0 Switcher, *46-48, 52*		
	(A) Nickel Plate Road, s-i-t, *46*	500	1875____
	(B) American Flyer Lines, s-i-t, *47*	115	477____
	(C) Same as (B), but DC	110	428____
	(D) American Flyer Lines, *48*	95	253____
	(E) American Flyer, *52*	105	223____
342AC	NKP 0-8-0 Switcher, *49-51*	100	237____
342DC	NKP 0-8-0 Switcher, *48-50*	100	263____
343	NKP 0-8-0 Switcher, *53-58*		
	(A) Reverse in tender, *53-54*	115	262____
	(B) Reverse on motor, *55-57*	135	378____
346	NKP 0-8-0 Switcher, *55*	205	442____
350	Royal Blue 4-6-2 Pacific Locomotive, *48-50*		
	(A) Wire handrails, *48*	85	133____
	(B) Cast handrails, *50*	43	90____
	(C) Cast handrails, Royal Blue on tender, *50*	750	1714 ____
353	AF Circus 4-6-2 Pacific Locomotive, *50-51*		
	(A) Wire handrails, *50*	183	513____
	(B) Cast handrails, *51*	150	513____

			Good	Exc
____	**354**	Silver Bullet 4-6-2 Pacific Locomotive, *54*	100	249
	355	C&NW Baldwin Locomotive, *56-57*		
____		(A) Unpainted green plastic	68	93
____		(B) Green, painted plastic	115	193
	356	Silver Bullet 4-6-2 Pacific Locomotive, *53*		
____		(A) Chrome finish	65	134
____		(B) Satin silver-painted	80	160
	360/61	Santa Fe PA/PB Diesel Set, *50-51*		
____		(A) Chrome finish, *50*	85	307
____		(B) Chrome finish with handrails, *50*	120	585
____		(C) Chrome finish with warbonnet, *50*	110	600
____		(D) Silver-painted with warbonnet, *51*	75	233
	360/64	Santa Fe PA/PB Diesel Set, *50-51*		
____		(A) Silver-painted, Santa Fe, *50*	75	209
____		(B) Other variations		NRS
	370	AF GM GP7 Diesel, *50-53*		
____		(A) Link coupler bars, *50-52*	81	98
____		(B) Knuckle couplers, *53*	65	159
____	**371**	AF GM GP7 Diesel, *54*	105	139
	372	Union Pacific GP7 Diesel, *55-57*		
____		(A) Built by Gilbert	115	185
____		(B) Made by American Flyer	156	199
	374/75	Texas & Pacific GP7 Diesel, *54-55*		
____		(A) Sheet metal frame, *54*	175	411
____		(B) Die-cast frame, *55*	160	323
____	**375**	AF GM GP7 Diesel, *53*	490	1398
____	**377/78**	Texas & Pacific GP7 Diesel, *56-57*	175	392
	405	Silver Streak PA Diesel, red stripe, *52*		
____		(A) Chrome finish	95	175
____		(B) Marblized chrome finish	110	290
____	**440**	Lamp	1	5
____	**441**	Lamp	1	5
____	**442**	Lamp	1	5
____	**443**	Lamp	1	10
____	**444**	Lamp	1	5
____	**451**	Lamp	1	8
____	**452**	Lamp	1	9
	453	Lamp, *46-48*		
____		(A) Single bulb	1	5
____		(B) 3 bulbs	1	9
____	**455**	Bulbs, 3 pieces	2	5
____	**460**	Bulbs, *51, 53-54*	34	257
____	**461**	Lamp	2	7
	466	AFL Comet PA Diesel, *53-55*		
____		(A) Chrome finish, *53*	103	164
____		(B) Silver-painted, decal, *54-55*	75	121
____		(C) Silver-painted, heat, stamped letters	90	203
____		(D) Silver-painted over Santa Fe lettering	85	203
____		(E) Silver-painted over Rocket lettering	90	250

		Good	Exc
467	AFL Comet PB Diesel, *55**		NRS____
470/71/73	SF PA/PB/PA Diesel Set, *53-58*		
	(A) Chrome finish, metal steps, *53*	135	389____
	(B) Silver-painted, metal steps, *54-57*	120	376____
	(C) Silver-painted, cast plastic steps	245	705____
472	Santa Fe PA Diesel, *56*	110	203____
474/75	Rocket PA/PA Diesel Set, *53-55*		
	(A) Chrome finish, *53*	140	383____
	(B) Silver-painted, *54-55*	120	274____
476	Rocket PB Diesel, *55**		NRS____
477/78	Silver Flash PA/PB Diesel Set, *53-54*		
	(A) Chrome finish, *53*	175	470____
	(B) Silver-painted, *54*	246	510____
479	Silver Flash PA Diesel, *55*	90	257____
480	Silver Flash PB Diesel, *55**	600	2146____
481	Silver Flash PA Diesel, *56*	136	374____
484/85/86	Santa Fe PA/PB/PA Diesel Set, *56-57*	215	519____
490/91/93	Northern Pacific PA/PB/PA Diesel Set, *56**	340	733____
490/92	Northern Pacific PA/PA Diesel Set, *57*	200	497____
494/95	New Haven PA/PA Diesel Set, *56*	270	513____
497	New Haven PA Diesel, *57*	105	233____
499	New Haven GE Electric, *56-57*	169	300____
500	AFL Combination Car, *52 u*		
	(A) Satin silver-painted	140	425____
	(B) Chrome finish	108	287____
501	AFL Coach, *52 u*		
	(A) Satin silver-painted	150	396____
	(B) Chrome finish	110	299____
502	AFL Vista Dome Car, *52 u*		
	(A) Satin silver-painted	145	428____
	(B) Chrome finish	110	303____
503	AFL Observation Car, satin silver-painted, *52 u*	155	515____
520	Knuckle Coupler Kit, *54-56*	1	7____
521	Knuckle Coupler Kit		26____
525	Knuckle Coupler Trucks		40____
526	Knuckle Coupler Trucks		45____
528	Knuckle Coupler Trucks		50____
529	Knuckle Coupler Trucks		49____
530	Knuckle Coupler Trucks		40____
531	Knuckle Coupler Trucks		46____
532	Knuckle Coupler Trucks		45____
541	Fuses, *46*		NRS____
561	Billboard Horn, *55-56*		
	(A) Santa Fe Freight Train in Desert	33	60____
	(B) Santa Fe Alco with Steam Engine on Bridge	51	63____
	(C) Santa Fe Alco with Steam Engine on Bridge, green base	51	65____
	(D) Santa Fe Freight Train in Desert, green base	55	65____

			Good	Exc
____	566	Whistling Billboard, *51-55*	16	39
____	568	Whistling Billboard, *56*	18	38
____	571	Truss Bridge, *55-56*	11	38
____	573	American Flyer Talking Station Record		10
	577	Whistling Billboard, *46-50*		
____		(A) Circus, *46, 47*	21	76
____		(B) Fox Mart, *47*	500	2650
____		(C) Trains, *50*	24	40
____	578	Station Figure Set, *46-52*	55	244
____	579	Single Street Lamp-green or silver, *46-49*	10	23
____	580	Double Street Lamp-green or silver, *46-49*	18	34
____	581	Girder Bridge, *46-56*	11	42
____	582	Blinker Signal, *46-48*	55	137
____	583	Electromatic Crane, *46-49*	65	100
____	583A	Electromatic Crane, *50-53*	84	145
____	584	Bell Danger Signal, *46-47*	250	860
____	585	Tool Shed, *46-52*	23	118
____	586F	Wayside Station, *46-56*	33	107
____	587	Block Signal, *46-47*	70	314
____	588	Semaphore Block Signal, *46-48*	650	3725
	589	Passenger and Freight Station, *46-56*		
____		(A) Green, painted roof	17	36
____		(B) Black, painted roof	15	61
____	590	Control Tower, *55-56*	26	124
____	591	Crossing Gate, *46-48*	25	72
____	592	Crossing Gate, *49-50*	24	39
____	592A	Crossing Gate, *51-53*	27	61
____	593	Signal Tower, *46-54*	41	146
____	594	Animated Track Gang, *46-47**	662	2130
____	596	Operating Water Tank, *46-56*	35	55
____	598	Talking Station Record, *46-56*	10	18
____	599	Talking Station Record, *56*	11	42
____	600	Crossing Gate with bell, *54-56*	30	64
____	605	American Flyer Lines FlatCar, silver or gray, *53*	11	24
____	606	American Flyer Lines Crane, *53*	25	42
____	607	AFL Work and Boom Car, gray base, *53*	9	35
____	609	American Flyer Lines FlatCar, *53*	10	23
____	612	Passenger and Freight Station with Crane, *46-51, 53-54*	55	90
____	613	Great Northern BoxCar, *53*	21	62
____	620	Southern Gondola, *53*	22	60
____	622	General American BoxCar, *53**	16	40
____	623	Illinois Central Reefer, *53**	11	22
	625	Shell Tank Car, *46-50*		
____		(A) Orange Tank, plastic or painted	370	563
____		(B) Black tank	10	18
____		(C) Silver tank	6	22
____	625	Gulf Tank Car, *51-53*	8	20
____	625G	Gulf Tank Car, *51-53 u*	9	20

		Good	Exc
627	AFL FlatCar, die-cast base, *50*	14	40____
627	C&NW FlatCar, plastic base, *46-50*	10	88____
628	C&NW FlatCar, *46-53*		
	(A) Metal or plastic	8	31____
	(B) Pressed wood	13	40____
629	Missouri Pacific Stock Car, *46-53*	15	23____
630	Reading Caboose, *46-52*	6	30____
630	American Flyer Caboose, *52*	12	36____
630	American Flyer Lines Caboose, *53*	8	23____
631	Texas & Pacific Gondola, *46-53*		
	(A) Unpainted green plastic	8	12____
	(B) Unpainted dark gray, *48 u*	85	295____
	(C) Red-painted, *52 u*	31	195____
	(D) Green, painted, *46-52*	4	19____
632	Virginian Hopper, gray or blue-gray, die-cast, *46*	30	108
			____
632	Lehigh New England Hopper, *46-53*		
	(A) Gray, painted, die-cast, *46*	30	216____
	(B) Black plastic, *46*	8	33____
	(C) Gray plastic, *47-49*	4	20____
	(D) White plastic, *50*	33	108____
	(E) Gray, painted plastic, *53*	9	30____
	(F) Black plastic, red filled circle in logo		250____
633	Baltimore & Ohio BoxCar, *46-52*	10	32____
633	Baltimore & Ohio Reefer, *46-52*		
	(A) Red, *52 u*	41	159____
	(B) Tuscan, *52 u*	51	260____
633F	G. Fox & Co. BoxCar, *47* u	990	1825____
634	C&NW Floodlight Car, "42597," *46-49, 53*		
	(A) Plastic base, *46*	20	83____
	(B) Die-cast base, *47-49*	11	27____
635	C&NW Crane, plastic base, *46*	15	68____
635	C&NW Crane, metal base, *47-49*		
	(A) Yellow cab	11	34____
	(B) Red cab	123	242____
	(C) Black roof		580____
636	Erie FlatCar, *48-53*		
	(A) AF-die-cast frame	13	30____
	(B) AFL-die-cast frame	50	235____
	(C) Pressed-wood frame, *53*	65	290____
637	MKT BoxCar, yellow-painted or yellow plastic, *49-53**	8	24
			____
638	American Flyer Caboose, *49-52*	6	10____
638	American Flyer Lines Caboose, *53*	5	10____
639	American Flyer BoxCar, *49-52*		
	(A) Unpainted yellow plastic	7	12____
	(B) Tuscan, painted	16	53____
	(C) Red-painted		555____
	(D) Yellow-painted	10	26____

		Good	Exc
639	American Flyer Reefer, *51-52*		
___	(A) Yellow-painted or unpainted yellow plastic	6	10
___	(B) Unpainted cream plastic	64	219
639	American Flyer Reefer, yellow-painted, *50-51*	10	19
___ **640**	Wabash Hopper, *53*	10	15
640	American Flyer Hopper, *49-53*		
___	(A) Gray plastic body, white lettering	4	11
___	(B) Gray plastic body, black lettering	4	10
___	(C) White plastic body, black lettering	14	54
641	American Flyer Gondola, *49-52*		
___	(A) Red-painted or unpainted red plastic	10	20
___	(B) Unpainted gray plastic, *51 u*	143	283
___ **641**	Frisco Gondola, *53*	11	20
___ **642**	American Flyer BoxCar, *51-52*	10	16
642	American Flyer Reefer, *52 u*		
___	(A) Unpainted red plastic	7	15
___	(B) Red-painted	10	20
___	(C) Tuscan, painted	25	27
___ **642**	Seaboard BoxCar, *53*	11	24
643	American Flyer Circus FlatCar, *50-53**		
___	(A) Yellow-metal, with door guides for load, *50*	100	525
___	(B) Yellow-metal	75	350
___	(C) Yellow-pressed wood	90	346
___	(D) Red-metal	120	1490
___	(E) Metal Car, no load	29	35
644	American Flyer Crane Car, *50-53*		
___	(A) Red cab-black boom, *50*	35	96
___	(B) Red cab-green boom, *50*	22	66
___	(C) Tuscan, painted cab, green boom, *50-51*	27	77
___	(D) Black cab-black boom	20	39
___ **645**	AF Work and Boom Car, *50*	16	52
___ **645A**	AF or AFL Work and Boom Car, *51-53*	16	29
646	Erie Floodlight Car, *50-53*		
___	(A) Green, painted, die-cast generator, *50*	47	177
___	(B) Red or green plastic generator	15	32
___	(C) Red or green painted generator	15	33
___ **647**	Northern Pacific Reefer, *52-53*	13	33
648	American Flyer FlatCar, red or tuscan, *52-54*	11	21
649	AF Circus Coach, *50-52*		
___	(A) Unpainted yellow plastic	23	65
___	(B) Yellow-painted	55	183
650	New Haven Pullman Car, *46-53*		
___	(A) Red or green, plastic frame	21	80
___	(B) Red or green, die-cast frame	22	39
___	(C) Red or green, sheet metal frame	15	25

		Good	Exc
651	New Haven Baggage Car, *46-53*		
	(A) Red or green, plastic frame	12	56____
	(B) Red or green, die-cast frame	12	29____
	(C) Red or green, sheet metal frame	11	31____
652	Pullman Car, *46-53*		
	(A) Red or green, long trucks	65	232____
	(B) Red-tuscan, or green, short trucks	41	110____
	(C) Red-maroon-or green, Pikes Peak	48	143____
653	Pullman Car, *46-53*		
	(A) Red or green, long trucks	65	208____
	(B) Red or green, short trucks	40	87____
654	Pullman Observation Car, *46-53*		
	(A) Red or green, long trucks	60	219____
	(B) Red or green, short trucks	41	88____
655	AFL Coach, *53*		
	(A) Red-painted	22	66____
	(B) Green, painted	32	62____
655	Silver Bullet Coach, *53*		
	(A) Chrome finish	25	63____
	(B) Satin silver-painted	20	125____
660	AFL Combination Car, *50-52*		
	(A) Aluminum body	18	49____
	(B) Chrome finish, plastic body	27	109____
661	AFL Coach, *50-52*		
	(A) Aluminum body	52	74____
	(B) Chrome finish, plastic body	44	78____
	(C) Satin silver-painted, plastic body	50	263____
662	AFL Vista Dome Car, *50-52*		
	(A) Aluminum body	22	61____
	(B) Chrome finish, plastic body	30	77____
663	AFL Observation Car, aluminum, *50-52*	22	79____
668	Manual Switch, left hand, *53-55*	5	9____
669	Manual Switch, right hand, *53-55*	5	9____
670	Track Trip, *55-56*	2	13____
678	Remote Control Switch, left hand, *53--56*	7	17____
679	Remote Control Switch, right hand, *53-56*	6	16____
690	Track Terminal, *46-56*		4____
691	Steel Pins, *46-48*		1____
692	Fiber Pins, *46-48*		3____
693	Track Locks, dozen, *48-56*		9____
694	Couplers, Trucks, Wheels, and Axles, *46-53*	2	18____
695	Reverse Loop Relay, *55-56*	26	115____
695	Track Trip, *46*	6	14____
696	Track Trip, *55-57*		
	(A) Plastic shoe	10	16____
	(B) Die-cast shoe	10	26____
697	Track Trip, *50-54*	4	15____
698	Reverse Loop Kit, *49-50, 52-54*	17	66____
700	Straight Track, *46-56*		2____

			Good	Exc
____	701	Straight Track, half section, *46-56*		2
____	702	Curved Track, *46-56*		2
____	703	Curved Track, half section, *46-56*		2
____	704	Manual Uncoupler, *52-56*		5
____	705	Remote Control Uncoupler, *46-47*	1	5
____	706	Remote Control Uncoupler, *48-56*	1	8
____	707	Track Terminal, *46-59*		2
____	708	Air Chime Whistle Control, *51-56*	3	35
____	709	Lockout Eliminator, *50-55*	2	19
____	710	Automatic Track Section, *46-47*	1	9
____	710	Steam Whistle Control, *55-56*	10	160
____	711	Mail Pickup, *46-47*	9	22
____	712	Special Rail Section, *47-56*		1
____	713	Special Rail Section with mail bag hook- *47-56*	8	30
____	714	Log Unloading Car, *51-54*	16	45
	715	American Flyer Lines FlatCar, *46-54*		
____		(A) Tootsietoy armored car	37	121
____		(B) Manoil coupe	25	46
____		(C) Tootsietoy racer		49
	716	American Flyer Lines Hopper, *46-51*		
____		(A) Between-rail pickup, *46*	6	36
____		(B) Outside rail pickup, *47-51*	6	29
____	717	American Flyer Lines FlatCar, *46-52*	15	31
____	718	AFL Mail Pickup Car, *49-54*		300
	718	New Haven Mail Pickup Car, *46-54*		
____		(A) Red body, red pickup arm	155	468
____		(B) Red or green body	31	112
____		(C) Maroon body		NRS
	719	CB&Q Hopper Dump Car, *50-54*		
____		(A) Tuscan, painted	25	57
____		(B) Red plastic	34	82
____	720	Remote Control Switches, *46-49*	19	59
____	720A	Remote Control Switches, *50-56*	23	47
____	722	Manual Switches, *46-51*	10	19
____	722A	Manual Switches, *52-56*	9	18
____	725	90-degree Crossing, *46-56*	3	14
____	725	90-degree Crossing with brass strips, *46*		100
____	726	Straight Rubber Roadbed, *50-56*	1	5
____	727	Curved Rubber Roadbed, *50-56*	1	3
____	728	Re-railer, *56*	3	24
	730	Bumper, *46-56*		
____		(A) Green plastic	11	19
____		(B) Red-51	35	95
____		(C) Green, painted	23	90
____	731	Pike Planning Kit, *52-56*	11	24
	732	AF Operating Baggage Car, *51-54*		
____		(A) Unpainted red or green	29	51
____		(B) Green, painted	34	98

		Good	Exc
734	American Flyer Operating BoxCar, *50-54*		
	(A) Red plastic	20	39____
	(B) Red painted	25	80____
	(C) Tuscan painted	20	48____
	(D) Tuscan painted, AFL	30	92____
735	NH Animated Station Coach, *52-54*	32	78____
736	Missouri Pacific Stock Car, *50-54*	10	34____
740	AFL Motorized HandCar, *52-54*		
	(A) No decals-no vent holes, black lettering, *52*	33	123____
	(B) Shield decal with stripes, *52*	20	58____
	(C) Shield decal with vent holes, no stripes	17	68____
741	AFL Handcar and Shed, motorized, *53-54*	75	102____
742	AFL Reversing HandCar, *55-56*	41	74____
743	Track Maintenance Car		2750____
747	Cardboard Trestle Set	7	22____
748	Girder, Trestle, and Tower Bridge, *58 u*	22	50____
748	Overhead Foot Bridge, *51-52*		
	(A) Gray/aluminum	17	32____
	(B) Bluish silver	28	51____
749	Street Lamp Set, *50-52*	6	26____
750	Trestle Bridge, *46-56*		
	(A) Black, painted	16	67____
	(B) Silver-painted	16	105____
	(C) Bluish gray, painted	25	110____
751	Log Loader, *46-50*	69	125____
751A	Log Loader, *52-53*	47	97____
752	Seaboard Coaler, *46-50*	100	220____
752A	Seaboard Coaler, *51-52*	115	165____
753	Mountain Tunnel and Pass Set, *60 u*	17	127____
753	Single Trestle Bridge, *52*	16	54____
754	Double Trestle Bridge, *50-52*	50	98____
755	Talking Station, *48-50*		
	(A) Green roof	50	68____
	(B) Blue roof	60	148____
758	Sam the Semaphore Man, *49*	29	55____
758A	Sam the Semaphore Man, *50-56*	36	113____
759	Bell Danger Signal, *53-56*	22	46____
760	Highway Flasher, *49-56*	9	27____
761	Semaphore, *49-56*	22	112____
762	Two-in-One Whistle, *49-50*	35	94____
763	Mountain Set, *49-50*	46	124____
764	Express Office, *50-51*	79	204____
766	Animated Station, *52-54*	68	157____
K766	Animated Station, *53-55*	55	142____
767	Roadside Diner, *50-54*		
	(A) Yellow plastic	39	75____
	(B) Yellow-painted	50	145____

			Good	Exc
	768	Oil Supply Depot, *50-53*		
___		(A) Shell	40	113
___		(B) Gulf	50	170
___	769	Aircraft Beacon, *50*	16	37
___	769A	Aircraft Beacon, *51-56*	19	55
___	770	Girder Trestle Set, *60 u*	4	18
___	770	Loading Platform, *50-52*	31	85
___	771	Operating Stockyard, *50-54**	44	59
___	K771	Stockyard and Car, *53-56*	50	84
	772	Water Tower, *50-56*		
___		(A) Small tank	30	59
___		(B) Small tank, with workman, *50*	207	505
___		(C) Large checkerboard tank, metal shack	49	122
	773	Oil Derrick, *50-52*		
___		(A) American Flyer, *50*	48	91
___		(B) Gulf logo		775
	774	Floodlight Tower, *51-56*		
___		(A) Red base, gray tower and platform	18	63
___		(B) Red base, gray tower and platform, with workman	80	324
___	775	Baggage Platform with boxCar, link couplers, *53-55*	24	78
___	K775	Baggage Platform with boxCar, knuckle couplers, *53-55*	35	131
___	778	Street Lamp Set, *53-56*	11	32
	779	Oil Drum Loader, *55-56*		
___		(A) Tan plastic base	55	120
___		(B) Gray, painted base	75	234
	780	Trestle Set, *53-56*		
___		(A) Black, *53*	15	26
___		(B) Orange	10	28
___	781	Abutment Set, *53*	22	115
___	782	Abutment Set, *53*	17	93
___	783	Hi-Trestle Sections, *53-56*	6	46
___	784	Hump Set, *55*	75	335
___	785	Coal Loader, *55-56*	123	190
___	787	Log Loader, *55-56*	73	142
___	788	Suburban Station, *56*	11	61
___	789	Station and Baggage Smasher, *56-57*	93	141
___	790	Trainorama, *53 u*	48	176
___	792	Terminal, *54-56*	65	137
___	793	Union Station, *55-56*	16	80
___	794	Union Station, *54*	32	129
___	795	Union Station and Terminal, *54*	110	352
___	799	Talking Station, *54-56*	35	174
___	801	Baltimore & Ohio Hopper, *56-57*	11	14
	802	Illinois Central Reefer, *56-57**		
___		(A) Orange plastic	16	21
___		(B) Orange-painted	100	242

GILBERT PRODUCTION 1946-1966

		Good	Exc
803	Santa Fe BoxCar, tuscan, unpainted, *56-57*	17	24____
804	Norfolk & Western Gondola, *56-57*	6	14____
805	Pennsylvania Gondola, tuscan, *56-57*	7	13____
806	American Flyer Lines Caboose, *56-57*	7	10____
807	Rio Grande BoxCar, *57*		
	(A) Unpainted, nonopening door	19	28____
	(B) Opening door		NRS____
	(C) White, painted, nonopening door		415____
900	NP Combination Car, *56-57**	100	238____
901	NP Coach, *56-57**	100	242____
902	NP Vista Dome Car, *56-57**	100	259____
903	NP Observation Car, *56-57**	100	235____
904	AFL Caboose, *56*	11	18____
905	AFL FlatCar, gray or blue-gray, *54*	11	34____
906	AFL Crane, gray or blue-gray, *54*	16	31____
907	AFL Work and Boom Car, *54*	13	36____
909	AFL FlatCar, gray or blue-gray, *54*	11	30____
910	Gilbert Chemical Tank Car, *54**	70	205____
911	C&O Gondola, *55-57*		
	(A) Silver pipes, black, painted or black body	10	39 ____
	(B) Brown pipes, black, painted body, *55*	39	195____
912	Koppers Tank Car, *55-57*		
	(A) Die-cast frame	38	62____
	(B) Plastic frame	25	59____
913	Great Northern BoxCar, *53-58*		
	(A) Decal goat logo	14	36____
	(B) Painted goat logo	14	30____
914	American Flyer Lines FlatCar, *53-57*	17	64____
915	American Flyer Lines FlatCar, *53-57*		
	(A) Black and red, yellow ramp, with TootsieToy racer	12	66 ____
	(B) gray, brown ramp, with Renwal gas truck	12	78 ____
916	Delaware & Hudson Gondola, *55-56*	9	34____
918	American Flyer Lines Mail Car, *53-58*		
	(A) American Flyer Lines	29	79____
	(B) New Haven	35	162____
919	CB&Q Dump Car, *53-56*	41	79____
920	Southern Gondola, *53-56*	14	31____
921	CB&Q Hopper, *53-56*	8	81____
922	General American BoxCar, *53-57**		
	(A) Decal	15	41____
	(B) Stamped	15	64____
923	Illinois Central Reefer, *54-55**	13	17____
924	Jersey Central Hopper, *53-56*	9	79____
925	Gulf Tank Car, *52-57*		
	(A) Early knuckle coupler, *52*	28	176____
	(B) Die-cast frame	15	33____
	(C) Plastic frame	10	20____

		Good	Exc
926	Gulf Tank Car, *55-57*		
_____	(A) Die-cast frame	10	74
_____	(B) Plastic frame	10	43
928	C&NW FlatCar, *52-54*		
_____	(A) Pressed-wood base, *52*	24	87
_____	(B) Die-cast base, *53-54*	9	23
_____ **928**	New Haven Log Car, *56 u*	17	32
_____ **928**	New Haven Lumber Car, *56-57*	11	32
929	Missouri Pacific Stock Car, *52-57*		
_____	(A) Closed slats, tuscan or red	10	31
_____	(B) Open slats, tuscan, *57*	100	1009
_____	(C) Early knuckle coupler, *52*	75	243
930	American Flyer Caboose, *52*		
_____	(A) Early knuckle coupler	28	112
_____	(B) Red	15	37
_____	(C) Tuscan	9	28
930	American Flyer Lines Caboose, *53-57*		
_____	(A) Type I or II body	22	46
_____	(B) Type III body	28	104
931	T&P Gondola, green, *52-55*		
_____	(A) Riveted couplers, *52*		1000
_____	(B) Nonriveted couplers	5	18
_____ **933**	B&O BoxCar, *53-54*	19	43
_____ **934**	American Flyer Lines Caboose, *54 u*	16	39
_____ **934**	C&NW Floodlight Car, "42597," gray or blue-gray, *53-54*	10	26
_____ **934**	Southern Pacific Floodlight Car, *54 u*	14	32
_____ **935**	AFL Bay Window Caboose, *57*	21	69
_____ **936**	Erie FlatCar, *53-54*	12	43
_____ **936**	Pennsylvania FlatCar, *55-57*	40	127
937	MKT BoxCar, *53-58**		
_____	(A) All yellow	10	40
_____	(B) Yellow and tuscan	10	34
_____ **938**	American Flyer Lines Caboose, *54-55*	5	16
_____ **940**	Wabash Hopper, *53-56*	7	17
_____ **941**	Frisco Lines Gondola, *53-56*	7	21
_____ **942**	Seaboard BoxCar, *54*	9	17
944	American Flyer Crane, *52-57*		
_____	(A) Gray die-cast body, black cab	22	47
_____	(B) Blue-gray die-cast body, black cab	30	59
945	AF or AFL Work and Boom Car, *52-57*		
_____	(A) Die-cast base, *52-56*	10	39
_____	(B) Plastic base, *57*	15	40
946	Erie Floodlight Car, *53-56*		
_____	(A) Red or green painted generator	13	41
_____	(B) Red-green, or yellow plastic generator	13	43
_____ **947**	Northern Pacific Reefer, *53-58*	21	41
_____ **948**	AFL FlatCar, *53-57*	11	30

		Good	Exc
951	AFL Baggage Car, *53-57*		
	(A) Red or maroon	15	47____
	(B) Green	18	58____
952	AFL Pullman Car, *53-58*		
	(A) No silhouettes, maroon or green	36	152____
	(B) Silhouettes, maroon	50	176____
953	AFL Combination Car, *53-58*		
	(A) No silhouettes, maroon or green	56	103____
	(B) Silhouettes, maroon	55	160____
954	AFL Observation Car, *53-56*		
	(A) No silhouettes, maroon or green	36	109____
	(B) Silhouettes, maroon	105	160____
955	AF or AFL Coach, *54-55*		
	(A) Satin silver-painted	30	81____
	(B) Green, painted	31	69____
	(C) Maroon-painted, silhouettes, "955"	21	80____
	(D) Maroon-painted, silhouettes, white, outlined windows	29	90 ____
956	Monon FlatCar, *56*	21	54____
957	Erie Operating BoxCar, *57 u*	47	557____
958	Mobilgas Tank Car, plastic or metal frame, *57 u*	23	90 ____
960	AFL Columbus Combination Car, *53-56*		
	(A) Satin silver	30	92____
	(B) Blue, green, or red band	56	114____
	(C) Chestnut band	75	153____
	(D) Orange band	50	131____
	(E) Chrome finish	50	114____
961	AFL Jefferson Pullman Car, *53-58*		
	(A) Satin silver	40	331____
	(B) Green or red band	45	111____
	(C) Chestnut band	108	410____
	(D) Orange band	65	159____
	(E) Chrome finish	50	105____
962	AFL Hamilton Vista Dome Car, *53-58*		
	(A) Satin silver	40	114____
	(B) Blue, green, or red band	41	98____
	(C) Chestnut band	90	238____
	(D) Orange band	65	164____
	(E) Chrome finish	50	113____
963	AFL Washington Observation Car, *53-58*		
	(A) Satin silver	40	107____
	(B) Blue, green, or red band	36	119____
	(C) Chestnut band	85	223____
	(D) Orange band	65	157____
	(E) Chrome finish	50	110____
969	Rocket Launcher FlatCar, *57 u*		
	(A) Black plastic	20	46____
	(B) Black, painted	80	285____

			Good	Exc
____	970	Seaboard Operating BoxCar, *56-57*	48	118
	971	Southern Pacific Lumber Unloading Car, *56-57*		
____		(A) Tuscan plastic	39	105
____		(B) Tuscan, painted plastic	50	620
____	973	Gilbert's Operating Milk Car, *56-57*	65	174
____	974	AFL Operating BoxCar, *53-54*	27	82
____	974	Erie Operating BoxCar, *55*	48	151
____	975	AFL Operating Coach, *54-55*	29	75
____	976	MP Operating Cattle Car, *53-62*	25	111
____	977	AFL Caboose, metal or rubber Man, *55-57*	26	44
____	978	AFL Grand Canyon Observation Car, *56-58*	148	413
____	979	AFL Bay Window Caboose, *57*	62	96
____	980	Baltimore & Ohio BoxCar, *56-57*	35	81
	981	Central of Georgia BoxCar, *56-57*		
____		(A) Shiny black paint	44	90
____		(B) Dull black paint	70	201
____	982	BAR BoxCar, *56-57*	42	98
____	983	MP BoxCar, *56-57*	48	96
____	984	New Haven BoxCar, *56-57*	30	64
____	985	B&M BoxCar, *57*	55	91
____	988	ART Reefer, *56-57*	49	82
____	989	Northwestern Reefer, *56-58*	73	133
____	994	Union Pacific Stock Car, *57*	66	135
____	C1001	White's Discount Centers BoxCar, *61* u*	345	1314
____	1023A	Trestle Set		220
____	1-1024A	Trestle Set, *52 u*	10	44
____	C2001	Post BoxCar, *62 u*	13	22
____	L2001	Game Train 4-4-0 Locomotive, *63*	15	42
____	L2002	Burlington Route 4-4-0 Locomotive, *63 u*	50	295
____	L2004	Rio Grande F9 Diesel, *62*	80	190
	C2009	Texas & Pacific Gondola, *62-64*		
____		(A) Unpainted dark green or dark green, painted		2000
____		(B) Unpainted light green	7	20
____	21004	PRR 0-6-0 Switcher, *57 u*	170	294
____	21005	PRR 0-6-0 Switcher, *57-58*	125	381
____	21084	C&NW 4-6-2 Pacific Locomotive, *57 u*	41	154
	21085	C&NW or CMStP&P 4-6-2 Pacific Locomotive, *58-65*		
____		(A) Plastic drivers	32	58
____		(B) Metal drivers	32	68
____	21088	FY&P Franklin 4-4-0 Locomotive, red, black, or green, *59-60*	53	77
____	21089	FY&PRR Washington 4-4-0 Locomotive, *60-61*	65	206
____	21095	NYNH&H 4-6-2 Pacific Locomotive, *57*		NRS
____	21099	NYNH&H 4-6-2 Pacific Locomotive, *58*	192	482
____	21100	Reading 4-4-2 Atlantic Locomotive, *57 u*	14	31

		Good	Exc
21105	Reading 4-4-2 Atlantic Locomotive, *57-60*		
	(A) Aluminum drive wheels	100	200____
	(B) Die-cast wheels with white tires	40	67____
	(C) Black plastic drive wheels	20	41____
21106	Reading 4-4-2 Atlantic Locomotive, *59 u*	105	253____
21107	PRR or BN 4-4-2 Atlantic Locomotive, *64-66 u*	10	20 ____
21115	PRR 4-6-2 Pacific Locomotive, *58*	215	1044____
21129	NYC 4-6-4 Hudson Locomotive, *58*	318	1354____
21130	NYC 4-6-4 Hudson Locomotive, *59-60*	140	335____
21139	UP 4-8-4 Northern Locomotive, *58-59*	353	1264____
21140	UP 4-8-4 Northern Locomotive, *60*	525	2014____
21145	NKP 0-8-0 Switcher, *58*	165	1020____
21155	0-6-0 Switcher, *58*	90	193____
21156	0-6-0 Switcher, *59*	75	200____
21158	0-6-0 Switcher, *60 u*	41	80____
21160	Reading 4-4-2 Atlantic Locomotive, *58-60 u*	15	26 ____
21161	Reading 4-4-2 Atlantic Locomotive, *60 u*		
	(A) American Flyer Lines	11	26____
	(B) Prestone Car Care Express	83	287____
21165	Erie 4-4-0 Locomotive, *61-62, 65-66 u*	10	26____
21166	Burlington Route 4-4-0 Locomotive, *63-65*		
	(A) White letters in black box	10	32____
	(B) Black letters in white box	85	204____
21168	Southern 4-4-0 Locomotive, *61-63*		
	(A) Knuckle coupler, *61*	25	64____
	(B) Pike Master couplers, *62-63*	10	44____
21205/-1	B&M Twin F9 Diesels, *61-62 u*		
	(A) Twin A units	110	252____
	(B) Single unit	75	177____
21206/-1	SF Twin F9 Diesels, *61-62 u*	105	352____
21207/-1	GN Twin F9 Diesels, *63-64*	100	395____
21210	Burlington F9 Diesel, *61*	65	262____
21215/-1	UP Twin F9 Diesels, *61-62*	95	228____
21215/16	UP Twin F9 Diesels, *61*		2100____
21234	Chesapeake & Ohio GP7 Diesel, *59-61*		
	(A) Long steps	145	411____
	(B) Short steps	165	694____
21551	Northern Pacific PA Diesel, *58*		
	(A) Plastic steps, portholes filled in	135	298____
	(B) Sheet, metal steps, portholes open	135	373____
21561	New Haven PA Diesel, *57-58*		
	(A) Plastic steps	125	226____
	(B) 1-rivet metal steps	125	328____
21573	New Haven GE Electric, *58-59*		
	(A) Shiny black, *58*	145	355____
	(B) Dull black, *59*	200	377____
21720	Santa Fe PB Diesel, *58 u*	275	1135____

		Good	Exc
21801	C&NW Baldwin Locomotive, *57-58*		
____	(A) Unpainted	42	109
____	(B) Painted	70	320
21801-1	C&NW Baldwin Locomotive, *58 u*		
____	(A) Unpainted	70	172
____	(B) Painted	85	290
____ **21808**	C&NW Baldwin Locomotive, *58 u*	61	97
21812	Texas & Pacific Baldwin Locomotive, *59-60*	75	105
____			
____ **21813**	M&StL Baldwin Locomotive, *58 u-60 u*	190	623
21831	Texas & Pacific GP7 Diesel, *58*		
____	(A) American Flyer Lines	150	323
____	(B) Texas & Pacific	185	541
21910/-1/-2	SF PA/PB/PA Diesel Set, *57-58*	370	768
____ **21918/-1**	Seaboard Baldwin Locomotive, *58*	320	488
____ **21920**	Missouri Pacific PA Diesel, *63-64*	185	527
____ **21920/-1**	Missouri Pacific PA/PA Diesel Set, *58**	340	1032
____ **21922/-1**	Missouri Pacific PA/PA Diesel Set, *59-60*	275	752
____ **21925/-1**	Union Pacific PA/PA Diesel Set, *59-60**	235	889
____ **21927**	Santa Fe PA Diesel, *60-62*	110	206
____ **22004**	Transformer, 40 watts, *59-64*	2	10
____ **22006**	Transformer, 25 watts, *63*	2	9
____ **22020**	Transformer, 50 watts, *57-64*	2	8
____ **22030**	Transformer, 100 watts, *57-64*	4	21
____ **22033**	Transformer, 25 watts, *65*	2	5
____ **22034**	Transformer, 50 watts, *65*	4	12
____ **22035**	Transformer, 175 watts, *57-64*	16	78
____ **22040**	Transformer, 110 watts, *57-58*	5	18
____ **22050**	Transformer, 175 watts, *57-58*	12	42
____ **22060**	Transformer, 175 watts, *57-58*	12	39
____ **22080**	Transformer, 300 watts, *57-58*	34	195
____ **22090**	Transformer, 350 watts, *59-64*	63	173
____ **23021**	Imitation Grass, *57-59*	6	22
____ **23022**	Scenery Gravel, *57-59*	6	78
____ **23023**	Imitation Coal, *57-59*	5	17
____ **23024**	Rainbow Wire, *57-64*	4	10
____ **23025**	Smoke Cartridges, *57-59*	4	25
____ **23026**	Service Kit, *59-64*	6	23
____ **23027**	Track Cleaning Fluid, *57-59*	1	4
____ **23028**	Smoke Fluid Dispenser, *60-64*	2	76
____ **23032**	Equipment Kit, *60-61*	33	112
____ **23036**	Money Saver Kit, *60, 62, 64*	32	295
____ **23040**	Mountain Tunnel and Pass Set, *58*		380
____ **23249**	Tunnel, *57-64*	9	48
____ **23561**	Billboard Horn, *57-59*	10	43
____ **23568**	Whistling Billboard, *57-64*	11	48
____ **23571**	Truss Bridge, *57-64*	7	33
____ **23581**	Girder Bridge, *57-64*	8	35

		Good	Exc
23586	Wayside Station, *57-59*	25	113____
23589	Passenger and Freight Station, *59 u*	15	55____
23590	Control Tower, *57-59*	20	110____
23596	Water Tank, *57-58*	25	103____
23598	Talking Station Record, *57-59*	5	19____
23599	Talking Station Record, *57*	9	36____
23600	Crossing Gate with bell, *57-58*	13	105____
23601	Crossing Gate, *59-62*	13	83____
23602	Crossing Gate, *63-64*	13	53____
23743	Track Maintenance Car, *60-64*	90	147____
23750	Trestle Bridge, *57-61*	26	75____
23758	Sam the Semaphore Man, *57*	29	85____
23759	Bell Danger Signal, *56-60*	12	86____
23760	Highway Flasher, *57-60*	9	54____
23761	Semaphore, *57-60*	22	79____
23763	Bell Danger Signal, *61-64*	11	81____
23764	Flasher Signal, *61-64*	12	51____
23769	Aircraft Beacon, *57-64*	13	75____
23771	Stockyard and Car, *57-61*	29	113____
23772	Water Tower, *57-64*	20	150____
23774	Floodlight Tower, *57-64*	16	109____
23778	Street Lamp Set, *57-64*	8	39____
23779	Oil Drum Loader, *57-61*	55	198____
23780	Gabe the Lamplighter-58-59		
	(A) Dark green base	294	604____
	(B) Light green base	650	900____
23785	Coal Loader, *57-60*	130	216____
23786	Talking Station, *57-59*	60	83____
23787	Log Loader, *57-60*	90	253____
23788	Suburban Station, *57-64*	10	60____
23789	Station and Baggage Smasher, *58-59*	55	217____
23791	Cow on Track, black/white or brown/white, *57-59*	28	90 ____
23796	Sawmill, *57-64*	105	168____
23830	Piggyback UnLoader, *59-60*	39	118____
24003	Santa Fe BoxCar, *58*		
	(A) Unpainted tuscan plastic	14	41____
	(B) Tuscan, painted		713____
24006	Great Northern BoxCar, *57-58*		2500____
24016	MKT BoxCar, *58*	260	673____
24019	Seaboard BoxCar, *58-61 u*	18	35____
24023	Baltimore & Ohio BoxCar, *58-59*	34	119____
24026	Central of Georgia BoxCar, *58*	32	132____
24029	BAR State of Maine Boxcar		
	(A) Knuckle couplers, *57-60*	58	91____
	(B) Pike Master couplers, *61*	100	180____
24030	MKT BoxCar, *60 u*		
	(A) Unpainted yellow plastic	10	17____
	(B) Yellow-painted plastic	50	607____

			Good	Exc
___	**24033**	Missouri Pacific BoxCar, *58*	48	122
___	**24036**	New Haven BoxCar, *58-60*	24	95
	24039	Rio Grande BoxCar, *59*		
___		(A) Unpainted white plastic	18	66
___		(B) Unpainted ivory plastic	10	41
___		(C) White, painted		228
___	**24043**	Boston & Maine BoxCar, *58-60*	33	79
___	**24045**	MEC Boxcar		NRS
___	**24047**	Great Northern BoxCar, *59*	55	182
___	**24048**	M&StL BoxCar, *59-62*	62	120
	24052	UFGE BoxCar, *61*		
___		(A) Unpainted yellow plastic	11	19
___		(B) Yellow-painted	150	208
	24054	Santa Fe BoxCar, *62-64, 66*		
___		(A) Red-painted plastic, *62-64*	20	54
___		(B) Unpainted red plastic, *66*	9	34
	24055	Gold Belt Line BoxCar, *60-61*		
___		(A) Opening with door	14	52
___		(B) Opening without door	14	35
	24056	Boston & Maine BoxCar, *61*		
___		(A) Blue-painted black plastic	70	283
___		(B) Unpainted blue plastic	27	136
	24057	Mounds BoxCar, *62*		
___		(A) White	5	11
___		(B) Ivory	9	19
	24058	Post BoxCar, white or ivory, *63-64*		
___		(A) Cereal	8	29
___		(B) Cereals	11	23
___	**24059**	Boston & Maine BoxCar, *63*	48	189
___	**24060**	M&StL BoxCar, *63-64*	39	130
	24065	NYC BoxCar, *60-64*		
___		(A) Knuckle couplers	41	167
___		(B) Pike Master couplers	25	75
___	**24066**	L&N BoxCar, blue-painted, *60*	80	165
___	**24067**	Keystone Line BoxCar, *60* * *u*	1350	2425
___	**24068**	Planters Peanuts BoxCar, *61* * *u*		NRS
	24076	Union Pacific Stock Car, *57-60*		
___		(A) Knuckle couplers	32	77
___		(B) Pike Master couplers	28	49
	24077	Northern Pacific Stock Car, *59-62*		
___		(A) Knuckle couplers	85	369
___		(B) Pike Master couplers	60	152
___	**24103**	Norfolk & Western Gondola, black plastic, *58, 63-64*	7	20
	24106	Pennsylvania Gondola, *60 u*		
___		(A) Unpainted tuscan plastic	7	19
___		(B) Tuscan, painted	43	160

		Good	Exc
24109	C&O Gondola with pipes, *57-60*		
	(A) Silver plastic or cardboard pipes	24	63____
	(B) Orange cardboard pipes	45	125____
24110	Pennsylvania Gondola, *59 u*		
	(A) Unpainted tuscan plastic	5	12____
	(B) Tuscan, painted	20	60____
24113	Delaware & Hudson Gondola, *57-59*	14	28____
24116	Southern Gondola, *57-60*	19	78____
24120	Texas & Pacific Gondola, *60 u*		
	(A) Unpainted green plastic	14	58____
	(B) Green, painted	100	300____
24124	Boston & Maine Gondola, *63-64*		
	(A) Unpainted blue	5	16____
	(B) Dark blue-painted	72	222____
24125	Bethlehem Steel Gondola, *60-66*		
	(A) Gray, painted with rail load	24	118____
	(B) Unpainted gray without load	9	21____
24126	Frisco Gondola, tuscan, *61*	33	136____
24127	Monon Gondola, *61-65*		
	(A) Knuckle couplers	5	14____
	(B) Pike Master couplers	4	11____
24130	Pennsylvania Gondola, *60 u*		
	(A) Pike Master couplers	9	18____
	(B) Fixed or operating knuckle couplers	4	12____
24203	Baltimore & Ohio Hopper, *58, 63-64*		
	(A) Unpainted black, *58*	20	30____
	(B) Black, painted, *58*	150	275____
	(C) Marbleized, *58*	150	275____
	(D) PM trucks and couplers, *63-64*	17	52____
24206	CB&Q Hopper, *58*	35	110____
24209	Jersey Central Hopper, *57-60*	27	121____
24213	Wabash Hopper, *58-60*	15	25____
24216	Union Pacific Hopper, *58-60*	22	66____
24219	Western Maryland Hopper, *58-59*	42	92____
24221	C&EI Hopper, *59-60*	35	162____
24222	Domino Sugar Hopper, *63-64**	138	383____
24225	Santa Fe Hopper, *60-65*		
	(A) Red-painted, knuckle couplers	15	43____
	(B) Red-painted, PM couplers	9	30____
24225	(C) Unpainted red plastic, PM couplers	25	42____
24230	Peabody Hopper, *61-64*		
	(A) Knuckle couplers	21	75____
	(B) Pike Master couplers	21	58____
24309	Gulf Tank Car, *57-58*	4	24____
24310	Gulf Tank Car, *58-60*	8	22____
24313	Gulf Tank Car, *57-60*		
	(A) Full tank	21	50____
	(B) Open-bottom tank		692____

			Good	Exc
	24316	Mobilgas Tank Car, *57-61, 65-66*		
____		(A) Knuckle couplers, complete tank	20	71
____		(B) Knuckle couplers, open-bottom tank	70	240
____		(C) Pike Master couplers	5	42
____	**24319**	PRR Salt Tank Car, *58**	155	524
	24320	Deep Rock Tank Car, *60-61*		
____		(A) Complete Tank, *60*	50	332
____		(B) Open-bottom Tank, *61*	100	459
____	**24321**	Deep Rock Tank Car, *59*	20	82
	24322	Gulf Tank Car, *59*		
____		(A) Full tank	15	21
____		(B) Open-bottom tank	25	99
	24323	Baker's Chocolate Tank Car, *59-60**		
____		(A) Type II frame white, white ends	480	939
____		(B) Type II frame white, gray, painted ends	118	379
____		(C) Type III frame white, open-bottom tank		2100
____	**24324**	Hooker Tank Car, *59-60*	31	116
	24325	Gulf Tank Car, *60*		
____		(A) Type II plastic frame	6	17
____		(B) Type III plastic frame, open-bottom tank	15	100
	24328	Shell Tank Car, *62-66*		
____		(A) Yellow plastic	7	22
____		(B) Yellow-painted	300	450
____	**24329**	Hooker Tank Car with platform, *61*	10	34
____	**24329**	Hooker Tank Car, no platform or number, *62-65 u*	9	27
____	**24330**	Baker's Chocolate Tank Car, *61-62*	54	96
	24403	Illinois Central Reefer		
____		(A) Unpainted orange plastic	18	23
____		(B) Orange-painted		341
____	**24409**	Northern Pacific Reefer, *58*	355	1322
____	**24413**	ART Reefer, *57-60*	38	141
____	**24416**	Northwestern Reefer, *58*	680	2027
____	**24419**	Canadian National Reefer, *58-59*	112	818
____	**24420**	Simmons Reefer, *58** *u*	660	1321
____	**24422**	Great Northern BoxCar, *63-65, 66 u*	50	148
	24422	Great Northern Reefer, *63-65, 66 u*		
____		(A) Unpainted green plastic, non-opening door	12	18
____		(B) Green, painted plastic, opening door	65	193
____		(C) Green, painted plastic, non-opening door	60	192
	24425	BAR Reefer, *60*		
____		(A) Knuckle couplers	175	639
____		(B) Pike Master couplers	200	473
____	**24426**	Rath Packing Reefer, *60-61*	215	303
____	**24516**	New Haven FlatCar, *57-59*	12	40
____	**24519**	Pennsylvania FlatCar, *58*	265	1204
____	**24529**	Erie Floodlight Car, *57-58*	10	52

		Good	Exc
24533	AFL Track Cleaning Car, *58-66*	10	27____
24536	Monon FlatCar, *58*	385	1705____
24537	New Haven FlatCar, *58 u*	10	38____
24539	New Haven FlatCar, *58-59, 63-64*		
	(A) Silver plastic or cardboard pipes, *58-59*	12	30____
	(B) Orange cardboard pipes, *63-64*	17	50____
	(C) Orange pipes, no number, *63-64*	25	57____
24540	New Haven FlatCar, *60 u*	44	305____
24543	American Flyer Lines Crane, *58*	11	44____
24546	AFL Work and Boom Car, *58-64*	10	55____
24547	Erie Floodlight Car, *58*	265	939____
24549	Erie Floodlight Car, *58-66*		
	(A) Yellow generator, knuckle couplers	15	47____
	(B) Red generator, PM couplers	12	25____
	(C) Yellow generator, PM couplers	8	37____
24550	Monon FlatCar, *59-64*	23	88____
24553	Rocket Transport FlatCar, *58-60*	22	85____
24556	Rock Island FlatCar, *59*	22	52____
24557	U.S. Navy Flatcar with jeeps, *59-61*	29	87____
24558	Canadian Pacific Flatcar with trees, *59-60*	102	469____
24559	New Haven FlatCar, *59 u*	80	245____
24561	American Flyer Lines Crane, *59-61*		
	(A) Gray, painted frame, knuckle couplers, *59*	10	40 ____
	(B) Unpainted gray frame, PM couplers, *60-61*	8	60 ____
24562	New York Central FlatCar, *60*	14	28____
24564	New Haven FlatCar, *60 u*		
	(A) Silver-gray plastic pipes	9	38____
	(B) Orange cardboard pipes	25	60____
24565	FY&PRR Flatcar with cannon, *60-61**	38	177____
24566	National Car FlatCar, *61-65*	26	118____
24566	New Haven FlatCar, *61-64*		
	(A) Unpainted black body, blue or red tractor	27	186 ____
	(B) Unpainted gray body, *61*	300	892____
24569	AFL Crane, *62-66*	11	28____
24572	U.S. Navy Flatcar with 2 jeeps, *61*		
	(A) Gray plastic or painted, knuckle couplers	38	146 ____
	(B) Gray plastic, Pike Master couplers	75	189____
24574	U.S. Air Force Flatcar with rocket fuel tanks, *60-61*		
	(A) Knuckle couplers	40	163____
	(B) Pike Master couplers	39	130____
24575	Borden's Milk FlatCar, unmarked, *66 u*	9	37____
24575	National Car Co. FlatCar, *60-66*		
	(A) Knuckle couplers	17	118____
	(B) Pike Master couplers	17	47____

		Good	Exc
24577	Illinois Central Flatcar with jet engine, *60-61, 63-64*		
____	(A) Knuckle couplers	48	266
____	(B) Pike Master couplers	42	175
____ **24578**	New Haven Flatcar with Corvette, *62-63*	113	277
24579	Illinois Central FlatCar, *60-61*		
____	(A) Silver pipes, knuckle couplers	45	164
____	(B) Orange pipes, PM couplers	50	210
24603	AFL Caboose, *57-58*		
____	(A) Unpainted red plastic	5	13
____	(B) Painted red plastic		NRS
____ **24610**	AFL Caboose, *58-60 u*	5	18
____ **24619**	AFL Bay Window Caboose, *58*	20	155
____ **24626**	AFL Caboose, *58*	9	29
____ **24627**	AFL Caboose, *59-60*	4	17
____ **24630**	AFL Caboose, *59-61 u*	4	18
24631	AFL Caboose, yellow-painted, *59-61, 63-65*		
	(A) Knuckle couplers, stripe, *59-61*	8	34
	(B) Pike Master couplers, stripe, *63-65*	6	29
	(C) Pike Master couplers, no stripe, *65*	80	165
____ **24632**	American Flyer Lines Caboose, *59*	28	62
____ **24633**	AFL Bay Window Caboose, *59-62*	30	67
24634	AFL Bay Window Caboose, *63-66*		
____	(A) Unpainted red plastic, illuminated	20	36
____	(B) Red-painted, illuminated	20	62
____	(C) Nonilluminated-plastic wheels	8	20
24636	American Flyer Lines Caboose, *60-66*		
____	(A) Red plastic	6	16
____	(B) Yellow-painted	171	470
____	(C) Red-painted		500
____ **24638**	AFL Bay Window Caboose, *62*	27	64
24720	FY&PRR Coach, *59-61*		
____	(A) Unpainted yellow	23	42
____	(B) Yellow-painted	29	56
24730	FY&PRR Overland Express Baggage Car, *59-60*		
____	(A) Unpainted yellow	20	39
____	(B) Yellow-painted	29	56
____ **24733**	AFL Pikes Peak Coach, *57*	145	611
____ **24739**	AFL Niagara Falls Combination Car, *57*		NRS
____ **24740**	Baggage Express Combination Car, *60*	28	41
____ **24750**	FY&PRR Combination Car, *60-61*	123	187
24773	AFL Columbus Combination Car, *57-58, 60-62*	65	152
____			
____ **24776**	AFL Columbus Combination Car, *59*	60	157
____ **24793**	AFL Jefferson Coach, *57-58, 60-62*	70	193
____ **24794**	AFL Jefferson Coach, *59*		1700
24813	AFL Hamilton Vista Dome Car, *57-58, 60-62*	60	140
____			

		Good	Exc
24816	AFL Hamilton Vista Dome Car, *59*	60	160____
24833	AFL Washington Observation Car, *57-58, 60-62*	60	127 ____
24836	AFL Washington Observation Car, *59*	60	121____
24837	Union Pacific Combination Car, *59-60**	85	245____
24838	Union Pacific Coach, *59-60**	90	347____
24839	Union Pacific Vista Dome Car, *59-60**	95	330____
24840	Union Pacific Observation Car, *59-60**	95	311____
24843	Northern Pacific Combination Car, no lights, *58*	90	255 ____
24846	Northern Pacific Coach, no lights, *58*	90	305____
24849	Northern Pacific Vista Dome Car, no lights, *58*	90	301 ____
24853	Northern Pacific Observation Car, no lights, *58*	90	240
24856	MP Eagle Hill Combination Car, *58, 63-64**	125	325____
24859	MP Eagle Lake Coach, *58, 63-64**	130	435____
24863	MP Eagle Creek Coach, *58, 63-64**	120	443____
24866	MP Eagle Valley Observation Car, *58, 63-64**	120	385 ____
24867	AFL Combination Car, no lights, *58 u, 60 u*	46	177____
24868	AFL Observation Car, no lights, *58 u, 60 u*	50	213____
24869	AFL Coach, no lights, *58 u, 60 u*	50	185____
24963	Car Assortment, *58*		NRS____
25003	American Flyer Log Car, *57-60*		
	(A) Number and lettering on bin	85	388____
	(B) No number or lettering on bin	20	66____
25005	Mail Car, *57*		NRS____
25016	Southern Pacific Lumber Unloading Car, *57-60*	44	125 ____
25019	Operating Milk Car, *57-60*	65	203____
25025	CB&Q Dump Car, *58-60*	75	191____
25031	AFL Caboose, *58*		NRS____
25042	Erie Operating BoxCar, *58*	70	215____
25045	Rocket Launcher FlatCar, *57-60*	16	60____
25046	Rocket Launcher Car, *60*	14	94____
25049	Rio Grande BoxCar, *58-60*	85	174____
25052	AFL Bay Window Caboose, *58*	53	118____
25056	USM Boxcar and Rocket Launcher FlatCar, *59*	125	319 ____
25057	TNT Exploding BoxCar, *60*	70	239____
25058	Southern Pacific FlatCar, *61-64*	48	152____
25059	Rocket Launcher FlatCar, *60-64*	21	82____
25060	CB&Q Dump Car, *61-64*	80	220____
25061	TNT Exploding BoxCar, *61*	100	365____
25062	Mine Carrier Exploding BoxCar, *62-64*		
	(A) Silver roof and ends	125	856____
	(B) Tuscan roof and ends	125	539____
25071	AF Tie-Jector Car, *61-64*	7	23____
25081	NYC Operating BoxCar, *61-64*	15	53____

			Good	Exc
_____ 25082	New Haven Operating BoxCar, *61-64*		11	64
25515	U.S. Air Force FlatCar, black, *60-63*			
_____	(A) Unpainted yellow sled		78	183
_____	(B) Yellow-painted sled		200	885
_____ 26101	Curved Track Panel, *65-66*		3	25
_____ 26121	Straight Track Panel, *65-66*		4	35
_____ 26122	Straight Panel with Whistle, *65-66*		7	104
_____ 26141	Switch Panel, right hand, *65-66*		7	54
_____ 26142	Switch Panel, left hand, *65-66*		7	54
_____ 26151	Crossover Panel, *65-66*		7	123
_____ 26261	Curved Snow Panel			94
_____ 26262	Straight Snow Panel			94
_____ 26263	Snow Switch, right hand			144
_____ 26264	Snow Switch, left hand			144
_____ 26265	Crossover Snow Panel			94
_____ 26300	PM Straight Track, *61-64*			1
_____ 26301	PM Straight Track, *61-64*			4
_____ 26302	PM Straight Track with Uncoupler, *61-64*			2
_____ 26310	PM Curved Track, *61-64*			1
_____ 26320	PM Remote Switch, right hand, *61-64*		6	13
_____ 26321	PM Remote Switch, left hand, *61-64*		7	12
_____ 26322	PM 90-degree Crossing, *61-64*		1	6
_____ 26323	PM Manual Switch, right hand, *61-64*		1	5
_____ 26324	PM Manual Switch, left hand, *61-64*		1	5
_____ 26340	PM Steel Track Pins, *61-64*			1
_____ 26341	PM Insulating Pins, *61-64*			8
_____ 26342	PM Adapter Pins, *61-64*			4
_____ 26343	PM Track Locks, *61-64*			14
_____ 26344	PM Track Terminal, *61-64*			1
_____ 26415	Track Assortment, *60-62*			NRS
_____ 26419	Accessory Package		4	15
_____ 26421	Accessory Package, *60*			403
_____ 26425	Track Assortment Pack, *60*		6	11
_____ 26426	Accessory Package, *60-61*			234
_____ 26428	Accessory Pack with box, *58 u*			410
_____ 26520	Knuckle Coupler Kit, *57-64*		1	5
_____ 26521	Knuckle Coupler Kit, *57-58*			24
_____ 26601	Fiber Roadbed, *59-62*			1
_____ 26602	Fiber Roadbed, *59-61-62*			1
_____ 26611	4-Level Trestle Display, *59-61*			600
_____ 26670	Track Trip, *57-58*		4	33
_____ 26671	Track Trip, *59*		3	42
_____ 26672	Track Trip, *60*		2	34
_____ 26673	Track Trip, *61-64*		2	26
_____ 26690	Track Terminal, with envelope, *57-59*		1	2
_____ 26691	Steel Pins, *57-60, 64*			5
_____ 26692	Fiber Pins, *57-60, 64*			5
_____ 26693	Track Locks, dozen, *57-60, 64*		2	6
_____ 26700	Straight Track, *57-64*			1

GILBERT PRODUCTION 1946-1966

		Good	Exc
26704	Manual Uncoupler,		1____
26708	Horn Control, *57-58*	4	9____
26710	Straight Track, half section, *57-64*		1____
26718	Remote Control Switch, left hand, *57*	6	17____
26719	Remote Control Switch, right hand, *57*	6	17____
26720	Curved Track, *57-64*		1____
26722	Curved Track, dozen	6	11____
26726	Straight Rubber Roadbed, half section, *58*	1	2____
26727	Rubber Roadbed, half section, *58*	1	2____
26730	Curved Track, half section, *57-64*		1____
26739	Whistle Control, *57-58*	13	43____
26742	Remote Control Switches, pair, *57*	9	50____
26744	Manual Switches, pair, *57-58*	4	16____
26745	Railroad Crossing, *57-64*	1	21____
26746	Rubber Roadbed, *57-64*		2____
26747	Rubber Roadbed, *57-64*		2____
26748	Re-railer, *57-64*	3	25____
26749	Bumper, *57-60*	2	18____
26751	Pike Planning Kit, *57-59*	8	24____
26752	Remote Control Uncoupler, *57-58, 60-61*	1	15____
26756	Bumper, *61-64*	5	17____
26760	Remote Control Switches, pair, *58-64*	11	41____
26761	Remote Control Switch, left hand, *58-64*	7	17____
26762	Remote Control Switch, right hand, *58-64*	7	17____
26770	Manual Switches, pair, *59-64*	4	15____
26781	Trestle Set, *57*	10	27____
26782	Trestle Set, *58-60*	4	24____
26783	Hi-Trestles, *57*	8	41____
26790	Trestle Set, *61-64*	13	30____
26810	Pow-R-Clips, *60-64*		6____
27441	Lamps-3 Bulbs, red	1	4____
27443	Lamps-3 Bulbs, green	1	3____
27458	Lamps-3 Bulbs, clear	1	12____
27460	Lamp Assortment, *59, 64*	10	191____
Unnumbered Items			
	Buffalo Hunt Gondola, *63-64*	4	14____
	Freight Ahead Caboose, *63*	3	7____

Mint

___	0700	Boxcar (NASG), *81 u*	113
___	2300	Oil Drum Loader, *83, 87*	65
___	2321	Operating Sawmill, *84, 86-87*	90
___	8150/52	Southern Pacific Alco PA1 Diesel, AA Set, *81*	363
___	8151	Southern Pacific Alco PA1 Diesel B-Unit, *82*	185
___	8153/55	Baltimore & Ohio Alco PA1 Diesel, AA Set, *81-83*	239
___	8154	Baltimore & Ohio Alco PA1 Diesel B-Unit *81-83*	100
___	8251/53	Erie Alco PA1 Diesel, AA Set, *82*	250
___	8252	Erie Alco PA1 Diesel B-Unit *82*	151
___	8350	Boston & Maine GP7 Diesel, *83*	300
___	8458	Southern GP9 Diesel, *84*	208
___	8459	Chessie System GP20 Diesel, *84*	271
___	8551	Santa Fe GP20 Diesel, *86*	205
___	8552	New York Central GP9 Diesel, *86*	188
___	9000	B&O Flatcar with trailers, *81, 83*	42
___	9002	B&M Flatcar with logs, *83*	83
___	9004	Southern Flatcar with trailers, *84*	41
___	9005	NYC Flatcar with trailers, *86*	33
___	9100	Gulf 1-D Tank Car, *79*	42
___	9101	Union 76 1-D Tank Car, *80*	35
___	9102	B&O 1-D Tank Car, *81-83*	27
___	9104	B&M 3-D Tank Car, *83*	92
___	9105	Southern 3-D Tank Car, *'84*	28
___	9106	NYC 3-D Tank Car, *86*	26
___	9200	Chessie System Hopper, with coal, *79*	38
___	9201	B&O Covered Hopper, *81, 83*	32
___	9203	Boston & Maine Hopper, *83*	78
___	9204	Southern Hopper, *84*	24
___	9205	Pennsylvania Covered Hopper, *84*	35
___	9206	New York Central Covered Hopper, *84*	29
___	9207	B&O Covered Hopper, *86*	30
___	9208	Santa Fe Covered Hopper, *86*	27
___	9209	New York Central Hopper, *86*	29
___	9300	Burlington Gondola, *80*	26
___	9301	B&O Gondola with canisters, *81, 83*	23
___	9303	Southern Gondola with canisters, *84*	27
___	9304	NYC Gondola with canisters, *86*	25
___	9400	Chessie System Bay Window Caboose, *80*	30
___	9401	B&O Bay Window Caboose, *81, 83*	31
___	9402	B&M Bay Window Caboose, *83*	68
___	9403	Southern Bay Window Caboose, *84*	35
___	9404	NYC Bay Window Caboose, *86*	34
___	9405	Santa Fe Bay Window Caboose, *86*	38
___	9500	Southern Pacific Combination Car, *81*	90
___	9501	Southern Pacific Coach, *81*	130

Mint

9502	Southern Pacific Vista Dome Car, *81*	123____
9503	Southern Pacific Observation Car, *81*	90____
9504	Erie Combination Car, *82*	55____
9505	Erie Coach, *82*	75____
9506	Erie Vista Dome Car, *82*	72____
9507	Erie Observation Car, *82*	55____
9700	Santa Fe Boxcar, *79*	
	(A) Door nibs	108____
	(B) No door nibs	50____
9701	Rock Island Boxcar, *80*	31____
9702	B&O Sentinel Boxcar, *81, 83*	36____
9703	Boston & Maine Boxcar, *83*	95____
9704	Southern Boxcar, *84*	38____
9705	Pennsylvania Boxcar, *84*	46____
9706	New York Central Pacemaker Boxcar, *84*	80____
9707	Railbox Boxcar, *84*	57____
9708	Conrail Boxcar, *84*	43____
9709	Baltimore & Ohio Boxcar, *86*	32____
9710	Santa Fe Boxcar, *86*	33____
9711	Southern Pacific Boxcar, *86*	31____
9712	Illinois Central Gulf Boxcar, *86*	34____
9713	New York Central Boxcar, *86*	35____
22678	B&M Baked Beans Boxcar (NETCA), *10*	45____
22997	Oil Drum Loader, *99*	102____
24213	Universal Lockon for S Gauge Track, *10*	4____
41000	Sierra Beer Boxcar (TTOS), *13*	90____
41001	Marathon Motors Boxcar (NASG), *12*	75____
41002	Green Bay & Western Reefer (SCSG), *13*	80____
41003	Aluminum Ore Covered Hopper (TCA), *13*	70____
41004	Lifesaver Caboose, (TTOS Cal-Stewart), *13*	80____
41005	Pennsylvania 3-bay Hopper (NASG), *13*	80____
41006	Reading Flatcar (TCA), *14*	80____
41007	Reading Boxcar (TCA), *14*	80____
41009	Milwaukee Road Boxcar (NASG), *14*	90____
41018	Candy Cane Tank Car (TTOS Cal-Stewart), *14*	65____
41019	D&H "I Love NY" Boxcar (TCA), *15*	65____
41020	Spreckels Sugar Hopper, (TCA Rocky Mountain), *15*	60____
41021	BNSF Boxcar (NASG), *15*	70____
41023	G. Fox & Co. Boxcar (NETCA)	138____
41023/1	Plibrico Flatcar (NASG), *16*	80____
41024	Forest Service/Smokey Bear Gondola (TTOS), *15*	60____
41025	Monsanto Chemical Tank Car, *15*	65____
41027	TTOS 50th Anniversary Mint Car, *16*	80____
41028	NASA Rocket Launching Car (TCA), *16*	75____
41029	NASA Unloading Boxcar (TCA), *16*	75____
41942	Youngstown Steel "Spirit of '76" Baldwin Diesel Switcher, *14*	290____
42169	KCS SD70ACe Diesel Locomotive "4042," CC, *12*	480____
42173	KCS SD70ACe Diesel Locomotive "4022," gray, *12*	480____
42500	UP "Building America" SD70ACe Diesel "8348," CC, *12*	460____

Mint

____	**42501**	UP "Building America" SD70ACe Diesel, nonpowered, *12*	240
____	**42502**	UP "Building America" SD70ACe Diesel "8461," CC, *12*	480
____	**42504**	KCS SD70ACe Diesel "4042," CC, *12*	480
____	**42505**	BNSF SD70ACe Diesel "9344," CC, *12*	480
____	**42506**	CSX SD70ACe Diesel "4847," CC, *12*	480
____	**42507**	KCS SD70ACe Diesel "4847," gray, *12*	480
____	**42508**	SP UP Heritage SD70ACe Diesel "1865," CC, *12*	480
____	**42509**	D&RGW UP Heritage SD70ACe Diesel "1870," CC, *12*	480
____	**42510**	C&NW UP Heritage SD70ACe Diesel "1859," CC, *12*	480
____	**42511**	MP UP Heritage SD70ACe Diesel "1851," CC, *12*	480
____	**42512**	Santa Fe U33C Diesel "8525," CC, *12-13*	480
____	**42513**	D&H U33C Diesel "761," CC, *12-13*	480
____	**42514**	IC U33C Diesel "5057," CC, *12*	480
____	**42515**	PC U33C Diesel "6560," CC, *12-13*	480
____	**42516**	Milwaukee Road U33C Diesel "5705," CC, *12-13*	480
____	**42519**	CNJ NS Heritage SD70ACe Diesel "1071," CC, *12*	480
____	**42520**	CNJ NS Heritage SD70ACe Diesel "1834," nonpowered, *12*	240
____	**42521**	DL&W NS Heritage SD70ACe Diesel "1074," CC, *12*	480
____	**42522**	DL&W NS Heritage SD70ACe Diesel "1856," nonpowered, *12*	240
____	**42523**	Erie NS Heritage SD70ACe Diesel "1068," CC, *12*	480
____	**42524**	Erie NS Heritage SD70ACe Diesel "1835," nonpowered, *12*	240
____	**42525**	Illinois Terminal NS Heritage SD70ACe Diesel "1072," CC, *12*	480
____	**42526**	Illinois Terminal NS Heritage SD70ACe Diesel "1899," nonpowered , *12*	240
____	**42527**	NYC NS Heritage SD70ACe Diesel "1066," CC, *12*	480
____	**42528**	NYC NS Heritage SD70ACe Diesel "1834," nonpowered, *12*	240
____	**42529**	PC NS Heritage SD70ACe Diesel "1073," CC, *12*	480
____	**42530**	PC NS Heritage SD70ACe Diesel "1971," nonpowered, *12*	240
____	**42531**	Reading NS Heritage SD70ACe Diesel "1067," CC, *13*	480
____	**42532**	Reading NS Heritage SD70ACe Diesel, nonpowered, *13*	240
____	**42533**	Savannah & Atlanta NS Heritage SD70ACe Diesel "1065," CC, *13*	480
____	**42534**	Savannah & Atlanta NS Heritage SD70ACe Diesel, nonpowered, *13*	240
____	**42535**	Virginian NS Heritage SD70ACe Diesel "1069," CC, *13*	480
____	**42536**	Virginian NS Heritage SD70ACe Diesel "1910," nonpowered, *13*	240
____	**42537**	Wabash NS Heritage SD70ACe Diesel "1070," CC, *13*	480
____	**42538**	Wabash NS Heritage SD70ACe Diesel "1880," nonpowered, *13*	240
____	**42542**	Central of Georgia NS Heritage ES44AC Diesel "8101," CC, *13-16*	515

42543	Central of Georgia NS Heritage ES44AC Diesel "1833," nonpowered, *13-16*	270 ____
42544	Conrail NS Heritage ES44AC Diesel "8098," CC, *13-16*	515 ____
42545	Conrail NS Heritage ES44AC Diesel "1976," nonpowered, *13*	270 ____
42546	Interstate NS Heritage ES44AC Diesel "8105," CC, *13-16*	515 ____
42547	Interstate NS Heritage ES44AC Diesel "1896," nonpowered, *13*	270 ____
42548	LV NS Heritage ES44AC Diesel "8104," CC, *13*	515 ____
42549	LV NS Heritage ES44AC Diesel "1847," nonpowered, *13*	270 ____
42550	Nickel Plate Road NS Heritage ES44AC Diesel "8100" CC, *13-16*	515 ____
42551	Nickel Plate Road NS Heritage ES44AC Diesel "1881," nonpowered, *13*	270 ____
42552	N&W NS Heritage ES44AC Diesel "8103," CC, *13-16*	515 ____
42553	N&W NS Heritage ES44AC Diesel "1838," nonpowered, *13*	270 ____
42554	PRR NS Heritage ES44AC Diesel "8102," CC, *13-16*	515 ____
42555	PRR NS Heritage ES44AC Diesel "1846," nonpowered, *13*	270 ____
42556	Southern NS Heritage ES44AC Diesel "8099," CC, *13*	515 ____
42557	Southern NS Heritage ES44AC Diesel "1894," nonpowered, *13*	270 ____
42558	Norfolk Southern NS Heritage ES44AC Diesel "8114," CC, *13-15*	515 ____
42559	Norfolk Southern NS Heritage ES44AC Diesel "1982," nonpowered, *13*	270 ____
42560	Monongahela NS Heritage ES44AC Diesel "8025," CC, *13*	515 ____
42561	Monongahela NS Heritage ES44AC Diesel "1901," nonpowered, *13*	270 ____
42562	NKP 2-8-4 Berkshire Locomotive "765," *15, 16*	350 ____
42563	Bethlehem Steel 0-6-0 Dockside Steam Switcher 71", *13-16*	95
42564	Reading 0-6-0 Dockside Steam Switcher "1242," *13, 16*	95 ____
42565	C&O 0-6-0 Dockside Steam Switcher "65," *13*	95 ____
42566	AFL 0-6-0 Dockside Steam Switcher "269," *13-16*	95 ____
42567	Christmas 0-6-0 Dockside Steam Locomotive "2013," *13-14*	98 ____
42569	C&O 2-8-4 Berkshire Locomotive "2687," *15-16*	350 ____
42570	D&H Alco PA A-A Diesel, Set "18-19," CC, *14, 17*	675 ____
42573	SP Alco PA A-A Diesel, Set "94-95," CC, *14, 17*	675 ____
42580	BNSF ES44AC Diesel "6438," CC, *13*	515 ____
42581	BNSF ES44AC Diesel "6423," CC, *14*	515 ____
42582	CP ES44AC Diesel "8744," CC, *14*	515 ____
42583	CP ES44AC Diesel "8730," CC, *14*	515 ____
42584	CSX ES44AC Diesel "924," CC, *14*	515 ____
42585	CSX ES44AC Diesel "937," CC, *14*	515 ____
42586	KCS ES44AC Diesel "4692," CC, *14*	515 ____
42587	KCS ES44AC Diesel "4696," CC, *14*	515 ____

Mint

____ 42588	UP ES44AC Diesel "7523," CC, *14*	515
____ 42589	UP ES44AC Diesel "7494," CC, *14*	515
____ 42590	UP Auto Carrier "ETTX 715001," *17*	75
____ 42591	CSX Auto Carrier "TTGX 150648," *17*	75
____ 42592	NS Auto Carrier "NS 171253," *17*	75
____ 42593	BNSF Auto Carrier "TTGX 965530," *17*	75
____ 42597	CP Baldwin Diesel Switcher "7070," *14-17*	283
____ 42598	UP Baldwin Diesel Switcher "1206," *14-17*	247
____ 42599	Youngstown Steel Diesel Switcher, "805," *15-17*	290
____ 44000	Flatcar "16001" (TCA), *17*	85
____ 44001	Flatcar "16002" (TCA), *17*	85
____ 44002	Deep-Rock 3-D Tank Car "24317" (GGAFC), *17*	80
____ 44003	Deep-Rock 3-D Tank Car "24318" (GGAFC), *17*	80
____ 44004	A&P Wood-sided Reefer "733" (TCA Atlantic), *17*	50
____ 44005	A&P Wood-sided Reefer "734" (TCA Atlantic), *17*	50
____ 44006	A&P Wood-sided Reefer "735" (TCA Atlantic), *17*	50
____ 44007	A&P Wood-sided Reefer "736" (TCA Atlantic), *17*	50
____ 44008	A&P Wood-sided Reefer "737" (TCA Atlantic), *17*	50
____ 44009	A&P Wood-sided Reefer "738" (TCA Atlantic), *17*	50
____ 44010	Gulf Tank Car (NASG), *17*	70
____ 44011	Gulf Tank Car (NASG), *18*	70
____ 44014	Coors Reefer "5400" (TCA Rocky Mountain) , *14*	70
____ 44014	NYC 2-Bay Hopper "870818," *18*	60
____ 44015	Coors Reefer "5403" (TCA Rocky Mountain), *15*	70
____ 44016	Coors Reefer "5408" (TCA Rocky Mountain), *16*	70
____ 44017	Coors Reefer "5413" (TCA Rocky Mountain), *17*	70
____ 44020	Nickel Plate Road 2-8-4 Berkshire Locomotive "765," FlyerChief, *17-18*	370
____ 44021	Nickel Plate Road 2-8-4 Berkshire Locomotive "759," FlyerChief, *17-18*	370
____ 44022	Pere Marquette 2-8-4 Berkshire Locomotive "1225," FlyerChief, *17-18*	370
____ 44023	Pere Marquette 2-8-4 Berkshire Locomotive "1223," FlyerChief, *17-18*	370
____ 44024	Erie 2-8-4 Berkshire Locomotive "3362," FlyerChief, *17-18*	370
____ 44025	C&O 2-8-4 Berkshire Locomotive "2696," FlyerChief, *17-18*	370
____ 44026	Southern 2-8-4 Berkshire Locomotive "2716," FlyerChief, *17-18*	370
____ 44039	Polar Express Steam Passenger Set, FlyerChief, *17-18*	450
____ 44044	Santa Fe Docksider Steam Freight Set, FlyerChief, *18*	330
____ 44050	Nickel Plate Road 3-Bay Hopper "78002," *17-18*	60
____ 44051	Nickel Plate Road 3-Bay Hopper "78126," *17-18*	60
____ 44052	Nickel Plate Road 3-Bay Hopper "78154," *17-18*	60
____ 44053	Nickel Plate Road 3-Bay Hopper "78257," *17-18*	60
____ 44054	Nickel Plate Road 3-Bay Hopper "78849," *17-18*	60
____ 44055	C&O 3-Bay Hopper "79090," *17-18*	60
____ 44056	C&O 3-Bay Hopper "79261," *17-18*	60
____ 44057	C&O 3-Bay Hopper "79419," *17-18*	60
____ 44058	C&O 3-Bay Hopper "79611," *17-18*	60

Mint

44059	C&O 3-Bay Hopper "79951," *17-18*	60____
44060	AT&SF 3-Bay Hopper "78705," *17-18*	60____
44061	AT&SF 3-Bay Hopper "78721," *17-18*	60____
44062	AT&SF 3-Bay Hopper "78730," *17-18*	60____
44063	AT&SF 3-Bay Hopper "78754," *17-18*	60____
44064	AT&SF 3-Bay Hopper "78792," *17-18*	60____
44065	Erie 3-Bay Hopper "38303," *17-18*	60____
44066	Erie 3-Bay Hopper "38327," *17-18*	60____
44067	Erie 3-Bay Hopper "38333," *17-18*	60____
44068	Erie 3-Bay Hopper "38410," *17-18*	60____
44069	Erie 3-Bay Hopper "38489," *17-18*	60____
44070	ACL Boxcar "20921," *17-18*	60____
44071	ACL Boxcar "21003," *17-18*	60____
44072	MILW Boxcar "2151," *17-18*	60____
44073	MILW Boxcar "2156," *17-18*	60____
44074	DL&W Boxcar "47897," *17-18*	60____
44075	DL&W Boxcar "47974," *17-18*	60____
44076	PRR Boxcar "567427," *17-18*	60____
44077	PRR Boxcar "568169," *17-18*	60____
44078	Reading Boxcar "113029," *17-18*	60____
44079	Reading Boxcar "113054," *18*	60____
44080	NS Waffle-sided Boxcar "407014," *18*	65____
44081	NS Waffle-sided Boxcar "407407," *18*	65____
44082	D&RGW Waffle-sided Boxcar "65327," *18*	65____
44083	D&RGW Waffle-sided Boxcar "65349," *18*	65____
44084	MEC Waffle-sided Boxcar "29213," *18*	65____
44085	MEC Waffle-sided Boxcar "29225," *18*	65____
44086	SCL Waffle-sided Boxcar "80008," *18*	65____
44087	SCL Waffle-sided Boxcar "80326," *18*	65____
44088	Southern Waffle-sided Boxcar "528641," *18*	65____
44089	Southern Waffle-sided Boxcar "531876," *18*	65____
44090	B&O 2-Bay Hopper "727056," *18*	60____
44091	B&O 2-Bay Hopper "727189," *18*	60____
44092	B&O 2-Bay Hopper "727237," *18*	60____
44093	B&O 2-Bay Hopper "727341," *18*	60____
44094	B&O 2-Bay Hopper "727412," *18*	60____
44095	GN 2-Bay Hopper "73202," *18*	60____
44096	GN 2-Bay Hopper "73313," *18*	60____
44097	GN 2-Bay Hopper "73456," *18*	60____
44098	GN 2-Bay Hopper "73510," *18*	60____
44099	GN 2-Bay Hopper "73614," *18*	60____
44100	NYC 2-Bay Hopper "870048," *18*	60____
44101	NYC 2-Bay Hopper "870289," *18*	60____
44102	NYC 2-Bay Hopper "870426," *18*	60____
44103	NYC 2-Bay Hopper "870614," *18*	60____
44105	Reading 2-Bay Hopper "88030," *18*	60____
44106	Reading 2-Bay Hopper "88075," *18*	60____
44107	Reading 2-Bay Hopper "88112," *18*	60____
44108	Reading 2-Bay Hopper "88174," *18*	60____
44109	Reading 2-Bay Hopper "88200," *18*	60____

Mint

____**44110**	GN Extended Vision Caboose "X-106," *17-18*	65
____**44111**	C&NW B-W Caboose "11225," *18*	70
____**44112**	Pere Marquette NE Caboose "A909," *17-18*	65
____**44113**	Reading NE Caboose "92902," *17-18*	65
____**44114**	Wabash Offset Cupola Caboose "2738," *18*	70
____**44115**	B&M EMD GP7 Diesel "1567," FlyerChief, *17-18*	250
____**44116**	NYC EMD GP7 Diesel "5628," FlyerChief, *17-18*	250
____**44117**	Reading EMD GP7 Diesel "619," FlyerChief, *17-18*	250
____**44118**	GN EMD GP7 Diesel "601," FlyerChief, *17-18*	250
____**44119**	C&NW Baldwin Diesel Switcher, "1260," FlyerChief, *18*	250
____**44120**	NS Baldwin Diesel Switcher "661," FlyerChief, *18*	250
____**44121**	PRR Baldwin Diesel Switcher "9221," FlyerChief, *18*	250
____**44122**	Patapsco & Back Rivers Baldwin Diesel Switcher "309," FlyerChief, *18*	250
____**44123**	Nickel Plate Road 2-8-4 Berkshire Locomotive "765," CC, *18*	500
____**44124**	Pere Marquette 2-8-4 Berkshire Locomotive "1225," CC, *18*	500
____**44125**	C&O 2-8-4 Berkshire Locomotive "759," CC, *18*	500
____**44126**	Erie 2-8-4 Berkshire Locomotive "3361," CC, *18*	500
____**44127**	American Railroads 2-8-4 Berkshire Locomotive "759," CC, *18*	500
____**44128**	RF&P 2-8-4 Berkshire Locomotive "752," CC, *18*	500
____**44129**	2018 American Flyer Christmas Boxcar, *18*	60
____**44130**	Polar Express Baggage Car, *18*	80
____**44131**	Polar Express Hot Chocolate Car, *18*	80
____**44132**	Polar Express Passenger Coach Add-on Car, *18*	80
____**44133**	AF Traveling Showroom Aquarium Car, *18*	95
____**44134**	Polar Express Aquarium Car, *18*	100
____**44135**	FGE Wood-sided Refrigerator Car "35205," *17-18*	65
____**44136**	FGE Wood-sided Refrigerator Car "35284," *17-18*	65
____**44137**	PFE Wood-sided Refrigerator Car "91022," *17-18*	65
____**44138**	PFE Wood-sided Refrigerator Car "91056," *17-18*	65
____**44139**	MDT Wood-sided Refrigerator Car "17177," *17-18*	65
____**44140**	MDT Wood-sided Refrigerator Car "17200," *17-18*	65
____**44141**	GN Wood-sided Refrigerator Car "67582," *17-18*	65
____**44142**	GN Wood-sided Refrigerator Car "67587," *17-18*	65
____**44143**	BAR Wood-sided Refrigerator Car "6507," *17-18*	65
____**44144**	BAR Wood-sided Refrigerator Car "6510," *17-18*	65
____**47900**	D&H Streamlined Coach 2-pack, *15-17*	160
____**47903**	D&H Streamlined Diner/Vista Dome 2-pack, *15-17*	160
____**47906**	D&H Streamlined Full Vista/Combo 2-pack, *15-17*	160
____**47909**	D&H Streamlined Baggage/Observation 2-pack, *15-17*	160
____**47912**	SP Streamlined Coach 2-pack, *15-17*	160
____**47915**	SP Streamlined Diner/Vista Dome 2-pack, *15-17*	160
____**47918**	SP Streamlined Combo/Observation 2-pack, *15-17*	160
____**47921**	Pere Marquette 2-8-4 Berkshire Locomotive "1225," *15-16*	350
____**47922**	Erie 2-8-4 Berkshire Locomotive "3360," *15-16*	350
____**47923**	Southern 2-8-4 Berkshire Locomotive "2716," *15-16*	350

Mint

Number	Description	Mint
47924	Northeast Ohio Mixed Freight Set, *17*	600____
47925	UP Mixed Freight Set, *17*	600____
47926	CP Mixed Freight Set, *17*	600____
47927	UP Auto Carrier "ETTX 715029," *17*	75____
47928	UP Auto Carrier "ETTX 715036," *17*	75____
47929	UP Auto Carrier "ETTX 715039," *17*	75____
47930	CSX Auto Carrier "TTGX 150643," *17*	75____
47931	CSX Auto Carrier "TTGX 150640," *17*	75____
47932	CSX Auto Carrier "TTGX 150654," *17*	75____
47933	NS Auto Carrier "NS 171257," *17*	75____
47934	NS Auto Carrier "NS 171260," *17*	75____
47935	NS Auto Carrier "NS 171265," *17*	75____
47936	BNSF Auto Carrier "TTGX 965537," *17*	75____
47937	BNSF Auto Carrier "TTGX 965542," *17*	75____
47938	BNSF Auto Carrier "TTGX 965521," *17*	75____
47940	FasTrack R20 Command/Remote Switch-right-hand, *15-18*	110____
47941	FasTrack R20 Command/Remote Switch-left-hand, *15-18*	110____
47941	UP B-W Caboose "24591," *16*	73____
47942	MKT UP Heritage SD70ACe Diesel "1988," CC, *16*	590____
47943	WP UP Heritage SD70ACe Diesel "1983," CC, *16*	590____
47944	UP SD70ACe Diesel "8444," CC, *16*	590____
47945	EMD Demonstrator SD70ACe Diesel "2012," CC, *16*	590____
47946	BNSF SD70ACe Diesel "9358," CC, *16*	590____
47947	KCS SD70ACe Diesel "4054," CC, *16*	590____
47948	NS SD70ACe Diesel "1030," CC, *16*	590____
47949	CSX UP SD70ACe Diesel "4817," CC, *16*	590____
47950	MILW 4-8-4 Northern Locomotive "265," FlyerChief, *16-17*	500____
47951	UP 4-8-4 Northern Locomotive "808," FlyerChief, *16-17*	500____
47952	Frisco 4-8-4 Northern Locomotive "4501," FlyerChief, *16-17*	500____
47953	NYC 4-8-4 Northern Locomotive "6015," FlyerChief, *16-17*	500____
47958	Pennsylvania Docksider Freight Set, *16*	320____
47959	Shell Tank Car, *16-17*	65____
47960	UP Boxcar "196881," *16-17*	65____
47961	NYC Boxcar "168245," *16-17*	65____
47963	PRR 2-bay Covered Hopper, *16-17*	60____
47964	NS Gondola with containers, *16-17*	65____
47965	NH Log Dump Car, *16-17*	75____
47966	NATX 3-D Tank Car, *16-17*	65____
47967	CSX Waffle-sided Boxcar "136156," *16-17*	65____
47968	C&NW Stock Car "14300," *16*	65____
47970	NYC B-W Caboose "20300," *16-18*	75____
47971	UP Extended Vision Caboose "24591," *17*	75____
47972	B&M Cupola Caboose "C-48," *16-18*	65____
47973	Nickel Plate Road Cupola Caboose "775," *16-18*	65____
47974	Christmas Boxcar, *16-17*	65____
47980	Suburban Station, *16-18*	80____

Mint

____ **47981**	AT&SF Extended Vision Caboose "999702," *16-18*	65
____ **47982**	Chessie Extended Vision Caboose "3181," *16-18*	65
____ **47983**	Piggyback Unloader with UP Flatcar "258258," w/2 UP Trailers, *17-18*	110
____ **47984**	NH Flatcar "40510," w/2 NH Trailers, *17*	65
____ **47985**	PRR Flatcar "46914," w/2 REA Trailers, *17-18*	65
____ **47986**	FasTrack 4.5" Straight Track, *17-18*	5
____ **47987**	FasTrack 1.75" Straight Track, *17-18*	5
____ **47988**	FasTrack 1.37" Straight Track, *17-18*	5
____ **47989**	MP Alco PA A-A Diesel, Set, CC, *17*	700
____ **47992**	NH Alco PA A-A Diesel, Set, CC, *17*	350
____ **47995**	PRR Alco PA A-A Diesel, Set, CC, *17*	700
____ **47998**	AT&SF Alco PA A-A Diesel, Set, "51-52," CC, *17*	700
____ **47999**	Santa Fe Alco PA AA Set, *17*	700
____ **48000**	Southern Pacific GP9 Diesel "8000," *87*	190
____ **48001**	Illinois Central Gulf GP20 Diesel "8001," *87*	195
____ **48002**	SP GP9 Diesel Dummy Unit "8002," *88*	135
____ **48003**	Santa Fe GP20 Diesel Dummy Unit "8553," *88*	122
____ **48004**	Chessie System GP20 Diesel Dummy Unit "8460," *88*	160
____ **48005**	Pennsylvania GP9 Diesel "8005," *89*	167
____ **48006**	Polar Express Billboard Pack, *17-18*	14
____ **48007**	Burlington Northern GP20 Diesel "8007," *90*	304
____ **48008**	New Haven EP-5 Electric Locomotive "8008," *91*	200
____ **48009**	American Flyer GM GP7 Diesel "8009," *91*	167
____ **48010**	MILW EP-5 Electric Locomotive "8010," *92*	209
____ **48013**	Conrail GP7 Diesel "5600," *95*	230
____ **48014**	Northern Pacific GP9 Diesel "8014," *95*	190
____ **48016**	"Merry Christmas" GP20 Diesel "1225," *95*	227
____ **48017**	Nickel Plate Road GP9 Diesel Set, *97*	289
____ **48018**	Polar Express Passenger Coach Add-on Car, *17*	70
____ **48019**	SP GP20 Diesel "4060," *98*	175
____ **48020**	Milwaukee Road GP9 Diesel "304," *98*	220
____ **48022**	AT&SF Tie Ejector Car "490284," *17*	85
____ **48023**	Santa Fe Merger GP9 Diesel "2927," *99*	362
____ **48024**	AT&SF Warbonnet Crane and Boom Car Combo, *17*	190
____ **48031**	AT&SF EMD GP7 Diesel "2849,"FlyerChief, *17-18*	250
____ **48032**	UP EMD GP7 Diesel "125," FlyerChief, *17-18*	250
____ **48033**	Rock Island GP9 Diesel "1272," *02*	250
____ **48034**	Seaboard Baldwin Switcher "1413," *03*	198
____ **48035**	Santa Fe Baldwin Switcher "2257," *03*	205
____ **48036**	NYC 2-8-2 Light Mikado Locomotive "1849," *04*	593
____ **48037**	Nickel Plate Road EMD GP7 Diesel "514," FlyerChief, *17-18*	250
____ **48038**	GN EP-5 Electric Locomotive "5011," *04-05*	205
____ **48039**	Baltimore & Ohio 0-6-0 Dockside Switcher, *05*	93
____ **48040**	Santa Fe 0-6-0 Dockside Switcher, *05*	100
____ **48041**	UP Light Mikado Locomotive "2549," RailSounds, *05*	510
____ **48042**	Southern Light Mikado Locomotive "4501," RailSounds, *05*	448
____ **48043**	NYC Baldwin Switcher, "8100," *04*	213

		Mint
48044	Southern Baldwin Switcher, *04*	200____
48045	North Pole Central EMD GP7 Diesel "25," FlyerChief, *17-18*	250 ____
48047	UP 4-8-4 Northern Locomotive "800," RailSound*s*, *06*	395 ____
48048	DM&IR SD9 Diesel, *05*	220____
48049	Southern Pacific SD9 Diesel, *05*	220____
48051	Burlington SD9 Diesel "373," *06*	153____
48052	Erie 4-6-2 Pacific Locomotive "2934," TMCC, *06*	555____
48053	Pennsylvania 2-8-2 Mikado "9628," CC, *06*	537____
48054	UP 4-8-4 Northern Locomotive "809," *06*	488____
48055	Bethlehem Steel 0-6-0 Dockside Switcher, *06*	100____
48056	NYC 0-6-0 Dockside Switcher, *06*	96____
48058	Chessie System SD9 Diesel, *06*	235____
48059	North Pole Central Switcher "25," *06*	100____
48060	C&O 2-8-2 Mikado Locomotive "1068," RailSound*s*, *07-09*	525 ____
48061	B&O 4-6-2 Pacific Locomotive "5213," RailSound*s*, *07-09*	475 ____
48062	PRR Dockside Switcher, *07-09*	103____
48063	UP Dockside Switcher, *07-09*	113____
48064	MILW 4-8-4 Northern Locomotive "261," RailSounds, *07-09*	382 ____
48065	American Flyer SD9 Diesel "1956," *07*	388____
48066	UP SD9 Diesel, *07*	288____
48067	C&NW Baldwin Switcher, "1044," *07*	265____
48070	UP 4-8-8-4 Big Boy Locomotive "4014," CC, *08-09*	682____
48071	CN GP9 Diesel "4232," *08*	275____
48072	ACL 4-6-2 Pacific Locomotive "1523," CC, *08*	650____
48075	NH EP-5 Electric Locomotive "378" 08-09	222____
48078	Commemorative Handcar and Shed, *09*	93____
48081	WP 2-8-2 Mikado Locomotive "319," CC, *10*	700____
48082	UP Challenger Steam Locomotive "3985," CC, *11*	1000____
48084	UP Greyhound Challenger Locomotive "3977," CC, *11*	1000 ____
48085	Denver & Rio Grande Western 4-6-6-4 Challenger, *10*	1000 ____
48087	Commemorative Dockside Switcher, "1958," *11-13*	110____
48088	Christmas GP9 Diesel, *11-12*	300____
48089	Clinchfield Challenger Steam Locomotive "675," CC, *11*	1000 ____
48090	NP Challenger Steam Locomotive "5121," CC, *11*	1000____
48091	WP Challenger Steam Locomotive "402," CC, *11*	1000____
48092	GN Challenger Steam Locomotive "4000," CC, *11*	1000____
48094	Spokane Portland & Seattle Steam Locomotive, *11*	1000____
48096	AF Christmas Handcar with shed, *12*	120____
48097	Clear 0-6-0 Dockside Steam Switcher, "1967," *12*	110____
48100/01	Wabash Alco PA1 AA Set, *88*	245____
48102/03	C&O Alco PA1 AA Set, *89*	334____
48106/07	UP Alco PA1 AA Set, *90*	477____
48112/13	MP Alco PA1 AA Set, *91*	452____
48114/15/16	NP Alco PA1 ABA Set, *92*	420____

		Mint
___ **48117**	NP Alco PA1 Diesel B Unit "8117," RailSounds, *92*	105
___ **48118**	MP Alco PA1 Diesel B-Unit "8118," RailSounds, *92 u*	110
___ **48119**	UP Alco PA1 Diesel B-Unit "8119," RailSounds, *92 u*	115
___ **48120/21**	WP Alco PA1 Diesel, AA Set, *93*	225
___ **48122**	WP Alco PA1 Diesel B-Unit, RailSounds, *93*	123
___ **48123**	SP Alco PA1 Diesel B-Unit "8123," RailSounds, *93*	140
___ **48126/27**	Silver Flash Alco Diesel, PA1 AB Set, *95*	522
___ **48128**	Silver Flash Alco PA1 Diesel B Unit "480," *95*	105
48129	Silver Flash Alco PA1 Diesel Dummy A Unit "479," *96*	115
___ **48130**	SF Alco PA1 and PB-1 Diesel Set, *97*	266
___ **48135**	NYC Alco PA Diesel, B Unit "4302," *03*	145
___ **48136**	Santa Fe Alco PB Diesel B-Unit, *04*	145
___ **48139**	Pennsylvania Alco PB Diesel B-Unit, RailSounds, *05*	135
___ **48141**	WM Baldwin Switcher "132," *06*	230
___ **48142**	Erie-Lackawanna U33C Diesel "3320," CC, *09*	370
___ **48144**	PRR Baldwin Switcher "5618," *08*	245
___ **48146**	SP U33C Diesel "8773," CC, *09*	370
___ **48147**	ATSF Alco PA Diesel AA Set, *09*	370
___ **48155**	D&RGW Alco PA Diesel AA Set, *10*	370
___ **48158**	Burlington Northern U33C Diesel, *10*	440
___ **48159**	Great Northern U33C Diesel, *10*	440
___ **48161**	Northern Pacific U33C Diesel, *10*	440
___ **48162**	Texas Special Alco PA Diesel, AA Set, *11, 13-14*	470
___ **48165**	M&StL Baldwin Diesel Switcher, *12-16*	290
___ **48166**	UP "Building America" SD70ACe Diesel "8348," *12-14*	500
___ **48167**	UP "Building America" SD70ACe Diesel, nonpowered, *12-13*	253
___ **48168**	UP "Building America" SD70ACe Diesel "8461," CC, *12-13*	480
___ **48169**	KCS SD70ACe Diesel "4042," CC, *12-13*	480
___ **48170**	NS SD70ACe Diesel "1011," CC, *12-13*	480
___ **48171**	BNSF SD70ACe Diesel "9344," CC, *12*	480
___ **48172**	CSX SD70ACe Diesel "4847," CC, *12-13*	480
___ **48173**	KCS SD70ACe Diesel "4022," gray, CC, *12*	480
___ **48174**	SP UP Heritage SD70ACe Diesel "1865," CC, *12-14*	480
___ **48175**	D&RGW UP Heritage SD70ACe Diesel "1870," CC, *12-14*	480
___ **48176**	C&NW UP Heritage SD70ACe Diesel "1859," CC, *12-13*	480
___ **48177**	MP UP Heritage SD70ACe Diesel "1851," CC, *12-13*	480
___ **48178**	AT&SF 2-8-8-2 Steam Locomotive "1795," CC, *12-13*	1000
___ **48179**	PRR 2-8-8-2 Steam Locomotive "374," CC, *12-13*	1000
___ **48180**	N&W 2-8-8-2 Steam Locomotive "2009," CC, *12-13*	1000
___ **48181**	UP 2-8-8-2 Steam Locomotive "3672," CC, *12-13*	1000
___ **48182**	Virginian 2-8-8-2 Steam Locomotive "741," CC, *12-13*	1000
___ **48185**	AT&SF U33C Diesel Locomotive "8522," CC, *12*	480
___ **48186**	AT&SF U33C Diesel Locomotive "8509," CC, *12*	480
___ **48187**	D&H U33C Diesel Locomotive "755," CC, *12*	480

Mint

48188	D&H U33C Diesel Locomotive "752," CC, 12	480____
48189	IC U33C Diesel Locomotive "5054," CC, 12	480____
48190	IC U33C Diesel Locomotive "5052," CC, 12	480____
48191	MILW U33C Diesel Locomotive "5702," CC, 12	480____
48192	MILW U33C Diesel Locomotive "8002," CC, 12	480____
48193	PC U33C Diesel Locomotive "6552," CC, 12	480____
48194	PC U33C Diesel Locomotive "6541," CC, 12	480____
48195	Christmas U33C Diesel "1225," CC, 12	480____
48197	Santa Fe 2-8-8-2 Steam Locomotive "1797," CC, 13	1000____
48198	N&W 2-8-8-2 Steam Locomotive "2020," CC, 13	1000____
48200	ATSF Boxcar (TCA), 97	107____
48203	NYC Reefer (TTOS), 97	45____
48204	D&RGW Boxcar (TCA), 97	70____
48205	Pacific Fruit Express Reefer (NASG), 97	52____
48208	New England Hopper, (TCA), 98	55____
48209	Cotton Belt Boxcar (TTOS), 98	105____
48210	New England Hopper, (TCA), 98	83____
48211	Magnolia Tank Car (NASG), 98	62____
48212	SP Tank Car (TTOS), 99	70____
48213	L&N Boxcar (TCA), 99 u	129____
48214	GN Caboose (NASG), 99 u	55____
48215	Monsanto Hopper, 99 u	90____
48217	SP Gondola (TTOS), 00	110____
48218	SP Crane Car (TTOS), 00	110____
48219	"Ship It on the Frisco" Boxcar (TCA), 01 u	75____
48220	Deep Rock Tank Car (NASG), 00 u	115____
48221	Norfolk Southern 2-bay Hopper, (TCA), 01	105____
48222	British Columbia Tank Car (TTOS), 00	75____
48223	Toy Train Museum 1-D Tank Car (TCA), 01 u	80____
48224	Gulf Tank Car (NASG), 01	80____
48225	Salt Lake Route Boxcar (TTOS), 02 u	91____
48226	Toy Train Museum Flatcar with wheel load (TCA), 02 u	109 ____
48227	D&S Hopper, (TTOS), 02 u	60____
48228	Cook Paint Tank Car (NASG), 02 u	117____
48229	D&RGW Tank Car (TTOS), 03	78____
48230	Toy Train Museum Gondola with pipe load (TCA), 03 u	60 ____
48231	Linde Boxcar (TTOS), 03	110____
48232	NH Flatcar with N.E. Transport trailer (NETCA), 03	110____
48233	UP 1-D Tanker (NASG), 03	87____
48234	Toy Train Museum Boxcar (TCA), 04	55____
48235	Forest Service/Smokey Bear Tank Car (TTOS), 04	112____
48236	BNSF Icicle Reefer (TTOS), 04	98____
48237	Poland Spring Boxcar (NETCA), 04	110____
48238	GE Cable Reel Car (NASG), 04	125____
48239	Gilbert's Milk Tank Car (TTOS), 05	70____
48240	Toy Train Museum Combination Car (TCA), 05	73____
48241	Las Vegas & Tonopah Boxcar (TTOS), 05	70____
48242	Fisk Tire Boxcar (NETCA), 05	110____
48243	GE Twin Searchlight Car (NASG), 05	90____

____	**48244** Ward Kimball Boxcar (TTOS Cal-Stewart), *05*	61
____	**48245** A.C. Gilbert Coach (TTOS), *06*	85
____	**48246** SP Flatcar with trailers (TTOS), *06*	92
____	**48247** Toy Train Museum Idler Caboose, (TCA), *06*	68
____	**48248** Indian Motocycle Boxcar (NETCA), *06*	250
____	**48249** Yule Marble Flatcar (TCA), *07*	106
____	**48250** GE Crane Car (NASG), *06*	86
____	**48253** Coors Reefer (TCA), *07*	91
____	**48254** Toy Train Museum Crane Car, *07*	90
____	**48255** PRR 2-bay Hopper, with coal load (TTOS), *07*	79
____	**48256** Forest Service/Smokey Bear Boxcar (TTOS), *08*	83
____	**48257** Oilzum Tanker 2-car Set (NETCA), *08*	100
____	**48260** Sacramento Northern Reefer (SVAFC), *07*	112
____	**48261** UP Generator Car (St. Louis S Gaugers), *07*	103
____	**48261X** C&NW Safety and Generator Car (St. Louis S Gaugers), *11*	90
____	**48262** Union Tank Car (TTOS), *07*	103
____	**48263** Cape Cod Potato Chip Boxcar (NETCA), *07*	103
____	**48264** GE Boom Car (NASG), *07*	81
____	**48265** Life Savers Tank Car (TTOS Cal-Stewart), *07*	86
____	**48267** Rutland Boxcar (TCA), *08*	80
____	**48268** Rutland Boxcar (TCA), *08*	80
____	**48269** ATSF Grand Canyon Reefer (TCA), *09*	85
____	**48270** GE Baldwin Diesel Switcher, *08*	345
____	**48271** Hoover Dam Power Co. Flatcar (TCA), *09*	50
____	**48272** Forest Service/Smokey Bear Flatcar with airplane (TTOS), *08*	127
____	**48273** Northwestern Reefer (TTOS), *09*	60
____	**48274** Western Pacific Stock Car (TTOS), *09*	85
____	**48275** Life Savers Wild Cherry Tank Car (TTOS Cal-Stewart), *08*	93
____	**48276** Bay State Beer Reefer (NETCA), *09*	73
____	**48281** GN Boxcar (Southeastern Michigan S Gaugers), *10*	75
____	**48284** Elgin-Joliet & Eastern Gondola with coil covers (NASG), *09*	97
____	**48285** Karo Tank Car (Southern California S Gaugers), *10*	125
____	**48286** Carling Black Label Beer Reefer #1 (TCA), *10*	80
____	**48287** Carling Black Label Beer Reefer #2 (TCA), *10*	80
____	**48288** Life Savers Pep-O-Mint Tank Car (TTOS Cal-Stewart), *09*	60
____	**48290** Life Savers Butter Rum Tank Car (TTOS Cal-Stewart), *10*	75
____	**48291** Jenney 3-D Tank Car (NASG), *10*	85
____	**48292** Sacramento Canning Tank Car (TCA), *11*	90
____	**48293** Charleston & West Carolina Boxcar (TTOS), *11*	95
____	**48294** Dixie Honey 1-D Tank Car (NASG), *11*	80
____	**48295** Flatcar with Howard Johnson trailers (NETCA), *11*	75
____	**48296** Life Savers Wint O Green Tank Car (TTOS Cal-Stewart), *12*	90
____	**48297** NS Flatcar with jet engines (TCA), *12*	70
____	**48298** Spreckels Sugar Hopper (TCA Rocky Mountain), *12*	65
____	**48299** Spreckels Sugar Hopper (TCA Rocky Mountain), *13*	80

Mint

48300	Southern Pacific Overnight Boxcar, *87*	41____
48301	D&RGW Boxcar, *87*	37____
48302	Canadian Pacific Boxcar, *87*	42____
48303	Chessie System Boxcar, *87*	42____
48304	Burlington Northern Boxcar, *87*	44____
48305	Wabash Boxcar, *88*	31____
48306	Seaboard Coast Line Boxcar, *88*	36____
48307	Western Pacific Boxcar, *88*	56____
48308	Maine Central Boxcar "8308," *90*	76____
48309	Christmas Boxcar "8309," *90 u*	206____
48310	MKT Boxcar "8310," *91*	36____
48311	Christmas Boxcar "8311," *91 u*	53____
48312	Missouri Pacific Boxcar "8312," *92*	45____
48313	BAR State of Maine Boxcar "8313," *92*	52____
48314	Christmas Boxcar "8314," *92 u*	68____
48316	Bangor & Aroostook Reefer "29425," *93*	31____
48317	Rath Packing Reefer "29426," *93*	29____
48318	A.C. Gilbert Boxcar "8318," *93*	51____
48319	Christmas Boxcar "8319," *93*	45____
48320	NKP Boxcar, *94*	34____
48321	Christmas Boxcar "8321," *94*	38____
48322	New Haven Boxcar, *95*	47____
48323	Christmas Boxcar, *95*	47____
48324	AF 50th Anniversary Boxcar "1946-1996," *96*	53____
48325	Holiday Boxcar, *96*	34____
48326	B&O Boxcar (TCA), *96*	67____
48327	AF Christmas Boxcar "900," *97*	42____
48328	GN Boxcar "900-197," *97*	32____
48329	ATSF Boxcar "900-297," map graphic, *97*	28____
48330	PRR Boxcar "900-397," *97*	30____
48332	MKT Boxcar "937," *98*	43____
48333	Bangor & Aroostook Boxcar "982," *98*	39____
48334	Seaboard Boxcar "942," *98*	25____
48335	Christmas Gondola, *98*	50____
48340	American Flyer Christmas Car, *00*	70____
48341	American Flyer Christmas Car, *99*	93____
48342	American Flyer Christmas Boxcar, *01*	49____
48343	Great Northern Boxcar, *01*	50____
48346	Christmas Boxcar, *02*	55____
48347	C&O Boxcar "2701," *02*	48____
48348	NP Boxcar "31226," *02*	57____
48349	Goofy Boxcar, *03*	28____
48351	Donald Duck Boxcar, *04-05*	31____
48352	Pennsylvania Boxcar "47133," *03*	50____
48353	American Flyer Christmas Boxcar, *03-04*	45____
48354	Southern Pacific Boxcar, *04*	50____
48355	American Flyer Christmas Boxcar, *05*	45____
48356	Pluto Boxcar, *05*	32____
48357	Winnie the Pooh Boxcar, *04-05*	23____
48358	Santa Fe Boxcar "272197," *05*	43____

			Mint
_____	**48359**	Holiday Boxcar, _05_	48
_____	**48362**	Burlington Boxcar "63114," _06_	55
_____	**48363**	Holiday Boxcar, _06_	55
_____	**48364**	Gilbert AF 60th Anniversary Boxcar, _06_	62
_____	**48365**	Western Maryland Boxcar, _06_	125
_____	**48366**	Jersey Central Boxcar "20958," _07_	43
_____	**48367**	CP Rail Stock Car "277315," _07_	55
_____	**48368**	American Flyer Holiday Boxcar, _07_	48
_____	**48370**	UPS Centennial Boxcar "1937," _07_	39
_____	**48372**	CN Boxcar "36298," _08_	60
_____	**48373**	UP Stock Car "48155D," _08_	60
_____	**48374**	American Flyer Holiday Boxcar, _08_	60
_____	**48375**	American Flyer Stock Car with reindeer, _08_	52
_____	**48376**	American Flyer Holiday Boxcar, _09_	70
_____	**48378**	IC Boxcar "400664," _09_	70
_____	**48379**	GN Stock Car, _09_	70
_____	**48380**	American Flyer Circus Stock Car "3636," _09_-10	48
_____	**48381**	1953 Catalog Art Boxcar, _09_	50
_____	**48383**	U.S. Mail Post Office Boxcar "8383," _09_-11	70
_____	**48384**	American Flyer Holiday Boxcar, _10_	55
_____	**48385**	American Flyer 1959 Catalog Art Boxcar, _10_	51
_____	**48386**	NYC Pacemaker Stock Car "23243," _10_	70
_____	**48387**	Airco Boxcar "4838," _10_	70
_____	**48388**	WP Boxcar "1955," _10_	70
_____	**48389**	Angela Trotta Thomas "Flyer Fantasy" Boxcar, _10_	55
_____	**48390**	American Flyer 1955 Catalog Art Boxcar, _11_	65
_____	**48391**	Timken Boxcar, _11_	70
_____	**48393**	Keystone Camera Boxcar, _11_	70
_____	**48394**	Holiday Boxcar, _11_	70
_____	**48395**	NP "Pig Palace" Stock Car, _11_-13	70
_____	**48396**	Coca-Cola Christmas Boxcar, _11_-14	53
_____	**48397**	Halloween Boxcar, _11_-13	70
_____	**48399**	Ringling Bros. Boxcar, _11_	70
_____	**48400**	SP 3-D Tank Car, _87_	34
_____	**48402**	Penn Salt 1-D Tank Car "24319," _92_	70
_____	**48403**	British Columbia 1-D Tank Car "8403," _93_	99
_____	**48404**	U.S. Army 1-D Tank Car, _94_	45
_____	**48405**	Shell 1-D Tank Car "8681," _95_	54
_____	**48406**	Celanese Chemicals Tank Car, _96_	51
_____	**48407**	Gilbert Chemicals Tank Car, _96_	47
_____	**48408**	Sunoco 1-D Tank Car "625," _97_	33
_____	**48410**	Tank Train 1-D Tank Car "44587," _99_	75
_____	**48411**	Gilbert Chemicals Tank Car "48411," _02_	67
_____	**48412**	Alaska 3-D Tank Car, _02_	50
_____	**48413**	Diamond Chemicals Tank Car "19418," _03_	44
_____	**48414**	Nestle Nesquik 1-D Tank Car "48414," _04_	48
_____	**48415**	Hooker Chemicals 3-D Tank Car "48515," _04_	49
_____	**48416**	Campbell's Soup 1-D Tank Car, _04_	46
_____	**48417**	Pillsbury 1-D Tank Car, _05_	49
_____	**48418**	Protex 3-D Tank Car "PDAX 1054," _05_	45

Mint

48419	Jack Frost 1-D Tank Car "107," *06*	55____
48420	Union Pacific 3-D Tank Car, *06*	43____
48421	Philadelphia Quartz 1-D Tank Car "806," *07*	43____
48422	Simonin's 3-D Tank Car "9565," *07*	57____
48423	2017 American Flyer Christmas Boxcar, *17*	65____
48424	American Flyer Candy Cane 1-D Tank Car, *08*	60____
48425	NYC 3-D Tank Car, *08*	60____
48426	American Flyer Commemorative Freight Car 3-pack, *08-09*	124 ____
48428	DM&IR 1-D Tank Car "817," *09*	70____
48430	Comet 1-D Tank Car, *09*	70____
48431	Sunoco 1-D Tank Car, *09-10*	49____
48433	Coca-Cola 1-D Tank Car, *10-11*	70____
48434	American Flyer Smoke Fluid 1-D Tank Car, *12-13*	70____
48435	Hershey's 1-D Tank Car, *11*	70____
48436	NYC Reefer "491" (NASG), *91 u*	70____
48436	NYMX Reefer (NASG), *91*	100____
48437	Gilbert Chemicals 3-D Tank Car, *11*	70____
48438	Cities Service 3-D Tank Car, *12-13, 15*	60____
48440	Track Cleaning Fluid 3-D Tank Car, *13-17*	60____
48442	AFL Air Service 1-D Tank Car, *13-17*	60____
48443	Union Starch 1-D Tank Car, *15-17*	60____
48459	Chessie GP20 Diesel, *07*	258____
48470	Jersey Central Boxcar (NASG), *88 u*	165____
48471	MKT 1-D Tank Car "120089" (NASG), *89 u*	243____
48472	Pennzoil 3-D Tank Car "390" (NASG), *90 u*	160____
48473	Central of Georgia Boxcar (TCA), *90 u*	68____
48474	C&NW Reefer "70165" (TCA), *91 u*	208____
48475	Boraxo Covered Hopper "591" (NASG), *91 u*	70____
48475	American Flyer Lines Smoking Caboose, *11*	80____
48477	Ralston Purina Boxcar "11492" (TCA), *92 u*	92____
48478	Burlington Boxcar "792" (NASG), *92 u*	101____
48479	NKP FlatCar "20602" withErtl trailer (NASG), *92 u*	127____
48480	Susquehanna Boxcar "993" (NASG), *93 u*	91____
48481	REA Reefer "893" (NASG), *93 u*	78____
48482	Great Northern Boxcar "3993" (TCA), *93 u*	79____
48483	A.C. Gilbert Society "Boys Club" Boxcar, *93 u*	65____
48484	A.C. Gilbert Society "Boys at the Gate" Boxcar, *93 u*	88____
48485	Northern Pacific Boxcar "1094" (NASG), *94 u*	74____
48486	NYNH&H Boxcar "1194" (NASG), *94 u*	51____
48487	Yorkrail Boxcar "1994" (TCA), *94 u*	93____
48489	Pennsylvania Dutch Boxcar "91653" (TCA), *97 u*	286____
48490	Western Pacific Boxcar "101645" (TTOS), *95 u*	70____
48491	BN Flatcar "1995" withtrailers (TCA), *95 u*	100____
48492	Northern Pacific Boxcar "1261" (TCA), *95 u*	74____
48493	SP TTUX Flatcar Set with trailers (NASG), *95 u*	75____
48494	LV Covered Grain Hopper "1295" (NASG), *95 u*	60____
48495	Monsanto 1-D Tank Car-white (St. Louis S Gaugers), *95 u*	187 ____
48496	Monsanto 1-D Tank Car-orange (St. Louis S Gaugers), *95 u*	1018 ____

_____ 48497	MKT 3-D Tank Car "117018" (TCA), *95 u*	105
_____ 48498	Western Pacific Boxcar "31337" (TTOS), *96 u*	117
_____ 48500	SP Gondola with canisters, *87*	25
_____ 48501	Southern Pacific Flatcar with trailers, *87*	41
_____ 48502	Wabash Flatcar with trailers, *88*	46
_____ 48503	Wabash Gondola with canisters, *88*	22
_____ 48505	IC Gulf Bulkhead Flatcar "8505," *90*	38
_____ 48507/08	U.S. Army Flatcars with 2 tanks, *95*	61
_____ 48509	AF Flatcar with 2 farm tractors, *95*	45
_____ 48510	Nickel Plate Road Gondola with canisters, *95*	34
_____ 48511	TTUX Triple Crown Flatcars with trailers, *96*	73
_____ 48513	CSX Flatcar with generator, *96*	28
_____ 48514	Intermodal TTUX Set with 2 cars and 2 trailers, *97*	53
_____ 48515	New Haven Flatcar, *97*	54
_____ 48516	SP Searchlight Car "627," *97*	47
_____ 48524	Borden's Flatcar, *01*	46
_____ 48525	Burlington Gondola, *01*	39
_____ 48526	Reading Gondola, "38708" withpipes, *02*	40
_____ 48527	Santa Fe Flatcar "90019" withjet rocket, *02*	46
_____ 48528	Conrail Flatcar with wheel loader, *02*	54
_____ 48529	NYC Flatcar with wheel load, *02*	48
_____ 48531	Chessie Depressed Center Flatcar with cable reel, *03*	59
_____ 48532	SP Flatcar "513183" withtrailers, *03*	48
_____ 48533	PFE Flatcar with trailers, *04-05*	42
_____ 48534	NYC Depressed Center Flatcar with cable reel, *04*	55
_____ 48535	GN Bulkhead Flatcar "48535," *04-05*	46
_____ 48536	Southern Flatcar with wheel load, *04*	65
_____ 48537	Nestle Nesquik Flatcar with milk containers, *04-05*	44
_____ 48538	Hood's Flatcar with milk containers, *04-05*	46
_____ 48539	REA Flatcar "TLCX2" with trailers, *05*	50
_____ 48540	B&O Flatcar "8652" with girder, *05*	49
_____ 48541	D&H Gondola "13903" with pipe load, *05*	45
_____ 48542	UPS Flatcar with trailer, *05*	45
_____ 48543	Supplee Flatcar with milk containers, *06*	55
_____ 48544	WM Flatcar "2632" with girder, *06*	55
_____ 48545	DM&IR Gondola "4290" with pipe load, *06*	55
_____ 48546	Alaska Depressed Center Flatcar with cable reel, *06*	60
_____ 48547	Chessie System Gondola, *06*	100
_____ 48548	PRR Flatcar "480078" with trailers, *07*	35
_____ 48549	UP Gondola with canisters, *07*	38
_____ 48550	GN Depressed Center Service Car, *07*	44
_____ 48553	AF Christmas Gondola with candy canes, *07*	55
_____ 48554	Bethlehem Steel Gondola with coil covers, *08*	50
_____ 48555	Reading Flatcar "9314" with wheel load, *08*	60
_____ 48559	Christmas Gondola with presents, *09*	36
_____ 48560	BNSF Flatcar with jet engine, *09-11*	53
_____ 48561	CNJ Flatcar with boat, *10*	70
_____ 48563	Reindeer Express Agency Flatcar with trailers, *10*	70
_____ 48565	Commemorative Flatcar with piggyback trailers, *11*	58
_____ 48566	Gondola with Christmas trees, *11*	70

		Mint
48568	Ringling Bros. Flatcar with piggyback trailers, *11*	70 ____
48569	Buttermilk Bay Creamery Flatcar with milk containers, *11*	70 ____
48570	PRR Gondola with coil covers, *12-13*	70 ____
48571	Flatcar with Santa's sleigh, *12-13*	70 ____
48572	Naughty or Nice Gondola-coil covers, *13-14*	70 ____
48576	AFL Gilbert Dairy Flatcar with milk containers, *13-17*	60 ____
48577	Flatcar with Santa's sleigh, *13-14*	70 ____
48579	AFL Depressed Center Flatcar with cable reel, *14-15*	50 ____
48580	U.S. Navy Flatcar with Jeeps, *14-15*	70 ____
48600	Southern Pacific Hopper, *87*	31 ____
48601	Union Pacific Covered Hopper, *87*	29 ____
48602	Erie Covered Hopper, *87*	29 ____
48603	Wabash Hopper, with coal load, *88*	26 ____
48604	Milwaukee Road Covered Hopper, *88*	31 ____
48605	Burlington Northern Covered Hopper, *88*	26 ____
48609	D&H Covered Hopper "8609," *93*	38 ____
48610	NKP Covered Hopper, *94*	35 ____
48611	Cargill Covered Grain Hopper, *95*	38 ____
48612	ADM 3-bay Covered Hopper, *97*	42 ____
48613	B&LE Hopper, 4-pack, *98*	234 ____
48614	B&LE Hopper, *98*	77 ____
48619	Union Pacific Hopper, *01*	40 ____
48620	B&O Hopper "435350," *02*	50 ____
48621	CN Covered Hopper, *02*	43 ____
48622	Burlington Hopper "170616," *03*	32 ____
48623	"Naughty & Nice" Hopper, 2-pack, *04-05*	88 ____
48627	Southern Hopper, with ballast load, *04*	55 ____
48628	DM&IR Hopper, *05*	51 ____
48629	CP Hopper, *06*	55 ____
48630	Milwaukee Road 3-bay Hopper, *07*	38 ____
48631	NYC 2-bay Hopper, *07*	30 ____
48632	Santa's Candy Shop 2-bay Hopper, *09-10*	70 ____
48633	UP 2-bay Hopper "82173," *09-10*	55 ____
48635	Hershey's Special Dark 2-Bay Hopper, *12*	70 ____
48636	WP 3-Bay Hopper, *12*	70 ____
48637	Santa Fe Midnight Chief 2-Bay Hopper, *13-17*	56 ____
48638	North Pole Express Hopper, *12, 15-16*	70 ____
48639	CN Scale Cylindrical Hopper "370708," *12, 15-16*	80 ____
48640	BN Scale Cylindrical Hopper "458856," *12, 15-16*	80 ____
48641	MP UP Heritage Scale Cylindrical Hopper "27421," *12, 15-16*	80 ____
48642	Saskatchewan Scale Cylindrical Hopper "397015," *12*	80 ____
48643	SP Scale Cylindrical Hopper "491020," *12, 15-16*	80 ____
48644	D&RGW UP Heritage Scale Cylindrical Hopper, *12*	80 ____
48645	C&NW UP Heritage Scale Cylindrical Hopper, *12, 15-16*	80 ____
48646	UP "Building America" Scale Cylindrical Hopper, *12, 15-16*	77 ____
48647	AFL Artificial Coal 3-Bay Hopper, *13-17*	60 ____

___ 48648	Alberta Cylindrical Hopper "396161," *12*, *15-16*	80
___ 48649	PRR Cylindrical Hopper "260411," *12*, *15-16*	80
48650 ___	Govt. of Canada Cylindrical Hopper "607002," *12*, *15-16*	80
___ 48651	NS Cylindrical Hopper "81022," *12*, *15-16*	80
48652 ___	CNJ NS Heritage Cylindrical Hopper "68110," *12*, *15-16*	80
48653 ___	DL&W NS Heritage Cylindrical Hopper "11254," *12*, *15-16*	80
48654 ___	Erie NS Heritage Cylindrical Hopper "91068," *12*, *15-16*	80
48655 ___	Illinois Terminal NS Heritage Cylindrical Hopper "107296," *12-16*	80
___ 48656	NYC NS Heritage Cylindrical Hopper "18292," *12*	80
48657 ___	PC NS Heritage Cylindrical Hopper "32428," *12*, *15-16*	80
___ 48658	Reading NS Heritage Cylindrical Hopper, *13*	80
48659 ___	Savannah & Atlanta NS Heritage Cylindrical Hopper "19065," *13-16*	80
___ 48660	Virginian NS Heritage Cylindrical Hopper, *13-16*	80
___ 48661	Wabash NS Heritage Cylindrical Hopper, *13-16*	80
___ 48662	AFL Scenery Gravel 3-Bay Hopper, *13-17*	60
___ 48664	Christmas Cylindrical Hopper, *13-17*	80
48665 ___	Central of Georgia NS Heritage Cylindrical Hopper, *13-16*	80
___ 48666	Conrail NS Heritage Cylindrical Hopper, *13*	80
48667 ___	Interstate NS Heritage Cylindrical Hopper "13488," *13-16*	80
___ 48668	LV NS Heritage Cylindrical Hopper, *13-16*	80
48669 ___	Nickel Plate Road NS Heritage Cylindrical Hopper, *13-16*	80
___ 48670	N&W NS Heritage Cylindrical Hopper, *13-16*	80
___ 48671	PRR NS Heritage Cylindrical Hopper, *13*	80
___ 48672	Southern NS Heritage Cylindrical Hopper, *13-16*	80
48673 ___	Norfolk Southern NS Heritage Cylindrical Hopper, *13-16*	80
___ 48674	Monongahela NS Heritage Cylindrical Hopper, *13-16*	80
___ 48700	SP Bay Window Caboose, *87*	35
___ 48701	Illinois Central Gulf Bay Window Caboose, *87*	40
___ 48702	Wabash Square Window Caboose, *88*	42
___ 48703	Union Pacific Square Window Caboose, *88*	36
___ 48705	Pennsylvania Square Window Caboose, *89*	47
___ 48706	BN Square Window Caboose "8706," *90*	98
___ 48707	NH Square Window Caboose "8707," *91*	41
___ 48710	Conrail Bay Window Caboose "21503," *95*	46
___ 48711	Northern Pacific Bay Window Caboose "8711," *95*	43
___ 48712	"Happy New Year" Bay Window Caboose "0101," *95*	48
___ 48713	Nickel Plate Road Caboose, *97*	50
___ 48714	SP Square Window Caboose "990," *97*	45
___ 48715	Milwaukee Road Caboose, *97*	53
___ 48718	C&NW Caboose, *98*	48
___ 48721	Santa Fe Caboose "999628," *99*	70
___ 48722	Rock Island Bay Window Caboose "17778," *02*	55

Mint

48723	Santa Fe Boom Car "206982," *03*	39____
48724	Seaboard Square Window Caboose "49658," *03*	54____
48725	NYC Caboose "17560," *03-04*	48____
48726	NYC Boom Car "48726," *04-05*	42____
48727	UP Bay Window Caboose "24554," *05*	71____
48728	Southern Bay Window Caboose "X545," *05*	48____
48729	Southern Boom Car, *04*	50____
48730	DM&IR Extended Vision Caboose "C-227," *05*	55____
48731	SP Bay Window Caboose "1338," *05*	55____
48732	UP Boom Car, *05*	55____
48733	Erie Caboose "C107" *06*	53____
48734	PRR Caboose "477810" 08	60____
48735	Burlington Extended Vision Caboose "13853," *06*	55____
48736	WM Caboose "1864," *06*	48____
48738	Chessie System Caboose, *06*	45____
48739	American Flyer Christmas Caboose, *06*	55____
48740	M.O.W. Boom Car "916," *07*	75____
48741	C&NW Extended Vision Caboose "13653," *07*	55____
48742	American Flyer Caboose, *07*	55____
48743	C&O Caboose "90877," *07*	55____
48746	ACL Caboose "0400" *08*	60____
48747	CN Extended Vision Caboose "79644," *08*	52____
48750	Erie-Lack. Extended Vision Caboose, *09*	60____
48751	Cotton Belt Bay Window Caboose, *09*	70____
48752	BN Extended View Caboose, *11*	70____
48754	WP Bay Window Caboose, *10-11*	70____
48755	NP Extended View Caboose, *11*	70____
48756	Conrail Extended View Caboose, *11*	70____
48757	GN Extended View Caboose, *11*	70____
48759	Clear Smoking Caboose "997," *12*	80____
48800	Wabash Reefer, *88*	36____
48801	Union Pacific Reefer, *88*	29____
48802	Pennsylvania Reefer, *88*	37____
48805	National Dairy Despatch Insulated Boxcar "8805," *90*	43____
48806	REA Reefer "8806," *94*	36____
48807	NKP Reefer "8807," *94*	35____
48808	PFE Reefer "30000," *03*	49____
48809	NP Reefer "139," *04*	36____
48814	Fruit Growers Express Reefer "40703," *06*	52____
48815	Needham Reefer "60500," *07-08*	55____
48823	Hershey's Reefer, *10*	70____
48824	Pacific Fruit Express Reefer "47760," *11*	70____
48825	Holiday Boxcar, *12-13*	70____
48826	American Flyer 1956 Catalog Art Boxcar, *12*	60____
48827	M&StL Boxcar, *12-13*	57____
48828	Mr. Goodbar Reefer, *12-14*	70____
48829	Pabst Beer Reefer, *12*	70____
48830	Schlitz Beer Reefer, *12*	70____
48831	Angela Trotta Thomas "Circus Comes to Town" Boxcar, *12-13*	70____

			Mint
____	48832	American Flyer 1951 Catalog Art Boxcar, *13-14*	50
____	48833	Christmas Boxcar, *13*	50
____	48835	Boy Scouts of America Cub Scout Boxcar, *13-14*	55
____	48836	Boy Scouts of America Eagle Scout Boxcar, *13-14*	55
____	48838	Penguin Seafood Reefer, *13-14*	50
____	48839	Smoke Cartridge Transport Boxcar, *13-14, 16-17*	60
____	48844	Christmas Mint Car, *13*	60
____	48845	Fort Knox Mint Car, *13-17*	65
____	48846	Gilbert Mines Mint Car, *13*	60
____	48847	New York Federal Reserve Mint Car, *13-17*	65
____	48848	San Francisco Federal Reserve Mint Car, *13-17*	63
____	48851	AFL Stock Car, *14-16*	60
____	48852	AT&SF Grand Canyon Line Boxcar, *14-17*	60
____	48854	Boston Federal Reserve Mint Car, *14-17*	70
____	48855	AFL Waffle-sided Boxcar, *14-17*	50
____	48856	NH Waffle-sided Boxcar, *14-17*	50
____	48857	C&NW Waffle-sided Boxcar, *14-18*	58
____	48858	BNSF 57' Mechanical Reefer "798879," *14*	80
____	48859	UP 57' Mechanical Reefer "455995," *14*	80
____	48860	PFE 57' Mechanical Reefer "458455," *14*	80
____	48861	GN 57' Mechanical Reefer "8870," *14*	80
____	48862	Govt. of Canada Cylindrical Hopper "106010," *14-16*	80
____	48863	CN Cylindrical Hopper "369290," *14-16*	80
____	48864	Santa Fe Cylindrical Hopper "300022," *14-15*	80
____	48865	Frisco Cylindrical Hopper "81028," *14-16*	80
____	48866	GN Cylindrical Hopper "71600," *14-16*	80
____	48867	U.S. Army Unloading Boxcar, *15-17*	80
____	48868	NP 57' Mechanical Reefer "794," *14-16*	80
____	48870	GN Boxcar-Steam RailSounds, *14-18*	170
____	48871	Erie Boxcar-Steam RailSounds, *14-18*	170
____	48874	2014 AF Christmas Boxcar, *14*	50
____	48875	North Pole Gondola with cocoa containers, *14*	50
____	48876	Reading 2-bay Hopper "81001," *15-17*	60
____	48877	U.S. Army Missile Launch Flatcar, *15-17*	70
____	48878	U.S. Army Flatcar with Rockets, *15-17*	60
____	48879	NH Gondola with pipes, *15-17*	65
____	48880	AFL Commemorative Work Caboose, *15-17*	65
____	48882	Christmas Boxcar, *15*	65
____	48900	C&O Combination Car, *89*	49
____	48901	C&O Coach, *89*	63
____	48902	C&O Vista Dome Car, *89*	58
____	48903	C&O Observation Car, *89*	49
____	48904	UP Combination Car "8904," *90*	54
____	48905	UP Coach "8905," *90*	90
____	48906	UP Vista Dome Car "8906," *90*	73
____	48907	UP Observation Car "8907," *90*	47
____	48908	UP Coach "8908," *90 u*	113
____	48909	UP Vista Dome Car "8909," *90 u*	122
____	48910	Missouri Pacific Combination Car "8910," *91*	50
____	48911	Missouri Pacific Vista Dome Car "8911," *91*	78

		Mint
48912	Missouri Pacific Coach "8912," *91*	78____
48913	Missouri Pacific Observation Car "8913," *91*	69____
48914	Missouri Pacific Coach "8914," *91*	82____
48915	Missouri Pacific Vista Dome Car "8915," *91*	71____
48920	Northern Pacific Combination Car "8920," *92*	55____
48921	Northern Pacific Coach "8921," *92*	67____
48922	Northern Pacific Vista Dome Car "8922," *92*	67____
48923	Northern Pacific Observation Car "8923," *92*	50____
48924	Northern Pacific Vista Dome Car "8924," *92*	67____
48925	Northern Pacific Coach "8925," *92*	72____
48926	WP California Zephyr Combination Car "801," *93*	37____
48927	WP California Zephyr Vista Dome Car "814," *93*	40____
48928	WP California Zephyr Vista Dome Car "815," *93*	40____
48929	WP California Zephyr Vista Dome Car "813," *93*	54____
48930	WP California Zephyr Vista Dome Car "811," *93*	60____
48931	WP California Zephyr Observation Car "882," *93*	37____
48932	WP California Zephyr Dining Car "842," *93*	43____
48933	Missouri Pacific Dining Car "8933," *94*	90____
48934	Northern Pacific Dining Car "8934," *94*	90____
48935	New Haven Combination Car, *95*	57____
48936	New Haven Vista Dome Car, *95*	55____
48937	New Haven Observation Car, *95*	57____
48938	Silver Flash Combination Car "960," *95*	75____
48939	Silver Flash Coach "961," *95*	67____
48940	Silver Flash Observation Car "963," *95*	79____
48941	Union Pacific Vista Dome Dining Car "8941," *95*	97____
48942	Vista Dome Car "962," *96*	140____
48943	New Haven Vista Dome Dining Car, *96*	65____
48944	ATSF Super Chief Passenger Car 4-pack, *97*	360____
48961	NYC Streamliner Passenger Car 2-pack, *02*	160____
48964	NYC Baggage Car "9149," *03*	50____
48965	B&O Passenger Car 2-pack, *03*	157____
48968	Santa Fe Passenger Car 2-pack, *04-05*	85____
48975	Pennsylvania Passenger Car 2-pack, *05*	130____
48976	Pennsylvania Baggage Car, *05*	75____
48977	Pennsylvania Dining Car, *05*	75____
48978	UP Heavyweight Passenger Car 4-pack, *06*	334____
48983	UP Heavyweight Passenger Car 2-pack, *06*	148____
48990	NYC Heavyweight Passenger Car 4-pack, *07*	265____
48991	NYC Heavyweight Passenger Car 2-pack, *07*	140____
48992	PRR Heavyweight Passenger Car 4-pack, *07*	265____
48993	Pennsylvania Heavyweight Passenger Car 2-Pack, *07*	140____
48994	Blue Comet Heavyweight Passenger Car 2-pack, *07*	140____
49001	NYC Searchlight Car "9001," *90*	47____
49002	B&M Flatcar with logs, *83*	83____
49003	Union Pacific Searchlight Car "9003," *91*	43____
49006	MILW Animated Square Window Caboose, *92*	47____
49009	AFL Flatcar with derrick, *96*	33____
49010	"Stable of Champions" Horse Car, *96*	32____
49011	UP Moe & Joe Animated Flatcar "15100," *03*	68____

		Mint
____ **49012**	Santa Fe Crane Car "199707," *03*	69
____ **49013**	PRR Depressed Center Searchlight Car, *04-05*	80
____ **49014**	NYC Crane Car "X-15," *04-05*	63
____ **49015**	Westside Lumber Moe & Joe Animated Flatcar, *04-05*	63
____ **49016**	Santa Fe Walking Brakeman Boxcar, *04-05*	65
____ **49017**	GN Animated Caboose "X84," *04-05*	62
____ **49019**	Southern Crane Car, *04*	65
____ **49021**	UP Crane Car "JPX-251," *05*	70
____ **49022**	M.O.W. Searchlight Car, *05*	70
____ **49023**	NYC Walking Brakeman Car "174226," *05*	68
____ **49024**	Pennsylvania Coal Dump Car "494979," *05*	74
____ **49025**	American Flyer Dump Car with presents, *05*	75
____ **49026**	American Flyer Operating Tie Car, *06*	58
____ **49027**	Pennsylvania Log Dump Car, *06*	80
____ **49028**	American Flyer Candy Cane Dump Car, *06*	78
____ **49029**	Santa Fe Animated Caboose, *06*	70
____ **49031**	GN Walking Brakeman Car, *06*	50
____ **49032**	Bethlehem Steel Depressed Center Searchlight Car, *06*	65
____ **49033**	NYC Coal Dump Car, *06*	74
____ **49035**	Southern Operating Coal Dump Car, *06*	65
____ **49037**	M.O.W. Crane Car "900," *07*	85
____ **49038**	D&RGW Walking Brakeman Car "69676," *07*	85
____ **49039**	Santa Fe Log Dump Car, *07-08*	85
____ **49040**	Chessie System Animated Caboose "3507," *07*	85
____ **49041**	C&O Tie Car, *07*	50
____ **49042**	Erie Coal Dump Car "05473," *07*	85
____ **49045**	American Flyer 915 Unloading Car, *08*	74
____ **49046**	American Flyer Santa Animated Caboose, *08*	73
____ **49047**	CP Rail Coal Dump Car "5522," *09*	90
____ **49048**	NYC Operating Boxcar "75509," *09*	68
____ **49049**	AF Commemorative Unloading Car, *10*	63
____ **49050**	Ringling Bros. Flatcar with Moe and Joe clowns, *11*	80
____ **49054**	GN Operating Log Dump Car, *10*	80
____ **49055**	Wabash Coal Dump Car, *10*	90
____ **49056**	NP Coal Dump Car, *11*	90
____ **49057**	WP Log Dump Car, *11*	85
____ **49060**	Ringling Bros. Searchlight Car, *11*	80
____ **49061**	Christmas Music Reefer, *12-13*	80
____ **49062**	Route of the Reindeer Animated Caboose, *12-14*	85
____ **49063**	Zombie Walking Brakeman Car, *13, 15-17*	80
____ **49064**	NH Boxcar, Diesel RailSounds, *13-18*	170
____ **49065**	UP Boxcar, Diesel RailSounds, *13- 17*	170
____ **49078**	Polar Express Elf Handcar, *14-17*	100
____ **49081**	70-Ton Truck with rotating bearing caps, pair, *14, 17-18*	25
____ **49082**	C&O Coal Dump Car, *14-17*	79
____ **49083**	Santa Fe Depressed Center Searchlight Car, *14-17*	80
____ **49084**	PRR Gas Unloading Car, *14-17*	80
____ **49085**	FasTrack Activator Rail, *14-18*	20

Mint

No.	Description	Mint
49086	Telephone Poles 6-pack, *15-18*	30
49088	SP Crane Car "7072," *15*	90
49089	SP Boom Car "7073," *15*	65
49600	Union Pacific Pony Express Set, *90*	570
49601	Missouri Pacific Eagle Set, *91*	618
49602	Northern Pacific North Coast Limited Set, *92*	699
49604	Western Pacific California Zephyr Set, *93*	448
49605	New Haven Passenger Car Set, *95*	193
49606	Silver Flash Passenger Car Set, *95*	658
49608	Domino Sugar Covered Hopper, *92*	57
49611	NYC Alco PA Diesel, Passenger Set, *02*	610
49612	B&O Passenger Car 4-pack, *03*	770
49613	Southern Baldwin Switcher Work Train Set, *04*	413
49614	Pennsylvania Alco PA Diesel, Passenger Set, *05*	575
49615	Chessie System SD9 Diesel, Freight Set, *06*	424
49616	Alton Limited Passenger Set, CC, *06*	740
49617	Blue Comet Steam Passenger Set, *07*	763
49618	NYC Dockside Switcher Freight Set, *07*	275
49621	American Flyer Christmas Steam Train, *09*	350
49622	Freedom Train Passenger Set, *08*	548
49624	American Flyer 959 Defender Freight Set, *10*	625
49625	Bakelite Plastics Freight Car 2-pack, *10*	135
49626	Ringling Bros. GP9 Diesel Circus Train Set, *11*	550
49627	Southern Crescent Limited Passenger Train Set, *11*	900
49632	Polar Express Berkshire Steam Passenger Set, *14-17*	400
49634	SP Dockside Switcher Steam Freight Set, *13-14*	270
49805	American Flyer 23780 Gabe the Lamplighter, *01*	114
49806	American Flyer 23796 Sawmill, *01*	75
49807	American Flyer 752 Seaboard Coaler, *01*	145
49808	American Flyer 594 Animated Track Gang Set, *06*	88
49809	American Flyer 772 Water Tower, *02*	53
49810	American Flyer 787 Log Loader, *04-05*	110
49811	American Flyer 773 Oil Derrick, *04-05*	53
49812	American Flyer 755 Talking Station, *04-05*	88
49813	American Flyer 789 Baggage Smasher, *04-05*	74
49814	American Flyer 774 Floodlight Tower, *04-05*	58
49815	American Flyer 741 Handcar and Shed, *04-05*	82
49818	American Flyer 23830 Piggyback Unloader and Flatcar, *04-05*	62
49819	American Flyer 583A Electromagnetic Crane, *04-05*	148
49820	American Flyer 758 Sam the Semaphore Man, *07-09*	95
49824	American Flyer 770 Loading Platform and Car, *05*	125
49825	American Flyer 571 Truss Bridge, *07-09*	27
49827	54" Curved Track, *07-11*	3
49828	10" Straight Track, *07-11*	3
49829	36" Straight Track, *07-11*	9
49830	Fiber Insulator Pins, *07-14*	2
49831	Steel Pins, *07-18*	3
49832	American Flyer 582 Blinking Signal, *07-08*	55
49833	American Flyer 587 Block Signal, *07-08*	55

		Mint
____ **49835**	American Flyer 588 Semaphore Block Signal, *07-09*	55
____ **49838**	American Flyer 792 Railroad Terminal, *08*	79
____ **49839**	American Flyer 793 Union Station, *08-10*	53
____ **49843**	Suburban Station, *09-10*	70
____ **49844**	Christmas Animated Billboard, *10-13*	35
____ **49845**	Truss Bridge, *10-15*	23
____ **49846**	American Flyer 773 Sunoco Oil Derrick, *10*	73
____ **49847**	American Flyer 774 Floodlight Tower, *10-12, 15-16*	94
____ **49848**	American Flyer Lines Girder Bridge, *10*	21
____ **49849**	Lackawanna Girder Bridge, *10*	18
____ **49850**	D&RGW Girder Bridge, *10-11*	21
____ **49851**	Gilbert Oil Storage Tank, *11*	72
____ **49852**	FasTrack 10" Straight Track, *12-18*	6
____ **49853**	FasTrack R20 Curved Track, *12-18*	7
____ **49854**	FasTrack 10" Terminal Track, *12-18*	9
____ **49855**	Illuminated Station Platform, *10*	35
____ **49856**	FasTrack R20 Switch-right hand, *12-14*	100
____ **49857**	FasTrack R20 Switch-left hand, *12-14*	100
____ **49858**	FasTrack Transition Track, *12-18*	10
____ **49859**	FasTrack R27 Wide-Radius Curved Track, *13-18*	9
____ **49860**	Sunoco Oil Storage Tank with light, *12*	73
____ **49861**	Classic Billboard Set, *12*	13
____ **49862**	FasTrack 30" Straight Track, *13-18*	16
____ **49863**	FasTrack 45-Degree Crossover , *13-18*	26
____ **49864**	FasTrack 90-Degree Crossover, *13-18*	26
____ **49865**	FasTrack Grade Crossing with Gates & Flashers, *13-14*	160
____ **49866**	FasTrack Straight Track with Illuminated Bumper, *13-18*	33
____ **49867**	FasTrack 5" Half Straight Track, *13-18*	6
____ **49868**	FasTrack R20 Manual Switch-left hand, *13-18*	50
____ **49869**	FasTrack R20 Manual Switch-right hand, *13-18*	50
____ **49870**	FasTrack R20 Manual Switch-left hand, CC, *13-14*	120
____ **49871**	FasTrack R20 Manual Switch-right hand, CC, *13-14*	120
____ **49872**	Telephone Poles, *13-17*	40
____ **49875**	American Flyer Replacement Wheel and Axle Packs, *13-17*	20
____ **49876**	Water Tower with shed, *13-17*	90
____ **49877**	Elevated Gilbert Oil Tank, *13-18*	76
____ **49878**	FasTrack R20 Half Curve, *13-18*	6
____ **49882**	Polar Express Girder Bridge, *14-17*	22
____ **49883**	FasTrack R27 Manual Switch-left-hand, *15-18*	69
____ **49884**	FasTrack R27 Manual Switch-right-hand, *15-18*	69
____ **49885**	FasTrack R27 Remote Switch-left-hand, *15-18*	150
____ **49886**	FasTrack R27 Remote Switch-right-hand, *15-18*	150
____ **49889**	FasTrack Figure-8 Add-On Track Pack, *14-18*	85
____ **49890**	FasTrack Inner Passing Loop Add-On Track Pack, *14-18*	127
____ **49891**	FasTrack 10" Grade Crossing, *14*	20
____ **49892**	FasTrack R27 Half Curve, *14-18*	8
____ **49893**	FasTrack Earthen Bumper-2 pieces, *14-18*	13

No.	Description	Mint
49895	FasTrack Uncoupling Section, *14-18*	43____
49896	FlyerChief Terminal Track, *15-18*	9____
49922	Freedom Train Heavyweight Passenger Car 2-pack, *08*	150 ____
49923	Alton Limited Heavyweight Passenger Car 2-pack, *08*	150 ____
49927	UP Streamlined Baggage Car "8944," *09*	75____
49928	MP Streamlined Baggage Car "8933," *09*	75____
49929	American Freedom Display Car "3510," *09*	73____
49930	ATSF Streamliner Passenger Car 3-pack, *09*	200____
49934	C&O Streamliner Baggage Car "48190," *10*	80____
49935	NP Streamliner Baggage Car "8929," *10*	80____
49936	D&RGW Streamliner Passenger Car 3-pack, *10*	250____
49940	ATSF Streamliner Full Vista Dome Car, *10*	80____
49941	UP Streamliner Full Vista Dome Car, *10*	83____
49942	NYC Streamliner Full Vista Dome Car, *10*	80____
49943	D&RGW Streamliner Full Vista Dome Car, *11-14*	80____
49944	Erie Streamliner Baggage Car, *11-15*	80____
49945	D&RGW Streamliner Baggage Car "754," *10*	80____
49946	SP Daylight Streamliner Baggage Car, *11-13*	80____
49947	SP Daylight Streamliner Full Vista Dome Car, *11-13*	80____
49948	Erie Streamliner Full Vista Dome Car, *11-15*	80____
49949	Texas Special Streamliner Passenger Car 3-Pack, *11-13*	250 ____
49950	Texas Special Streamlined Combination Car, *12-13*	80____
49951	Texas Special Streamlined Vista Dome Car, *12-13*	80____
49952	Texas Special Streamlined Observation Car, *12-13*	80____
49953	Union Refrigerator Transit Co. Bananas Wood-sided Refrigerator Car, *17*	65 ____
49954	Columbia Soups Wood-sided Refrigerator Car, *17*	65____
49955	Monarch Finer Foods Wood-sided Refrigerator Car, *17*	65 ____
49956	Texas Special Streamlined Full Vista Dome Car, *12-14*	80 ____
49957	Texas Special Streamlined Baggage Car, *12-14*	80____
49958	AT&SF Streamlined Full Vista Dome Car, *12-14*	80____
49959	PRR Streamlined Vista Dome Car, *12-15*	80____
49960	North Pole Express Streamliner 3-Pack, *12-14*	250____
49972	Polar Express Abandoned Toy Car, *14-17*	70____
49973	Polar Express Baggage Car, *14-17*	70____
49977	American Flyer Work Crew People Pack, *14-18*	27____
49978	AF Classic Catalogs Billboard Set, *15-17*	13____
49979	Winter Station, *14-18*	80____
49990	FasTrack Outer Passing Loop Add-On Track Pack, *14-16*	155 ____
49991	FasTrack Siding Track Add-On Track Pack, *14-18*	100____
52009	WP Stock Car (SVAFC), *09*	120____
52094	Ann Arbor Covered Grain Hopper "1496" (NASG), *96 u*	55 ____
52095	Mobil 1-D Tank Car "1596" (NASG), *96 u*	85____

Retail

____	**100**	40' Boxcar	47
____	**102**	B&O 40' Boxcar	47
____	**103**	Cotton Belt 40' Boxcar	47
____	**105**	D&RGW 40' Boxcar	47
____	**108**	GN 40' Boxcar	47
____	**112**	Soo Line 40' Boxcar	47
____	**113**	NYC 40' Boxcar	47
____	**114**	PRR 40' Boxcar	47
____	**115**	ATSF 40' Boxcar	47
____	**116**	Seaboard 40' Boxcar	47
____	**116C**	Seaboard "Silver Comet" 40' Boxcar	47
____	**116L**	Seaboard "Robert E. Lee" 40' Boxcar	47
____	**117**	SP 40' Boxcar	47
____	**118**	UP 40' Boxcar	47
____	**119**	C&O 40' Boxcar	47
____	**119B**	C&O 40' Boxcar	47
____	**121**	NYC Pacemaker 40' Boxcar	46
____	**122**	Rutland 40' Boxcar	50
____	**123**	PRR Merchandise Service 40' Boxcar	49
____	**125**	P&LE 40' Boxcar	48
____	**126**	NP 40' Boxcar	49
____	**128**	NH 40' Boxcar	47
____	**129**	GN 40' Boxcar	47
____	**130**	GM&O 40' Boxcar	47
____	**131**	N&W 40' Boxcar	47
____	**132**	CP 40' Boxcar	47
____	**133**	M&StL 40' Boxcar	47
____	**134**	Erie-Lackawanna 40' Boxcar	47
____	**135**	SP 40' Boxcar	48
____	**136**	Susquehanna 40' Boxcar	49
____	**137**	C&NW 40' Boxcar	47
____	**138**	Conrail 40' Boxcar	47
____	**139**	Southern 40' Boxcar	47
____	**140**	MP 40' Boxcar	47
____	**141**	NYC 40' Boxcar	47
____	**142**	Rock Island 40' Boxcar	47
____	**143**	Virginian 40' Boxcar	47
____	**144**	SP 40' Boxcar, silver	44
____	**145**	CNJ 40' Boxcar	47
____	**146**	Wabash 40' Boxcar	47
____	**147**	Central of Georgia 40' Boxcar	48
____	**148**	B&M 40' Boxcar	48

No.	Description	Retail	
149	Soo Line 40' Boxcar	47	___
150	D&RGW 40' Boxcar	47	___
151	B&O Sentinel 40' Boxcar	47	___
152	MKT 40' Boxcar	47	___
153	Texas & Pacific 40' Boxcar	47	___
175	Illinois Central Gulf 40' Boxcar	49	___
176	Reading 40' Boxcar	49	___
177	Akron, Canton & Youngstown 40' Boxcar	47	___
178	BN 40' Boxcar	47	___
179	Burlington 40' Boxcar	50	___
180G	NP 40' Boxcar, green	48	___
180R	NP 40' Boxcar, red	48	___
200	2-bay Rib-sided Hopper	40	___
201	C&O 2-bay Rib-sided Hopper	40	___
202	WM 2-bay Rib-sided Hopper	40	___
204	Erie 2-bay Rib-sided Hopper	40	___
205	N&W 2-bay Rib-sided Hopper	40	___
206	NYC 2-bay Rib-sided Hopper	40	___
207	PRR 2-bay Rib-sided Hopper	40	___
208	Peabody 2-bay Rib-sided Hopper	40	___
209	Southern 2-bay Rib-sided Hopper	40	___
210	UP 2-bay Rib-sided Hopper	40	___
211	SP 2-bay Rib-sided Hopper	40	___
212	D&RGW 2-bay Rib-sided Hopper	40	___
213	Virginian 2-bay Rib-sided Hopper	40	___
214	Reading 2-bay Rib-sided Hopper	40	___
215	CB&Q 2-bay Rib-sided Hopper	40	___
216	LV 2-bay Rib-sided Hopper	40	___
217	Interstate 2-bay Rib-sided Hopper	40	___
218	BN 2-bay Rib-sided Hopper	40	___
223	Burlington Express 40' Plug Door Boxcar	31	___
250	2-bay Offset-sided Hopper	40	___
251	ATSF 2-bay Offset-sided Hopper	40	___
252	CP 2-bay Offset-sided Hopper	40	___
253	GN 2-bay Offset-sided Hopper	40	___
254	NP 2-bay Offset-sided Hopper	40	___
255	IC 2-bay Offset-sided Hopper	40	___
256	NYC 2-bay Offset-sided Hopper	40	___
257	L&N 2-bay Offset-sided Hopper	40	___
258	MILW 2-bay Offset-sided Hopper	40	___
259	UP 2-bay Offset-sided Hopper	40	___
260	Frisco 2-bay Offset-sided Hopper	40	___
261	LNE 2-bay Offset-sided Hopper	40	___
262	D&H 2-bay Offset-sided Hopper	40	___
263	NKP 2-bay Offset-sided Hopper	40	___

____ 264	MP 2-bay Offset-sided Hopper	40
____ 265	Conrail 2-bay Offset-sided Hopper	40
____ 266	C&NW 2-bay Offset-sided Hopper	40
____ 267	Monon 2-bay Offset-sided Hopper	40
____ 268	B&O 2-bay Offset-sided Hopper	40
____ 352	CP 2-bay Offset-sided Hopper	40
____ 355	IC 2-bay Offset-sided Hopper	40
____ 359	UP 2-bay Offset-sided Hopper	40
____ 361	LNE 2-bay Offset-sided Hopper	40
____ 364	MP 2-bay Offset-sided Hopper	40
____ 366	C&NW 2-bay Offset-sided Hopper	40
____ 368	B&O 2-bay Offset-sided Hopper	40
____ 420	BN Gondola	43
____ 500	Tank Car	48
____ 501	Corn Products Tank Car	48
____ 502	GATX Tank Car	48
____ 503	Cargill Tank Car	48
____ 504	J.M. Huber Tank Car	48
____ 505	Englehard Tank Car	48
____ 506	Georgia Kao Tank Car	48
____ 507	New Jersey Zinc Tank Car	48
____ 508	BASF Wyandotte Tank Car	48
____ 509	American Maize Tank Car	48
____ 510	B.F. Goodrich Tank Car	48
____ 511	Elcor Chemical Tank Car	48
____ 512	Domino Sugar Tank Car	48
____ 513B	American Models Tank Car	48
____ 513G	American Models Tank Car, green	48
____ 514	Aeron Tank Car	48
____ 515	DuPont Tank Car	48
____ 517	Sinclair Diesel Tank Car	48
____ 518	Sinclair Gas Tank Car	48
____ 519	Texaco Tank Car	48
____ 520	Sunoco Tank Car	48
____ 521	Dow Tank Car	48
____ 772	Automatic Water Tower	80
____ 774	Floodlight Tower	80
____ 1100	40' Boxcar	31
____ 1100	WFE 40' Boxcar, Premium Series	32
____ 1102	B&O 40' Boxcar	47
____ 1103	Cotton Belt 40' Boxcar	31
____ 1105	BN/WFE 40' Boxcar	33
____ 1105	D&RGW 40' Boxcar	46
____ 1108	GN 40' Boxcar, Classic Series	50
____ 1112	Soo Line 40' Boxcar	25

		Retail	
1113	NYC 40' Boxcar	47	____
1114	PRR 40' Boxcar	47	____
1115	ATSF 40' Boxcar	47	____
1116	Seaboard 40' Boxcar	47	____
1117	SP 40' Boxcar	47	____
1118	UP 40' Boxcar	47	____
1119	C&O 40' Boxcar	47	____
1121	NYC 40' Boxcar, Classic Series	50	____
1122	Rutland 40' Boxcar, Classic Series	50	____
1125	P&LE 40' Boxcar, Premium Series	48	____
1126	NP 40' Boxcar, Premium Series	48	____
1128	NH 40' Boxcar	47	____
1129	GN 40' Boxcar	47	____
1130	GM&O 40' Boxcar	47	____
1131	N&W 40' Boxcar	47	____
1132	CP 40' Boxcar	47	____
1133	M&StL 40' Boxcar	47	____
1133	NYC 40' Boxcar	47	____
1134	Erie-Lackawanna 40' Boxcar	47	____
1135	SP 40' Boxcar, Premium Series	48	____
1136	Susquehanna 40' Boxcar, Classic Series	49	____
1137	C&NW 40' Boxcar	47	____
1138	Conrail 40' Boxcar	47	____
1500	50' Rib-sided Boxcar	40	____
1501	Railbox 50' Rib-sided Boxcar	40	____
1502	Evergreen 50' Rib-sided Boxcar	40	____
1503	MEC 50' Rib-sided Boxcar	40	____
1504	C&NW 50' Rib-sided Boxcar	40	____
1505	UP 50' Rib-sided Boxcar	42	____
1506	Conrail 50' Rib-sided Boxcar	40	____
1507	BN 50' Rib-sided Boxcar	40	____
1508	Tropicana 50' Rib-sided Boxcar	40	____
1509	D&RGW 50' Rib-sided Boxcar	40	____
1510	Rail Link 50' Rib-sided Boxcar	40	____
1511	CSX Link 50' Rib-sided Boxcar	41	____
1512	Soo Line 50' Rib-sided Boxcar	40	____
1513	Miller 50' Rib-sided Boxcar	40	____
1514	PRR 50' Rib-sided Boxcar	43	____
1515	NYC 50' Rib-sided Boxcar	40	____
1516	Amtrak 50' Rib-sided Boxcar	42	____
1516P3	Amtrak 50' Rib-sided Boxcar, Phase III	45	____
1517	NS 50' Rib-sided Boxcar	41	____
1518B	Rock Island 50' Rib-sided Boxcar, blue	40	____
1518W	Rock Island 50' Rib-sided Boxcar, white	40	____
2002	RI City of Chicago Observation (TCA)	55	____

_____ **2003**	RI City of Los Angeles Pullman Coach (TCA)	55
_____ **2004**	RI Redman/Fraley Pullman Combine (TCA)	55
_____ **2005**	RI 4-6-2 Pacific Locomotive (TCA)	380
_____ **2006**	RI City of San Antonio Post Office Car	75
_____ **2200**	40' Plug Door Boxcar	42
_____ **2202**	PFE 40' Boxcar, Premium Series	43
_____ **2203**	ART 40' Boxcar, Premium Series	43
_____ **2204**	FGE 40' Boxcar, Premium Series	43
_____ **2206**	Dubuque 40' Boxcar, Premium Series	43
_____ **2207**	WP 40' Plug Door Boxcar	40
_____ **2208**	CN 40' Plug Door Boxcar	40
_____ **2209**	DT&I 40' Boxcar, Premium Series	43
_____ **2210**	ATSF 40' Boxcar, Premium Series	43
_____ **2211**	PRR 40' Plug Door Boxcar	40
_____ **2212**	Soo Line 40' Plug Door Boxcar	40
_____ **2213**	Milwaukee Road 40' Plug Door Boxcar	40
_____ **2215**	NYC 40' Boxcar, Premium Series	43
_____ **2216**	BN 40' Boxcar, Premium Series	43
_____ **2217**	GN 40' Plug Door Boxcar	45
_____ **2218**	CP 40' Plug Door Boxcar	45
_____ **2219**	Pacific Great Eastern 40' Plug Door Boxcar	42
_____ **2220**	B&A 40' Boxcar, Classic Series	42
_____ **2221**	NP 40' Boxcar, Classic Series	42
_____ **2222**	Miller 40' Plug Door Boxcar	39
_____ **2223**	Burlington 40' Plug Door Boxcar, Classic Series	45
_____ **2224**	CP 40' Plug Door Boxcar, Classic Series	45
_____ **2225**	Frisco 40' Plug Door Boxcar, Classic Series	45
_____ **2226**	ADM 40' Plug Door Boxcar	39
_____ **2227**	State of Maine 40' Plug Door Boxcar	42
_____ **2228**	Reading 40' Plug Door Boxcar	43
_____ **2229**	Milwaukee Road 40' Plug Door Boxcar	43
_____ **3200**	2-bay Rib-sided Hopper	40
_____ **3201**	C&O 2-bay Rib-sided Hopper	40
_____ **3202**	WM 2-bay Rib-sided Hopper	40
_____ **3203**	B&O 2-bay Rib-sided Hopper	40
_____ **3204**	Erie 2-bay Rib-sided Hopper	40
_____ **3205**	N&W 2-bay Rib-sided Hopper	40
_____ **3206**	NYC 2-bay Rib-sided Hopper	40
_____ **3206R**	NYC 2-bay Rib-sided Hopper, red	40
_____ **3207**	PRR 2-bay Rib-sided Hopper	40
_____ **3208**	Peabody 2-bay Rib-sided Hopper	40
_____ **3209**	Southern 2-bay Rib-sided Hopper	40
_____ **3211**	SP 2-bay Rib-sided Hopper	40
_____ **3213**	Virginia 2-bay Rib-sided Hopper	40
_____ **3214**	Reading 2-bay Rib-sided Hopper	40

3215	CB&Q 2-bay Rib-sided Hopper	40	____
3216	LV 2-bay Rib-sided Hopper	40	____
3217	Interstate RR 2-bay Rib-sided Hopper	40	____
3218	Burlington 2-bay Rib-sided Hopper	40	____
3218	D&RGW 2-bay Rib-sided Hopper	40	____
3219	NH 2-bay Rib-sided Hopper	40	____
3220	Texas & Pacific 2-bay Offset-sided Hopper	40	____
3250	2-bay Offset-sided Hopper	40	____
3251	ATSF 2-bay Offset-sided Hopper	40	____
3252	CP 2-bay Offset-sided Hopper	40	____
3253	GN 2-bay Offset-sided Hopper	40	____
3254	NP 2-bay Offset-sided Hopper	40	____
3255	IC 2-bay Offset-sided Hopper	40	____
3256	NYC 2-bay Offset-sided Hopper	40	____
3257	L&N 2-bay Offset-sided Hopper	40	____
3258	MILW 2-bay Offset-sided Hopper	40	____
3259	UP 2-bay Offset-sided Hopper	40	____
3260	Frisco 2-bay Offset-sided Hopper	40	____
3261	LNE 2-bay Offset-sided Hopper	40	____
3262	D&H 2-bay Offset-sided Hopper	40	____
3263	NKP 2-bay Offset-sided Hopper	40	____
3264	MP 2-bay Offset-sided Hopper	40	____
3265	Conrail 2-bay Offset-sided Hopper	40	____
3266	C&NW 2-bay Offset-sided Hopper	40	____
3267	Monon 2-bay Offset-sided Hopper	40	____
3268	B&O 2-bay Offset-sided Hopper	40	____
3269	ACL 2-bay Offset-sided Hopper	40	____
3270	GM&O 2-bay Offset-sided Hopper	40	____
3271	Reading 2-bay Offset-sided Hopper	40	____
3272	Southern 2-bay Offset-sided Hopper	40	____
3273	Reading Blue Coal 2-bay Offset-sided Hopper	46	____
3274	Rock Island 2-bay Offset-sided Hopper	40	____
3275	CNJ 2-bay Offset-sided Hopper	40	____
3276	C&O 2-bay Offset-sided Hopper	40	____
3300	PS-2 CD 3-bay Hopper	50	____
3301	ADM PS-2 CD 3-bay Hopper	50	____
3302	BN PS-2 CD 3-bay Hopper	50	____
3303	Cargill PS-2 CD 3-bay Hopper	50	____
3304	C&NW PS-2 CD 3-bay Hopper	50	____
3305	Conrail PS-2 CD 3-bay Hopper	50	____
3306	GN PS-2 CD 3-bay Hopper	50	____
3307	IC PS-2 CD 3-bay Hopper	50	____
3308	PRR PS-2 CD 3-bay Hopper	50	____
3309	Pillsbury PS-2 CD 3-bay Hopper	50	____
3310	D&RGW PS-2 CD 3-bay Hopper	50	____

____ 3311	The Rock PS-2 CD 3-bay Hopper	50
____ 3312	ATSF PS-2 CD 3-bay Hopper	50
____ 3313	UP PS-2 CD 3-bay Hopper	50
____ 3351	Santa Fe 3-bay Offset-sided Hopper	43
____ 3352	Burlington 3-bay Offset-sided Hopper	43
____ 3353	B&M 3-bay Offset-sided Hopper	43
____ 3354	B&LE 3-bay Offset-sided Hopper	43
____ 3357	C&NW 3-bay Offset-sided Hopper	43
____ 3358	C&O 3-bay Offset-sided Hopper	43
____ 3359	CN 3-bay Offset-sided Hopper	43
____ 3360	CP 3-bay Offset-sided Hopper	43
____ 3362	Erie 3-bay Offset-sided Hopper	43
____ 3364	GTW 3-bay Offset-sided Hopper	43
____ 3365	IC 3-bay Offset-sided Hopper, orange	43
____ 3366	IC 3-bay Offset-sided Hopper	43
____ 3367	MP 3-bay Offset-sided Hopper	43
____ 3368	B&O 3-bay Offset-sided Hopper	43
____ 3369	NYC 3-bay Offset-sided Hopper	43
____ 3370	NKP 3-bay Offset-sided Hopper	43
____ 3371	P&LE 3-bay Offset-sided Hopper	43
____ 3372	Peabody 3-bay Offset-sided Hopper	43
____ 3373	Reading Blue Coal 3-bay Offset-sided Hopper	43
____ 3375	Rock Island 3-bay Offset-sided Hopper	43
____ 3377	Southern 3-bay Offset-sided Hopper	43
____ 3378	SP 3-bay Offset-sided Hopper	43
____ 3379	UP 3-bay Offset-sided Hopper	43
____ 3400	4-bay Offset-sided Hopper	40
____ 3401	B&O 4-bay Offset-sided Hopper	40
____ 3402	C&O 4-bay Offset-sided Hopper	40
____ 3403	IC 4-bay Offset-sided Hopper	40
____ 3404	NH 4-bay Offset-sided Hopper	40
____ 3405	MP 4-bay Offset-sided Hopper	40
____ 3406	Peabody Coal 4-bay Offset-sided Hopper	40
____ 3407	Rock Island 4-bay Offset-sided Hopper	40
____ 3408	ATSF 4-bay Offset-sided Hopper	40
____ 3409	WM 4-bay Offset-sided Hopper	40
____ 3410	NYC 4-bay Offset-sided Hopper	40
____ 3411	NP 4-bay Offset-sided Hopper	40
____ 3412	MKT 4-bay Offset-sided Hopper	40
____ 3414	Reading Blue Coal 4-bay Offset-sided Hopper	40
____ 3415	B&M 4-bay Offset-sided Hopper	40
____ 3451	BN 4-bay Rib-sided Hopper	40
____ 3452	CB&Q 4-bay Rib-sided Hopper	40
____ 3453	C&NW 4-bay Rib-sided Hopper	40
____ 3454	Conrail 4-bay Rib-sided Hopper	40

		Retail	
3455	CSX 4-bay Rib-sided Hopper	40	____
3456	D&RGW 4-bay Rib-sided Hopper	40	____
3457	GN 4-bay Rib-sided Hopper	40	____
3458B	GN 4-bay Rib-sided Hopper	40	____
3458C	PRR 4-bay Rib-sided Hopper, brown	40	____
3458R	PRR 4-bay Rib-sided Hopper	40	____
3459	UP 4-bay Rib-sided Hopper	40	____
3460	SP 4-bay Rib-sided Hopper	40	____
3461	Virginian 4-bay Rib-sided Hopper	40	____
3463	LV 4-bay Rib-sided Hopper	40	____
4400	Gondola	43	____
4401	Frisco Gondola	43	____
4402	Wabash Gondola	43	____
4403	Southern Gondola	43	____
4404	PRR Gondola	43	____
4405	GN Gondola	43	____
4406	LV Gondola	43	____
4407	B&O Gondola	43	____
4408	C&O Gondola	43	____
4409	Milwaukee Road Gondola	43	____
4410	SP Gondola	43	____
4411	WM Gondola	43	____
4412	Soo Line Gondola	43	____
4413	Lackawanna Gondola	43	____
4414	IC Gondola	43	____
4415	NYC Gondola	43	____
4416	NKP Gondola	43	____
4417	N&W Gondola	43	____
4418	UP Gondola	43	____
4419	ATSF Gondola	43	____
4420	BN Gondola	43	____
4421	CP Gondola	43	____
4422	NP Gondola	43	____
4423	D&H Gondola	43	____
4424	Reading Gondola	43	____
4425	D&RGW Gondola	43	____
4426	C&NW Gondola	43	____
4427	Conrail Gondola	43	____
4428	MP Gondola	43	____
4429	CB&Q Gondola	43	____
4430	NH Gondola	43	____
4430B	NH Gondola, black	43	____
4431	P&LE Gondola	43	____
4432	Rock Island Gondola	43	____
4433	NS Gondola, black	43	____

____	4433R	NS Gondola, red	43
____	4434	Virginian Gondola	43
____	4435	IC Gondola	43
____	4436G	MKT Gondola, green	43
____	4436R	MKT Gondola, red	43
____	4437	Texas& Pacific Gondola	43
____	4599	Chevron Tank Car (TCA)	43
____	6000	USRA 46' Flatcar	48
____	6001	B&O USRA 46' Flatcar	48
____	6002	Burlington USRA 46' Flatcar	48
____	6003	BN USRA 46' Flatcar	48
____	6004	Conrail USRA 46' Flatcar	48
____	6005	C&NW USRA 46' Flatcar	48
____	6006	C&O USRA 46' Flatcar	48
____	6007	CSX USRA 46' Flatcar	48
____	6008	CP USRA 46' Flatcar	48
____	6009	D&RGW USRA 46' Flatcar	48
____	6010	GN USRA 46' Flatcar	48
____	6011	IC USRA 46' Flatcar	48
____	6012	NH USRA 46' Flatcar	48
____	6013	NYC USRA 46' Flatcar	48
____	6014	NP USRA 46' Flatcar	48
____	6015	N&W USRA 46' Flatcar	48
____	6016	MP USRA 46' Flatcar	48
____	6017	PRR USRA 46' Flatcar	48
____	6018	ATSF USRA 46' Flatcar	48
____	6019	Southern USRA 46' Flatcar	48
____	6020	SP USRA 46' Flatcar	48
____	6021	UP USRA 46' Flatcar	48
____	6022	Frisco USRA 46' Flatcar	48
____	6023	Milwaukee Road USRA 46' Flatcar	48
____	6024	Rock Island USRA 46' Flatcar	48
____	6025	B&M USRA 46' Flatcar	48
____	6026	MKT USRA 46' Flatcar	48
____	6027	Texas & Pacific USRA 46' Flatcar	48
____	7500	Wood-sided Caboose	55
____	7501	ATSF Wood-sided Caboose	55
____	7502	ACL Wood-sided Caboose	55
____	7503	B&O Wood-sided Caboose	55
____	7504	CP Wood-sided Caboose	55
____	7505	CB&Q Wood-sided Caboose	55
____	7506	C&O Wood-sided Caboose	55
____	7507	C&NW Wood-sided Caboose	55
____	7508	D&RGW Wood-sided Caboose	55
____	7509	Erie Wood-sided Caboose	55

7510	Frisco Wood-sided Caboose	55 ____
7511	GN Wood-sided Caboose	55 ____
7512	GM&O Wood-sided Caboose	55 ____
7513	IC Wood-sided Caboose	55 ____
7514	Lackawanna Wood-sided Caboose	55 ____
7515	Milwaukee Road Wood-sided Caboose	55 ____
7516	MP Wood-sided Caboose	55 ____
7517	NH Wood-sided Caboose	55 ____
7518	NYC Wood-sided Caboose	55 ____
7519	N&W Wood-sided Caboose	55 ____
7520	NP Wood-sided Caboose	55 ____
7521	PRR Wood-sided Caboose	55 ____
7522	Rock Island Wood-sided Caboose	55 ____
7523	Southern Wood-sided Caboose	55 ____
7524	SP Wood-sided Caboose	55 ____
7525	UP Wood-sided Caboose	55 ____
7526	Rio Grande 4-stripe Wood-sided Caboose	55 ____
7527	NYC Pacemaker Wood-sided Caboose	55 ____
7528	Pere Marquette Wood-sided Caboose	55 ____
7529	LV Wood-sided Caboose	55 ____
7530	Cotton Belt Wood-sided Caboose	55 ____
7531	WM Wood-sided Caboose	55 ____
7532	MKT Wood-sided Caboose	55 ____
7533	Texas & Pacific Wood-sided Caboose	55 ____
7700	Bay Window Caboose	45 ____
7701	Chessie Bay Window Caboose	45 ____
7702	Erie Bay Window Caboose	45 ____
7703	Erie-Lackawanna Bay Window Caboose, red	45 ____
7704	Conrail Bay Window Caboose	45 ____
7705	C&NW Bay Window Caboose	45 ____
7706	Southern Bay Window Caboose	45 ____
7707	NYC Bay Window Caboose	45 ____
7708	PRR Bay Window Caboose	45 ____
7709	Norfolk & Western Bay Window Caboose	45 ____
7710	ATSF Bay Window Caboose	45 ____
7711	SP Bay Window Caboose	45 ____
7712	GN Bay Window Caboose	45 ____
7713	NP Bay Window Caboose	45 ____
7714	UP Bay Window Caboose	45 ____
7715	NH Bay Window Caboose	45 ____
7716	CP Bay Window Caboose	45 ____
7717	Virginian Bay Window Caboose, Premium	50 ____
7718	Erie-Lack. Bay Window Caboose, Premium	50 ____
7719	BN Bay Window Caboose	45 ____

____ 7720	Burlington Bay Window Caboose, Premium	50
____ 7721	Milwaukee Road Bay Window Caboose	45
____ 7722	Frisco Bay Window Caboose, Premium	50
____ 7723	MP Bay Window Caboose	45
____ 7724	CSX Bay Window Caboose	45
____ 7725	NYC Bay Window Caboose	45
____ 7726	SP Bay Window Caboose	45
____ 7728	Virginian Bay Window Caboose	45
____ 7729	CNJ Bay Window Caboose	45
____ 7730	Wabash Bay Window Caboose	45
____ 7731	WP Bay Window Caboose	45
____ 46000-UndecAC	USRA 4-6-2 Pacific Locomotive, full sound	426
____ 46000-UndecHR	USRA 4-6-2 Pacific, hi-rail	380
____ 46000-UndecL	USRA 4-6-2 Pacific, limited sound	400
____ 46000-UndecS	USRA 4-6-2 Pacific, scale	380
____ 46000-ATSFAC	ATSF 4-6-2 Pacific Locomotive, full sound	426
____ 46000-ATSFHR	ATSF 4-6-2 Pacific, hi-rail	380
____ 46000-ATSFL	ATSF 4-6-2 Pacific, limited sound	400
____ 46000-ATSFS	ATSF 4-6-2 Pacific, scale	380
____ 46000-CBQAC	CB&Q 4-6-2 Pacific Locomotive, full sound	426
____ 46000-CBQHR	CB&Q 4-6-2 Pacific Locomotive, hi-rail	380
____ 46000-CBQL	CB&Q 4-6-2 Pacific, limited sound	400
____ 46000-CBQS	CB&Q 4-6-2 Pacific, scale	380
____ 46000-GNAC	GN 4-6-2 Pacific Locomotive, full sound	426
____ 46000-GNHR	GN 4-6-2 Pacific, hi-rail	380
____ 46000-GNL	GN 4-6-2 Pacific, limited sound	400
____ 46000-GNS	GN 4-6-2 Pacific, scale	380
____ 46000-KATYAC	MKT 4-6-2 Pacific Locomotive, full sound	426
____ 46000-KATYHR	MKT 4-6-2 Pacific, hi-rail	380
____ 46000-KATYL	MKT 4-6-2 Pacific, limited sound	400
____ 46000-KATYS	MKT 4-6-2 Pacific, scale	380
____ 46000-NHAC	NH 4-6-2 Pacific Locomotive, full sound	426
____ 46000-NHHR	NH 4-6-2 Pacific, hi-rail	380
____ 46000-NHL	NH 4-6-2 Pacific, limited sound	400
____ 46000-NHS	NH 4-6-2 Pacific, scale	380
____ 46000-NYCAC	NYC 4-6-2 Pacific Locomotive, full sound	426
____ 46000-NYCHR	NYC 4-6-2 Pacific, hi-rail	380
____ 46000-NYCL	NYC 4-6-2 Pacific, limited sound	400
____ 46000-NYCS	NYC 4-6-2 Pacific, scale	380
____ 46000-PMAC	Pere Marquette 4-6-2 Pacific Locomotive, full sound	426
____ 46000-PMHR	Pere Marquette 4-6-2 Pacific, hi-rail	380
____ 46000-PML	Pere Marquette 4-6-2 Pacific, limited sound	400
____ 46000-PMS	Pere Marquette 4-6-2 Pacific, scale	380
____ 46000-PRRAC	PRR 4-6-2 Pacific Locomotive, full sound	426

Retail

46000-PRRHR	PRR 4-6-2 Pacific, hi-rail	380 ____
46000-PRRL	PRR 4-6-2 Pacific, limited sound	400 ____
46000-PRRS	PRR 4-6-2 Pacific, scale	380 ____
46000-SPAC	SP 4-6-2 Pacific Locomotive, full sound	426 ____
46000-SPHR	SP 4-6-2 Pacific, hi-rail	380 ____
46000-SPL	SP 4-6-2 Pacific, limited sound	400 ____
46000-SPS	SP 4-6-2 Pacific, scale	380 ____
46000-UPAC	UP 4-6-2 Pacific Locomotive, full sound	426 ____
46000-UPHR	UP 4-6-2 Pacific, hi-rail	380 ____
46000-UPL	UP 4-6-2 Pacific, limited sound	400 ____
46000-UPS	UP 4-6-2 Pacific, scale	380 ____
46001	B&O USRA 4-6-2 Locomotive	350 ____
46003AC	MILW 4-6-2 Pacific Locomotive, full sound	426 ____
46003HR	MILW 4-6-2 Pacific, hi-rail	380 ____
46003L	MILW 4-6-2 Pacific, limited sound	400 ____
46003S	MILW 4-6-2 Pacific, scale	380 ____
46006AC	Southern 4-6-2 Pacific Locomotive, full sound	426 ____
46006HR	Southern 4-6-2 Pacific, hi-rail	380 ____
46006L	Southern 4-6-2 Pacific, limited sound	400 ____
46006S	Southern 4-6-2 Pacific, scale	380 ____
46007AC	Rock Island 4-6-2 Pacific Locomotive, full sound	426 ____
46007HR	Rock Island 4-6-2 Pacific, hi-rail	380 ____
46007L	Rock Island 4-6-2 Pacific, limited sound	400 ____
46007S	Rock Island 4-6-2 Pacific, scale	380 ____
46200AC	LV 4-6-2 Pacific Locomotive, full sound	426 ____
46200HR	LV 4-6-2 Pacific, hi-rail	380 ____
46200L	LV 4-6-2 Pacific, limited sound	400 ____
46200S	LV 4-6-2 Pacific, scale	380 ____
46500	USRA 4-6-2 Locomotive	620 ____
46500AC	4-6-2 Pacific Steam Passenger Set	700 ____
46500HR	4-6-2 Pacific Steam Passenger Set, hi-rail	620 ____
46500S	4-6-2 Pacific Steam Passenger Set, scale	620 ____
46501	B&O USRA 4-6-2 Locomotive	620 ____
46502	Southern USRA 4-6-2 Locomotive	620 ____
46502AC	Southern 4-6-2 Pacific Steam Passenger Set	700 ____
46502HR	Southern 4-6-2 Pacific Steam Passenger Set, hi-rail	620 ____
46502S	Southern 4-6-2 Pacific Steam Passenger Set, scale	620 ____
46503AC	MILW 4-6-2 Pacific Steam Passenger Set	660 ____
46503HR	MILW 4-6-2 Pacific Steam Passenger Set, hi-rail	600 ____
46503S	MILW 4-6-2 Pacific Steam Passenger Set, scale	600 ____
46504AC	NH 4-6-2 Pacific Steam Passenger Set	700 ____
46504HR	NH 4-6-2 Pacific Steam Passenger Set, hi-rail	620 ____

___	46504S	NH 4-6-2 Pacific Steam Passenger Set, scale	620
___	48400	4-8-4 Northern Locomotive	500
___	48400-6	4-8-4 Northern Locomotive, coal tender	500
___	48401	Santa Fe 4-8-4 Northern Locomotive	500
___	48402	Rock Island 4-8-4 Northern Locomotive	500
___	48403	LV 4-8-4 Northern Locomotive	500
___	48404	CB&Q 4-8-4 Northern Locomotive	500
___	48405	WM 4-8-4 Northern Locomotive	500
___	48406	Cotton Belt 4-8-4 Northern Locomotive	500
___	48407	SP 4-8-4 Northern Locomotive	500
___	48408	C&O 4-8-4 Northern Locomotive	500
___	48409	Lackawanna 4-8-4 Northern Locomotive	500
___	48410	MILW 4-8-4 Northern Locomotive	500
	95247	CB&Q USRA 46' Flatcar with Burlington trailer (S Fest)	90
___	547798	C&NW 4-bay Hopper (TCA)	85
___	BD8RPO	Budd Railway Post Office Car	60
___	BD8200	Budd Coach, silver	95
___	BD8200C	Budd Coach, chrome	95
___	BD8201	B&O Budd Coach	95
___	BD8202	Southern Budd Coach	95
___	BD8203	UP Budd Coach	95
___	BD8204	New Haven Budd Coach	95
___	BD8205	NYC Budd Coach	95
___	BD8206	ATSF Budd Coach	95
___	BD8209	PRR Budd Coach	95
___	BD8214	ACL Budd Coach	95
___	BD8215	Burlington Budd Coach	95
___	BD8216	Rock Island Budd Coach	95
___	BD8217	IC Budd Coach	95
___	BD8218	Central of Georgia Budd Coach	95
___	BD8223	MP Colorado Eagle Budd Coach	95
___	BD8224	SP Budd Coach	95
___	BD8225	Texas Special Budd Coach	95
___	BDBS00	Budd 4-Car Set, silver	340
___	BDBS00C	Budd 4-Car Set, chrome	340
___	BDBS01	B&O Budd 4-Car Set	340
___	BDBS02	Southern Budd 4-Car Set	340
___	BDBS03	UP Budd 4-Car Set	340
___	BDBS04	New Haven Budd 4-Car Set	340
___	BDBS05	NYC 4-Car Budd Set	340
___	BDBS06	ATSF Budd 4-Car Set	340
___	BDBS09	PRR Budd 4-Car Set	340
___	BDBS14	ACL Budd 4-Car Set	340
___	BDBS15	Burlington Budd 4-Car Set	340

Code	Description	Retail	
BDBS16	Rock Island Budd 4-Car Set	340	___
BDBS17	IC Budd 4-Car Set	340	___
BDBS18	Central of Georgia Budd 4-Car Set	340	___
BDBS23	MP Colorado Eagle Budd 4-Car Set	340	___
BDBS24	SP Budd 4-Car Set	340	___
BSSC1	Conrail Trailer Hauler Freight Set	300	___
BSSC4	SP Trailer Hauler Freight Set	300	___
CB208S	Ground Throw	5	___
DXF211AB	B&O FA Diesel AB Set, sound	370	___
DXF211ABA	B&O FA Diesel ABA Set, sound	500	___
DXF211ABPW	B&O FA Diesel AB Set, powered B Unit	370	___
DXF214AB	RI FA Diesel AB Set, sound	370	___
DXF214ABA	RI FA Diesel ABA Set, sound	500	___
DXF214ABPW	RI FA Diesel AB Set, powered B Unit	370	___
DXF710AB	ACL FP7 Diesel AB Set, sound	370	___
DXF710ABA	ACL FP7 Diesel AB Set, sound	500	___
DXF710ABPW	ACL FP7 Diesel AB Set, powered B Unit	370	___
DXF711AB	B&O FP7 Diesel AB Set, sound	370	___
DXF711ABA	B&O FP7 Diesel ABA Set, sound	500	___
DXF711ABPW	B&O FP7 Diesel AB Set, powered B Unit	370	___
DXF712AB	C&O FP7 Diesel AB Set, sound	370	___
DXF712ABA	C&O FP7 Diesel ABA Set, sound	500	___
DXF712ABPW	C&O FP7 Diesel AB Set, powered B Unit	370	___
DXF713AB	D&RGW FP7 Diesel AB Set, sound	370	___
DXF713ABA	D&RGW FP7 Diesel ABA Set, sound	500	___
DXF713ABPW	D&RGW FP7 Diesel AB Set, powered B Unit	370	___
DXF714AB	RI FP7 Diesel AB Set, sound	370	___
DXF714ABA	RI FP7 Diesel ABA Set, sound	500	___
DXF714ABPW	RI FP7 Diesel AB Set, powered B Unit	370	___
DXF715AB	Southern FP7 Diesel AB Set, sound	500	___
DXF715ABA	Southern FP7 Diesel ABA Set, sound	370	___
DXFA2011	B&O FA Diesel A Unit	250	___
DXFA2014	Rock Island FA Diesel A Unit	250	___
DXFA211DNS	B&O FA Diesel B Unit, sound	250	___
DXFB211PW	B&O FA Diesel B Unit, powered	250	___
DXFB214PW	Rock Island B Unit, powered	250	___
DXFB214SND	Rock Island B Unit, sound	250	___
DXFB710PW	ACL FP7 Diesel B Unit, powered	250	___
DXFB711PW	B&O FP7 Diesel B Unit, powered	250	___
DXFB711SND	B&O FP7 Diesel B Unit, sound	250	___
DXFB712PW	C&O FP7 Diesel B Unit, powered	250	___
DXFB712SND	C&O FP7 Diesel B Unit, sound	250	___
DXFB713PW	D&RGW FP7 Diesel B Unit, powered	250	___
DXFB713SND	D&RGW FP7 Diesel B Unit, sound	250	___
DXFB714	Rock Island FP7 Diesel A Unit	250	___

	Product	Description	Retail
___	DXFB714PW	Rock Island FP7 Diesel B unit, powered	250
___	DXFB714SND	Rock Island FP7 Diesel B Unit, sound	250
___	DXFB715PW	Southern FP7 Diesel B Unit, powered	250
___	DXFB715SND	Southern FP7 Diesel B Unit, sound	250
___	DXFP7010	ACL FP7 Diesel A Unit	250
___	DXFP7011	B&O FP7 Diesel A Unit	250
___	DXFP7012	C&O FP7 Diesel A Unit	250
___	DXFP7013	D&RGW FP7 Diesel A Unit	250
___	DXFP715	Southern FP7 Diesel A Unit	250
___	DXFP7B710SND	ACL FP7 Diesel B Unit, sound	250
___	E800	E8 Diesel, DC scale or hi-rail	280
___	E800AA	E8 Diesel AA Set, DC scale or hi-rail	490
___	E803	NYC E8 Diesel, DC scale or hi-rail	280
___	E803AA	NYC E8 Diesel AA Set, DC scale or hi-rail	490
___	E805	PRR E8 Diesel, DC scale or hi-rail, red	280
___	E805AA	PRR E8 Diesel AA Set, DC scale or hi-rail, red	490
___	E806	PRR E8 Diesel, DC scale or hi-rail, green	280
___	E806AA	PRR E8 Diesel AA Set, DC scale or hi-rail, green	490
___	E808	UP E8 Diesel, DC scale or hi-rail	280
___	E808AA	UP E8 Diesel AA Set, DC scale or hi-rail	490
___	E811	B&O E8 Diesel, DC scale or hi-rail	280
___	E811AA	B&O E8 Diesel AA Set, DC scale or hi-rail	490
___	E818	ATSF E8 Diesel, DC scale or hi-rail	280
___	E818AA	ATSF E8 Diesel AA Set, DC scale or hi-rail	490
___	E819	Burlington E8 Diesel, DC scale or hi-rail	280
___	E819AA	Burlington E8 Diesel AA Set, DC scale or hi-rail	490
___	E820	IC E8 Diesel, DC scale or hi-rail	280
___	E820AA	IC E8 Diesel AA Set, DC scale or hi-rail	490
___	E821	Central of Georgia E8 Diesel, DC scale or hi-rail	280
___	E821AA	Central of Georgia E8 Diesel AA Set, DC scale or hi-rail	490
___	E822	Lackawanna E8 Diesel, DC scale or hi-rail	280
___	E822AA	Lackawanna E8 Diesel AA Set, DC scale or hi-rail	490
___	E823	MP E8 Diesel, DC scale or hi-rail	280
___	E823AA	MP E8 Diesel AA Set, DC scale or hi-rail	490
___	E824	SP E8 Diesel, DC scale or hi-rail	280
___	E824AA	SP E8 Diesel AA Set, DC scale or hi-rail	490
___	ESE01	Empire State Express Set	700
___	F40PIIAC	Amtrak F40 Diesel, phase II	170
___	F40PIIIAC	Amtrak F40 Diesel, phase III	170
___	F200AB	FA2 Diesel AB Set, sound	350
___	F200ABA	FA2 Diesel ABA Set, sound	500
___	F200ABPW	FA2 Diesel AB Set, powered	350
___	F201AB	CP FA2 Diesel AB Set, sound	390
___	F201ABA	CP FA2 Diesel ABA Set, sound	540

Retail

F201ABPW	CP FA2 Diesel AB Set, powered	390 ___
F202AB	GN FA2 Diesel AB Set, sound	390 ___
F202ABA	GN FA2 Diesel ABA Set, sound	540 ___
F202ABPW	GN FA2 Diesel AB Set, powered	390 ___
F203AB	NH FA2 Diesel AB Set, sound	390 ___
F203ABA	NH FA2 Diesel ABA Set, sound	540 ___
F203ABPW	NH FA2 Diesel AB Set, powered	390 ___
F204AB	NYC FA2 Diesel AB Set, sound	390 ___
F204ABA	NYC FA2 Diesel ABA Set, sound	540 ___
F204ABPW	NYC FA2 Diesel AB Set, powered	390 ___
F205AB	UP FA2 Diesel AB Set, sound	390 ___
F205ABA	UP FA2 Diesel ABA Set, sound	540 ___
F205ABPW	UP FA2 Diesel AB Set, powered	390 ___
F206AB	PRR FA2 Diesel AB Set, sound	390 ___
F206ABA	PRR FA2 Diesel ABA Set, sound	540 ___
F206ABPW	PRR FA2 Diesel AB Set, powered	390 ___
F700AB	FP7 Diesel AB Set, sound	360 ___
F700ABA	FP7 Diesel ABA Set, sound	500 ___
F700ABPW	FP7 Diesel AB Set, powered	360 ___
F701AB	BN FP7 Diesel AB Set, sound	390 ___
F701ABA	BN FP7 Diesel ABA Set, sound	540 ___
F701ABPW	BN FP7 Diesel AB Set, powered	390 ___
F702AB	GN FP7 Diesel AB Set, sound	390 ___
F702ABA	GN FP7 Diesel ABA Set, sound	540 ___
F702ABPW	GN FP7 Diesel AB Set, powered	390 ___
F703AB	NYC FP7 Diesel AB Set, sound	360 ___
F703ABA	NYC FP7 Diesel ABA Set, sound, gray	540 ___
F703ABPW	NYC FP7 Diesel AB Set, powered, gray	390 ___
F704AB	NP FP7 Diesel AB Set, sound	390 ___
F704ABA	NP FP7 Diesel ABA Set, sound	540 ___
F704ABPW	NP FP7 Diesel AB Set, powered	390 ___
F705AB	PRR FP7 Diesel AB Set, sound	390 ___
F705ABA	PRR FP7 Diesel ABA Set, sound, red	540 ___
F705ABPW	PRR FP7 Diesel AB Set, powered, red	390 ___
F706AB	PRR FP7 Diesel AB Set, sound	390 ___
F706ABA	PRR FP7 Diesel ABA Set, sound, green	540 ___
F706ABPW	PRR FP7 Diesel AB Set, powered, green	390 ___
F707AB	SP FP7 Diesel AB Set, sound	390 ___
F707ABA	SP FP7 Diesel ABA Set, sound	540 ___
F707ABPW	SP FP7 Diesel AB Set, powered	390 ___
F708AB	UP FP7 Diesel AB Set, sound	390 ___
F708ABA	UP FP7 Diesel ABA Set, sound	540 ___
F708ABPW	UP FP7 Diesel AB Set, powered	390 ___
F709AB	NYC FP7 Diesel AB Set, sound	390 ___
F709ABA	NYC FP7 Diesel ABA Set, sound, black	540 ___

____	F709ABPW	NYC FP7 Diesel AB Set, powered, black	390
____	F7B00PW	FP7 Diesel B Unit, powered	190
____	F7B00SND	FP7 Diesel B Unit, sound	190
____	F7B01PW	BN FP7 Diesel B Unit, powered	390
____	F7B01SND	BN FP7 Diesel B Unit, sound	190
____	F7B02PW	GN FP7 Diesel B Unit, powered	190
____	F7B02SND	GN FP7 Diesel B Unit, sound	190
____	F7B03PW	NYC FP7 Diesel B Unit, powered, gray	190
____	F7B03SND	NYC FP7 Diesel B Unit, sound, gray	190
____	F7B04PW	NP FP7 Diesel B Unit, powered	190
____	F7B04SND	NP FP7 Diesel B Unit, sound	190
____	F7B05PW	PRR FP7 Diesel B Unit, powered, red	190
____	F7B05SND	PRR FP7 Diesel B Unit, sound, red	190
____	F7B06PW	PRR FP7 Diesel B Unit, powered, green	190
____	F7B06SND	PRR FP7 Diesel B Unit, sound, green	190
____	F7B07PW	SP FP7 Diesel B Unit, powered	190
____	F7B07SND	SP FP7 Diesel B Unit, sound	190
____	F7B08PW	UP FP7 Diesel B Unit, powered	190
____	F7B08SND	UP FP7 Diesel B Unit, sound	190
____	F7B09PW	NYC FP7 Diesel B Unit, powered, black	190
____	F7B09SND	NYC FP7 Diesel B Unit, sound, black	190
____	FA2000	Alco FA2 Diesel	250
____	FA2001	CP Alco FA2 Diesel	250
____	FA2002	GN Alco FA2 Diesel	250
____	FA2003	NH Alco FA2 Diesel	250
____	FA2004	NYC Alco Diesel FA2	250
____	FA2005	UP Alco Diesel FA2	250
____	FA2006	PRR Alco Diesel FB2	250
____	FB200PW	FA2 Diesel B Unit, powered	190
____	FB200SND	FA2 Diesel B Unit, sound	190
____	FB201PW	CP FA2 Diesel B Unit, powered	190
____	FB201SND	CP FA2 Diesel B Unit, sound	190
____	FB202PW	GN FA2 Diesel B Unit, powered	190
____	FB202SND	GN FA2 Diesel B Unit, sound	190
____	FB203PW	NH FA2 Diesel B Unit, powered	190
____	FB203SND	NH FA2 Diesel B Unit, sound	190
____	FB204PW	NYC FA2 Diesel B Unit, powered	190
____	FB204SND	NYC FA2 Diesel B Unit, sound	190
____	FB205PW	UP FA2 Diesel B Unit, powered	190
____	FB205SND	UP FA2 Diesel B Unit, sound	190
____	FB206PW	PRR FA2 Diesel B Unit, powered	190
____	FB206SND	PRR FA2 Diesel B Unit, sound	190
____	FB2000	Alco FB2 Diesel	190
____	FB2001	CP Alco FB2 Diesel	190
____	FB2002	GN Alco FB2 Diesel	190

AMERICAN MODELS 1981-2019

Retail

FB2003	NH Alco FB2 Diesel	190	____
FB2004	NYC Alco FB2 Diesel	190	____
FB2005	UP Alco FB2 Diesel	190	____
FB2006	PRR Alco FB2 Diesel	190	____
FB7000	FB-7 Diesel	250	____
FB7001	BN FB-7 Diesel	250	____
FB7002	GN FB-7 Diesel	250	____
FB7003	NYC FB-7 Diesel	250	____
FB7004	NP FB-7 Diesel	250	____
FB7005	PRR FB-7 Diesel, tuscan	250	____
FB7006	PRR FB-7 Diesel, green	250	____
FB7007	SP FB-7 Diesel	250	____
FB7008	UP FB-7 Diesel	250	____
FP7000	FP7 Diesel	250	____
FP7001	BN FP7 Diesel	250	____
FP7002	GN FP7 Diesel	250	____
FP7003	NYC FP7 Diesel	250	____
FP7004	NP FP7 Diesel	250	____
FP7005	PRR FP7 Diesel, tuscan	250	____
FP7006	PRR FP7 Diesel, green	250	____
FP7007	SP FP7 Diesel	250	____
FP7008	UP FP7 Diesel	250	____
GG1200	GG1 Electric Locomotive	310	____
GG1201	PRR GG1 Electric Locomotive, green	310	____
GG1202	PRR GG1 Electric Locomotive, tuscan	310	____
GGCCAC	PRR Congressional GG1 Electric Locomotive, chrome	280	____
GGCSAC	PRR Congressional GG1 Electric Locomotive, silver	280	____
GGGIAC	PRR GG1 Electric Locomotive, green, 1-stripe	280	____
GGGSAC	PRR GG1 Electric Locomotive, green, 5-stripe	280	____
GGR6AC	PRR GG1 Electric Locomotive, tuscan, 5-stripe	280	____
GGRIAC	PRR GG1 Electric Locomotive, tuscan, 1-stripe	280	____
GP9000AC	GP9 Diesel	210	____
GP9001AC	Conrail GP9 Diesel	210	____
GP9002AC	Erie-Lackawanna GP9 Diesel	210	____
GP9003AC	NH GP9 Diesel	210	____
GP9004AC	NYC GP18 Diesel	210	____
GP9005AC	N&W GP9 Diesel	210	____
GP9006AC	PRR GP9 Diesel	210	____
GP9007AC	ATSF GP9 Diesel	210	____
GP9008AC	SP GP9 Diesel	210	____
GP9009AC	UP GP9 Diesel	210	____
GP9010AC	C&O GP9 Diesel	210	____
GP35000AC	GP35 Diesel	210	____
GP35001AC	C&O GP35 Diesel	210	____

Retail

____	GP35002AC	C&NW GP35 Diesel	210
____	GP35003AC	Conrail GP35 Diesel	210
____	GP35004AC	Erie-Lackawanna GP35 Diesel	210
____	GP35005AC	GN GP35 Diesel	210
____	GP35006AC	MP GP35 Diesel	210
____	GP35007AC	NYC GP35 Diesel	210
____	GP35008AC	PRR GP35 Diesel	210
____	GP35010AC	SP GP35 Diesel	210
____	GP35011AC	UP GP35 Diesel	210
____	GP35012AC	BN GP35 Diesel	210
____	GP35013AC	CSX GP35 Diesel	210
____	GP35014AC	ATSF GP35 Diesel, warbonnet	210
____	GP35015AC	Soo Line GP35 Diesel	210
____	GP35016AC	D&RGW GP35 Diesel	210
____	GP35017AC	Ann Arbor GP35 Diesel	210
____	HA8000	80' Passenger Lightweight Set	250
____	HA8001	GN 80' Passenger Lightweight Set	250
____	HA8002	NP 80' Passenger Lightweight Set	250
____	HA8003	NYC 80' Passenger Lightweight Set	250
____	HA8004	PRR 80' Passenger Lightweight Set	250
____	HA8006	UP 80' Passenger Lightweight Set	250
____	HA8100	Baggage-Dormitory Car	45
____	HA8101	NP Baggage-Dormitory Car	45
____	HA8103	NYC Baggage-Dormitory Car	45
____	HA8104	PRR Baggage-Dormitory Car	45
____	HA8106	UP Baggage-Dormitory Car	45
____	HA8111	GN Baggage-Dormitory Car	45
____	HA8200	60-seat Coach	45
____	HA8201	NP 60-seat Coach	45
____	HA8203	NYC 60-seat Coach	45
____	HA8204	PRR 60-seat Coach	45
____	HA8206	UP 60-seat Coach	45
____	HA8211	GN 60-seat Coach	45
____	HA8300	Vista Dome Car	45
____	HA8301	NP Vista Dome Car	45
____	HA8303	NYC Vista Dome Car	45
____	HA8304	PRR Vista Dome Car	45
____	HA8306	UP Vista Dome Car	45
____	HA8311	GN Vista Dome Car	45
____	HA8400	4-16 Duplex Sleeper Car	45
____	HA8401	NP 4-16 Duplex Sleeper Car	45
____	HA8403	NYC 4-16 Duplex Sleeper Car	45
____	HA8404	PRR 4-16 Duplex Sleeper Car	45
____	HA8406	UP 4-16 Duplex Sleeper Car	45
____	HA8411	GN 4-16 Duplex Sleeper Car	45

HA8500	Observation Lounge Car	45	____
HA8501	NP Observation Lounge Car	45	____
HA8503	NYC Observation Lounge Car	45	____
HA8504	PRR Observation Lounge Car	45	____
HA8506	UP Observation Lounge Car	45	____
HA8511	GN Observation Lounge Car	45	____
HW8000	72' Heavyweight Passenger Set	330	____
HW8001	C&NW 72' Heavyweight Passenger Set	330	____
HW8002	Southern Crescent 72' Heavyweight Passenger Set	330	____
HW8003	UP 72' Heavyweight Passenger Set	330	____
HW8004	NH 72' Heavyweight Passenger Set	330	____
HW8005	NYC 72' Heavyweight Passenger Set	330	____
HW8006	ATSF 72' Heavyweight Passenger Set	330	____
HW8007	D&RGW 72' Heavyweight Passenger Set	330	____
HW8008	C&NW 72' Heavyweight Passenger Set	330	____
HW8009	PRR 72' Heavyweight Passenger Set	290	____
HW8010	PRR 72' Heavyweight Passenger Set	330	____
HW8011	MILW 72' Heavyweight Passenger Set	330	____
HW8012	SP 72' Heavyweight Passenger Set	330	____
HW8013	Heavyweight Passenger Set, Pullman green, no lettering	330	____
HW8014	Heavweight Passenger Set, Pullman green, green roof	330	____
HW8015	SP 72' Heavyweight Passenger Set, gray	330	____
HW8016	C&O 72' Heavyweight Passenger Set	330	____
HW8017	CNJ 72' Heavyweight Passenger Set	330	____
HW8018	NH 72' Heavyweight Passenger Set	330	____
HW8019	Lackawanna 72' Heavyweight Passenger Set	330	____
HW8020	MKT 72' Heavyweight Passenger Set	330	____
HW8200	Heavyweight Coach	70	____
HW8201	C&NW Heavyweight Coach	70	____
HW8202	Southern Crescent Heavyweight Coach	70	____
HW8203	UP Heavyweight Coach	70	____
HW8204	NH Heavyweight Coach	70	____
HW8205	NYC Heavyweight Coach	70	____
HW8206	ATSF Heavyweight Coach	70	____
HW8207	D&RGW Heavyweight Coach	70	____
HW8208	C&NW Heavyweight Coach	70	____
HW8209	PRR Heavyweight Coach	70	____
HW8210	PRR Pullman Heavyweight Coach	70	____
HW8211	MILW Heavyweight Coach	70	____
HW8212	SP Heavyweight Coach	70	____
HW8213	Heavweight Pullman, black roof	70	____
HW8215	SP Heavyweight Passenger Coach, gray	70	____
HW8216	C&O Heavyweight Passenger Coach	70	____

	Item	Description	Retail
____	**HW8217**	CNJ Heavyweight Coach	70
____	**HW8218**	NH Heavyweight Coach	70
____	**HW8220**	MKT Heavyweight Coach	70
____	**HX8100**	80' Pullman Heavyweight 12-1 Sleeper Car	70
____	**HX8200**	80' Pullman Heavyweight 10-1 Sleeper Car	70
____	**HX8300**	80' Pullman Heavyweight Cafe	70
____	**HX8301**	80' Pullman Heavyweight Cafe	70
____	**HX8302**	NYC 80' Pullman Heavyweight Cafe	70
____	**HX8303**	PRR 80' Pullman Heavyweight Cafe	70
____	**HX8304**	CN 80' Pullman Heavyweight Cafe	70
____	**J3a**	NYC J3a Class Hudson 4-6-4 Locomotive, tender	360
____	**K46201**	PRR K4 4-6-2 Torpedo Locomotive, DC, bronze	400
____	**K46201AC**	PRR K4 4-6-2 Torpedo Locomotive, AC, bronze	400
____	**K46202**	PRR K4 4-6-2 Torpedo Locomotive, DC, green	400
____	**K46202AC**	PRR K4 4-6-2 Torpedo Locomotive, AC, green	400
____	**PABA400**	Alco PA1 Diesel ABA Set	565
____	**PABA401**	PRR Alco PA1 Diesel ABA Set, freight scheme, green	565
____	**PABA402**	ATSF Alco PA1 Diesel ABA Set, warbonnet, tuscan	565
____	**PABA403**	NYC Alco PA1 Diesel ABA Set	565
____	**PABA404**	NYC Alco PA2 Diesel ABA Set	565
____	**PABA405**	NYC System Alco PA1 Diesel ABA Set	565
____	**PABA406**	D&RGW Alco PA1 Diesel ABA Set	565
____	**PABA407**	NH Alco PA1 Diesel ABA Set, McGuiness scheme	565
____	**PABA408**	UP Alco PA1 Diesel ABA Set	565
____	**PABA409**	ATSF Alco PA1 Diesel ABA Set, warbonnet scheme	565
____	**PABA410**	ATSF Alco PA1 Diesel ABA Set, freight scheme	565
____	**PABA411**	D&H Alco PA1 Diesel ABA Set	565
____	**PABA412**	SP Daylight Alco PA1 Diesel ABA Set	585
____	**RS3000**	Alco RS3 Diesel	210
____	**RS3001**	Conrail Alco RS3 Diesel	210
____	**RS3002**	Cotton Belt Alco RS3 Diesel	210
____	**RS3003**	Erie-Lackawanna Alco RS3 Diesel	210
____	**RS3004**	GN Alco RS3 Diesel	210
____	**RS3005**	NH Alco RS3 Diesel	210
____	**RS3006**	NYC Alco RS3 Diesel	210
____	**RS3007**	PRR Alco RS3 Diesel	210
____	**RS3014**	Rock Island RS3 Diesel	210
____	**S1200**	Baldwin S12 Diesel	180
____	**S1201**	NH Baldwin S12 Diesel	200
____	**S1202**	C&NW Baldwin S12 Diesel	180
____	**S1203**	Conrail Baldwin S12 Diesel	180
____	**S1204**	Erie-Lackawanna Baldwin S12 Diesel	180

Retail

S1205	Erie-Lackawanna Baldwin S12 Diesel	180 ____
S1206	Southern Baldwin S12 Diesel	200 ____
S1207	NYC Baldwin S12 Diesel	180 ____
S1208	PRR Baldwin S12 Diesel	180 ____
S1209	ATSF Baldwin S12 Diesel	200 ____
S1210	SP Baldwin S12 Diesel	180 ____
S1211	UP Baldwin S12 Diesel	180 ____
S1212	D&RGW Baldwin S12 Diesel	180 ____
S1213	D&RGW Baldwin S12 Diesel	180 ____
S1214	CB&Q Baldwin S12 Diesel	180 ____
S1215	BN Baldwin S12 Diesel	200 ____
S1216	BN Baldwin S12 Diesel	200 ____
S1217	BN Baldwin S12 Diesel	200 ____
S1218	BN Baldwin S12 Diesel	200 ____
S1219	B&O Baldwin S12 Diesel	180 ____
S1220	IC Baldwin S12 Diesel	180 ____
S1221	IC Baldwin S12 Diesel	180 ____
S1222	CP Baldwin S12 Diesel	180 ____
S1223	CP Baldwin S12 Diesel	180 ____
S1224	SP Baldwin S12 Diesel	180 ____
SC65T	Trailer Train 5-Unit Spine Set	160 ____
SD60EMD	SD60 Diesel, long nose	250 ____
SD60EMDAA	SD60 Diesel AA Set, long nose	450 ____
SD6000	SD60 Diesel, long nose	250 ____
SD6000AA	SD60 Diesel AA Set, long nose	450 ____
SD6000Low	SD60 Diesel, low nose	250 ____
SD6000LowAA	SD60 Diesel AA Set, low nose	450 ____
SD6000M	SD60 Diesel, wide cab	250 ____
SD6000MAA	SD60 Diesel AA Set, wide cab	450 ____
SD6002	C&NW SD60 Diesel, long nose	250 ____
SD6002AA	C&NW SD60 Diesel AA Set, long nose	450 ____
SD6003M	Conrail SD60 Diesel, wide cab	250 ____
SD6003MAA	Conrail SD60 Diesel AA Set, wide cab	450 ____
SD6011	UP SD60 Diesel, long nose	250 ____
SD6011AA	UP SD60 Diesel AA Set, long nose	450 ____
SD6011M	UP SD60 Diesel, wide cab	250 ____
SD6011MAA	UP SD60 Diesel AA Set, wide cab	450 ____
SD6012	BN SD60 Diesel, long nose	250 ____
SD6012AA	BN SD60 Diesel AA Set, long nose	450 ____
SD6012M	BN SD60 Diesel, wide cab	250 ____
SD6012MAA	BN SD60 Diesel AA Set, wide cab	450 ____
SD6013	CSX SD60 Diesel, long nose	250 ____
SD6013AA	CSX SD60 Diesel AA Set, long nose	450 ____
SD6013M	CSX SD60 Diesel, wide cab	250 ____
SD6013MAA	CSX SD60 Diesel AA Set, wide cab	450 ____

		Retail
____ **SD6015**	Soo Line SD60 Diesel, long nose	250
____ **SD6015AA**	Soo Line SD60 Diesel AA Set, long nose	450
____ **SD6015M**	Soo Line SD60 Diesel, wide cab	250
____ **SD6015MAA**	Soo Line SD60 Diesel AA Set, wide cab	450
____ **SD6024**	NS SD60 Diesel, long nose	250
____ **SD6024AA**	NS SD60 Diesel AA Set, long nose	450
____ **SD6025M**	BNSF SD60 Diesel, wide cab	250
____ **SD6025MAA**	BNSF SD60 Diesel AA Set, wide cab	450
____ **SDK2053**	Transformer	110
____ **SLBSP2**	Amtrak Superliner Set, phase II	370
____ **SLBSP3**	Amtrak Superliner Set, phase III	370
____ **T-1**	UP 40' Semi Trailer	15
____ **T-2**	Southern 40' Semi Trailer	15
____ **T-3**	BN 40' Semi Trailer	15
____ **T-4**	CSX 40' Semi Trailer	15
____ **T-5**	D&RGW 40' Semi Trailer	15
____ **T-6**	ATSF 40' Semi Trailer	15
____ **T-7**	SP 40' Semi Trailer	15
____ **T-8**	Quantum 40' Semi Trailer	15
____ **T-9**	IC 40' Semi Trailer	15
____ **T-10**	CN&W 40' Semi Trailer	15
____ **T-11**	Conrail 40' Semi Trailer	15
____ **T-12**	American President Line 40' Semi Trailer	15
____ **T-13**	K-Line 40' Semi Trailer	15
____ **T-14**	Evergreen 40' Semi Trailer	15
____ **T-15**	N&W 40' Semi Trailer	15
____ **T-16**	Transamerica 40' Semi Trailer	15
____ **T-17**	MP 40' Semi Trailer	15
____ **T-18**	SP 40' Semi Trailer	15
____ **T-19**	NP 40' Semi Trailer	20
____ **T-20**	MKT 40' Semi Trailer	20
____ **T148B**	Bumper 2-pack	14
____ **T148C30**	30-degree Crossing	25
____ **T148C75**	75-degree Crossing	20
____ **T148L**	27"-radius Turnout, left hand, throw bar	35
____ **T148L-HT**	27"-radius Turnout, left hand, hand throw	40
____ **T148L-PW**	27"-radius Turnout, left hand, powered	50
____ **T148R**	27"-radius Turnout, right hand, throw bar	35
____ **T148R-HT**	27"-radius Turnout, right hand, hand throw	40
____ **T148R-PW**	27"-radius Turnout, right hand, powered	50
____ **T148UNC**	Electric Uncoupler	19
____ **T710**	Rail Joiners, 16 pieces	4
____ **T710INS**	Rail Joiners, insulated, 16 pieces	4
____ **T711**	Terminal with wire	3
____ **T14812**	12" Straight Track	4

Retail

T14821	21"-radius S-42 Track	4 ____
T14824	24"-radius S-48 Track	5 ____
T14827	27"-radius S-54 Track	5 ____
T14836	3' Flex Track	11 ____
TM00AC	FM H-24-66 Diesel	270 ____
TM00DC	FM H-24-66 Diesel, scale or hi-rail	250 ____
TM00AAAC	FM H-24-66 Diesel AA Set	500 ____
TM00AADC	FM H-24-66 Diesel AA Set, scale or hi-rail	470 ____
TM01AC	C&NW FM H-24-66 Diesel	270 ____
TM01DC	C&NW FM H-24-66 Diesel, scale or hi-rail	250 ____
TM01AAAC	C&NW FM H-24-66 Diesel AA Set	500 ____
TM01AADC	C&NW FM H-24-66 Diesel AA Set, scale or hi-rail	470 ____
TM02AC	Lackawanna FM H-24-66 Diesel	270 ____
TM02DC	Lackawanna FM H-24-66 Diesel, scale or hi-rail	250 ____
TM02AAAC	Lackawanna FM H-24-66 Diesel AA Set	500 ____
TM02AADC	Lackawanna FM H-24-66 Diesel AA Set, scale or hi-rail	470 ____
TM03AC	Pennsylvania FM H-24-66 Diesel	270 ____
TM03DC	Pennsylvania FM H-24-66 Diesel, scale or hi-rail	250 ____
TM03AAAC	Pennsylvania FM H-24-66 Diesel AA Set	500 ____
TM03AADC	Pennsylvania FM H-24-66 Diesel AA Set, scale or hi-rail	470 ____
TM04AC	Reading FM H-24-66 Diesel	270 ____
TM04DC	Reading FM H-24-66 Diesel, scale or hi-rail	250 ____
TM04AAAC	Reading FM H-24-66 Diesel AA Set	500 ____
TM04AADC	Reading FM H-24-66 Diesel AA Set, scale or hi-rail	470 ____
TM05AC	SP FM H-24-66 Diesel	270 ____
TM05DC	SP FM H-24-66 Diesel, scale or hi-rail	250 ____
TM05AAAC	SP FM H-24-66 Diesel AA Set	500 ____
TM05AADC	SP FM H-24-66 Diesel AA Set, scale or hi-rail	470 ____
TM06AC	Virginian FM H-24-66 Diesel	270 ____
TM06DC	Virginian FM H-24-66 Diesel, scale or hi-rail	250 ____
TM06AAAC	Virginian FM H-24-66 Diesel AA Set	500 ____
TM06AADC	Virginian FM H-24-66 Diesel AA Set, scale or hi-rail	470 ____
TM07AC	CNJ FM H-24-66 Diesel	270 ____
TM07DC	CNJ FM H-24-66 Diesel, scale or hi-rail	250 ____
TM07AAAC	CNJ FM H-24-66 Diesel AA Set	500 ____
TM07AADC	CNJ FM H-24-66 Diesel AA Set, scale or hi-rail	470 ____
TM08AC	CP FM H-24-66 Diesel	270 ____
TM08DC	CP FM H-24-66 Diesel, scale or hi-rail	250 ____
TM08AAAC	CP FM H-24-66 Diesel AA Set	500 ____
TM08AADC	CP FM H-24-66 Diesel AA Set, scale or hi-rail	470 ____

	Code	Description	Retail
___	**TM09AC**	NH FM H-24-66 Diesel	270
___	**TM09DC**	NH FM H-24-66 Diesel, scale or hi-rail	250
___	**TM09AAAC**	NH FM H-24-66 Diesel AA Set	500
___	**TM09AADC**	NH FM H-24-66 Diesel AA Set, scale or hi-rail	470
___	**TM10AC**	Wabash FM H-24-66 Diesel	270
___	**TM10DC**	Wabash FM H-24-66 Diesel, scale or hi-rail	250
___	**TM10AAAC**	Wabash FM H-24-66 Diesel AA Set	500
___	**TM10AADC**	Wabash FM H-24-66 Diesel AA Set, scale or hi-rail	470
___	**TMC-L**	Left Hand Turnout Powering Kit	20
___	**TMC-R**	Right Hand Turnout Powering Kit	20
___	**TMDAC**	Demonstrator FM H-24-66 Diesel	270
___	**TMDDC**	Demonstrator FM H-24-66 Diesel, scale or hi-rail	250
___	**TMDAAAC**	Demonstrator FM H-24-66 Diesel AA Set	500
___	**TMDAADC**	Demonstrator FM H-24-66 Diesel AA Set, scale or hi-rail	470
___	**TML**	Turnout Motor Kit, left hand	14
___	**TMR**	Turnout Motor Kit, right hand	14
___	**TSP**	Throw Bar Spring	1
___	**TWS103**	Rail Weathering Solution, 3 oz.	11
___	**U2500AC**	U25B Diesel	230
___	**U2500DC**	U25B Diesel	190
___	**U2500AC-DUAL**	U25B Diesel Set	430
___	**U2500DC-DUAL**	U25B Diesel Set	370
___	**U2501AC**	Burlington U25B Diesel	230
___	**U2501DC**	Burlington U25B Diesel	190
___	**U2501AC-DUAL**	Burlington U25B Diesel Set	430
___	**U2501DC-DUAL**	Burlington U25B Diesel Set	370
___	**U2502AC**	C&O U25B Diesel	230
___	**U2502DC**	C&O U25B Diesel	190
___	**U2502AC-DUAL**	C&O U25B Diesel Set	430
___	**U2502DC-DUAL**	C&O U25B Diesel Set	370
___	**U2503AC**	Erie-Lack. U25B Diesel	230
___	**U2503DC**	Erie-Lack. U25B Diesel	190
___	**U2503AC-DUAL**	Erie-Lack. U25B Diesel Set	430
___	**U2503DC-DUAL**	Erie-Lack. U25B Diesel Set	370
___	**U2504AC**	Frisco U25B Diesel	230
___	**U2504DC**	Frisco U25B Diesel	190
___	**U2504AC-DUAL**	Frisco U25B Diesel Set	430
___	**U2504DC-DUAL**	Frisco U25B Diesel Set	370
___	**U2505AC**	GN U25B Diesel	230
___	**U2505DC**	GN U25B Diesel	190
___	**U2505AC-DUAL**	GN U25B Diesel Set	430
___	**U2505DC-DUAL**	GN U25B Diesel Set	370
___	**U2506AC**	NH U25B Diesel	230

Retail

U2506DC	NH U25B Diesel	190 ____
U2506AC-DUAL	NH U25B Diesel Set	430 ____
U2506DC-DUAL	NH U25B Diesel Set	370 ____
U2507AC	RI U25B Diesel	230 ____
U2507DC	RI U25B Diesel	190 ____
U2507AC-DUAL	RI U25B Diesel Set	430 ____
U2507DC-DUAL	RI U25B Diesel Set	370 ____
U2508AC	Santa Fe U25B Diesel	230 ____
U2508DC	Santa Fe U25B Diesel	190 ____
U2508AC-DUAL	Santa Fe U25B Diesel Set	430 ____
U2508DC-DUAL	Santa Fe U25B Diesel Set	370 ____
U2509AC	SP U25B Diesel	230 ____
U2509DC	SP U25B Diesel	190 ____
U2509AC-DUAL	SP U25B Diesel Set	430 ____
U2509DC-DUAL	SP U25B Diesel Set	370 ____

Unnumbered Items

Limited Run	Wisconsin Central GP35 "728"	220 ____

Retail

____	**35-1001**	15" Straight Track, 6-pack	40
____	**35-1002**	10" Straight Track, 6-pack	35
____	**35-1003**	5" Straight Track, 6-pack	30
____	**35-1004**	40" Flex Track, 6-pack	60
____	**35-1005**	40" Flex Track, 24-pack	220
____	**35-1006**	20" Radius 30 Degree Curved Track, 6-pack	35
____	**35-1007**	20" Radius 15 Degree Half Curved Track, 6-pack	30
____	**35-1008**	25" Radius 30 Degree Curved Track, 6-pack	38
____	**35-1009**	25" Radius 15 Degree Half Curved Track, 6-pack	33
____	**35-1010**	30" Radius 30 Degree Curved Track, 6-pack	40
____	**35-1011**	30" Radius 15 Degree Half Curved Track, 6-pack	35
____	**35-1012**	STrax Railjoiner, 36-pack	10
____	**35-1013**	STrax Railjoiner, insulated,36-pack	10
____	**35-1014**	Flex Track Railjoiner, 36-pack	8
____	**35-1016**	American Flyer Railjoiner Adapter, 36-pack	10
____	**35-1017**	STrax Railjoiner Feeder Wire,12-pack	10
____	**35-1018**	No. 3 Remote Control Switch, right hand	70
____	**35-1019**	No. 3 Remote Control Switch, left hand)	70
____	**35-1020**	Switch Controller with 40" harness extension	15
____	**35-1021**	5" Bumper with operating warning light	22
____	**35-1022**	5" Operating Uncoupler Track	25
____	**35-1023**	5" Operating Accessory Track	25
____	**35-1101**	AAR 70-Ton Friction Bearing Truck, hi-rail	20
____	**35-1102**	AAR 70-Ton Friction Bearing Truck, scale	20
____	**35-1103**	AAR Type Y Truck, hi-rail	20
____	**35-1104**	AAR Type Y Truck, scale	20
____	**35-1105**	Barber S2 70 Ton Roller Bearing Truck, hi-rail	20
____	**35-1106**	Barber S2 70 Ton Roller Bearing Truck, scale	20
____	**35-1107**	American Flyer Compatible Freight Car Coupler	5
____	**35-1108**	33" Insulated Wheel 4-pack, hi-rail	13
____	**35-1109**	Code 110 33" Insulated Wheel 4-pack, scale	13
____	**35-1110**	Kadee Compatible Freight Car Coupler, scale	7
____	**35-90001**	No. 23796 Saw Mill	120
____	**35-90002**	No. 23772 Water Tower with bubbling pipe	120
____	**35-90003**	No. 23769 Revolving Aircraft Beacon	120
____	**35-90004**	No. 23774 Floodlight Tower	120
____	**35-90005**	No. 787 Log Loader	200
____	**35-90006**	Lamplighter	180
____	**35-20001-1**	Jersey Central F3 Diesel A Unit "52"	380
____	**35-20002-1**	Jersey Central F3 Diesel A Unit "55"	380
____	**35-20003-3**	Jersey Central F3 Diesel A Unit "56," nonpowered	200
____	**35-20004-1**	Jersey Central F3 Diesel B Unit "D"	360
____	**35-20005-3**	Jersey Central F3 Diesel B Unit "B," nonpowered	190
____	**35-20006-1**	New York Central F3 Diesel A Unit "1608"	380
____	**35-20007-1**	New York Central F3 Diesel A Unit "1635"	380

Item	Description	Price	
35-20008-3	New York Central F3 Diesel A Unit "1616," nonpowered	200	____
35-20009-1	New York Central F3 Diesel B Unit "2413"	360	____
35-20010-3	New York Central F3 Diesel B Unit "2408," nonpowered	190	____
35-20011-1	Pennsylvania F3 Diesel A Unit "9508"	380	____
35-20012-1	Pennsylvania F3 Diesel A Unit "9509"	380	____
35-20013-3	Pennsylvania F3 Diesel A Unit "9517," nonpowered	200	____
35-20014-1	Pennsylvania F3 Diesel B Unit "9512B"	360	____
35-20015-3	Pennsylvania F3 Diesel B Unit "9508," nonpowered	190	____
35-20016-1	Seaboard F3 Diesel A Unit "4024"	380	____
35-20017-1	Seaboard F3 Diesel A Unit "4027"	380	____
35-20018-3	Seaboard F3 Diesel A Unit "4029," nonpowered	200	____
35-20019-1	Santa Fe F3 Diesel A Unit "18"	380	____
35-20020-1	Santa Fe F3 Diesel A Unit "19C"	380	____
35-20021-3	Santa Fe F3 Diesel A Unit "24," nonpowered	200	____
35-20022-1	Santa Fe F3 Diesel B Unit "18A"	360	____
35-20023-3	Santa Fe F3 Diesel B Unit "24B," nonpowered	190	____
35-20024-1	Union Pacific F3 Diesel A Unit "1404A"	380	____
35-20025-1	Union Pacific F3 Diesel A Unit "1407A"	380	____
35-20026-3	Union Pacific F3 Diesel A Unit "1441A," nonpowered	200	____
35-20027-1	Union Pacific F3 Diesel B Unit "1471B"	360	____
35-20028-3	Union Pacific F3 Diesel B Unit "1446B," nonpowered	190	____
35-70001	Milwaukee Road PS2 Hopper 6-Car Set	330	____
35-70002	Norfolk Southern PS2 Hopper 6-Car Set	330	____
35-70003	BNSF PS2 Hopper 6-Car Set	330	____
35-70004	Southern PS2 Hopper 6-Car Set	330	____
35-70005	Bessemer & Lake Erie PS2 Hopper 6-Car Set	330	____
35-70006	Detroit Toledo & Ironton PS2 Hopper 6-Car Set	330	____
35-70007	Lehigh Valley PS2 Hopper 6-Car Set	330	____
35-70008	Maryland Midland PS2 Hopper 6-Car Set	330	____
35-70009	Milwaukee Road Ore Car 6-Car Set	330	____
35-70010	Duluth Missabe & Iron Range Ore Car 6-Car Set	330	____
35-70011	Chicago & North Western Ore Car 6-Car Set	330	____
35-70012	Canadian Pacific Ore Car 6-Car Set	330	____
35-70013	SOO Line Ore Car 6-Car Set	330	____
35-70014	Canadian National Ore Car 6-Car Set	330	____
35-70015	Bessemer & Lake Erie Ore Car 6-Car Set	330	____
35-70016	Great Northern Ore Car 6-Car Set	330	____
35-74000	Baltimore & Ohio Steel Rebuilt Boxcar "466013"	55	____
35-74001	Christmas Steel Rebuilt Boxcar "2013"	60	____
35-74002	Boston & Maine Steel Rebuilt Boxcar "73022"	60	____
35-74003	Boston & Maine Steel Rebuilt Boxcar "73025"	60	____
35-74004	New Haven Steel Rebuilt Boxcar "36454"	60	____
35-74005	New Haven Steel Rebuilt Boxcar "36450"	60	____
35-74006	New York Central Steel Rebuilt Boxcar "174992"	60	____
35-74007	New York Central Steel Rebuilt Boxcar "174995"	60	____
35-74008	Norfolk & Western Steel Rebuilt Boxcar "43628"	60	____

____ **35-74009**	Norfolk & Western Steel Rebuilt Boxcar "43630"	60
____ **35-74010**	Western Maryland Steel Rebuilt Boxcar "29076"	60
____ **35-74011**	Western Maryland Steel Rebuilt Boxcar "29083"	60
____ **35-74012**	Santa Fe Steel Rebuilt Boxcar "145002"	60
____ **35-74013**	Santa Fe Steel Rebuilt Boxcar "145005"	60
____ **35-74014**	Union Pacific Steel Rebuilt Boxcar "181679"	60
____ **35-74017**	Chesapeake & Ohio Rebuilt Steel Boxcar	60
____ **35-74018**	Nevada Southern Railway Rebuilt Steel Boxcar	60
35-74020 ____	Bicycle Playing Cards Rebuilt Steel Boxcar (Hi-Rail Wheels) "1985"	80
____ **35-74015**	Union Pacific Steel Rebuilt Boxcar "181680"	60
____ **35-75001**	Milwaukee Road PS2 Hopper "99618"	60
____ **35-75002**	Milwaukee Road PS2 Hopper "99614"	60
____ **35-75003**	Norfolk Southern PS2 Hopper "233548"	60
____ **35-75004**	Norfolk Southern PS2 Hopper "233635"	60
____ **35-75005**	Maryland Midland PS2 Hopper "5152"	60
____ **35-75006**	Maryland Midland PS2 Hopper "5186"	60
____ **35-75007**	Lehigh Valley PS2 Hopper "50835"	60
____ **35-75008**	Lehigh Valley PS2 Hopper "50879"	60
____ **35-75009**	Bessemer & Lake Erie PS2 Hopper "3732"	60
____ **35-75010**	Bessemer & Lake Erie PS2 Hopper "3735"	60
____ **35-75011**	Southern PS2 Hopper "95420"	60
____ **35-75012**	Southern PS2 Hopper "95462"	60
____ **35-75013**	Detroit Toledo & Ironton PS2 Hopper "11120"	60
____ **35-75014**	Detroit Toledo & Ironton PS2 Hopper "11135"	60
____ **35-75015**	BNSF PS2 Hopper "405600"	60
____ **35-75016**	BNSF PS2 Hopper "405619"	60
____ **35-75017**	Bessemer & Lake Erie Ore Car "20090"	60
____ **35-75018**	Bessemer & Lake Erie Ore Car "20093"	60
____ **35-75019**	Canadian National Ore Car "123060"	60
____ **35-75020**	Canadian National Ore Car "123064"	60
____ **35-75021**	Canadian Pacific Ore Car "377120"	60
____ **35-75022**	Canadian Pacific Ore Car "377128"	60
____ **35-75023**	Chicago & North Western Ore Car "111542"	60
____ **35-75024**	Chicago & North Western Ore Car "111548"	60
____ **35-75025**	Duluth Missabe & Iron Range Ore Car "31050"	60
____ **35-75026**	Duluth Missabe & Iron Range Ore Car "31056"	60
____ **35-75027**	Great Northern Ore Car "89001"	60
____ **35-75028**	Great Northern Ore Car "89003"	60
____ **35-75029**	Milwaukee Road Ore Car "76712"	60
____ **35-75030**	Milwaukee Road Ore Car "76730"	60
____ **35-75031**	SOO Line Ore Car "81950"	60
____ **35-75032**	SOO Line Ore Car "81956"	60
____ **35-76002**	B&O Flatcar "8775" with 48' trailer	70
____ **35-76003**	B&O Flatcar "8780" with 48' trailer	70
____ **35-76004**	Great Northern Flatcar "60250" with 48' trailer	70
____ **35-76005**	Great Northern Flatcar "60252" with 48' trailer	70
____ **35-76006**	Western Maryland Flatcar "2620" with 48' trailer	70
____ **35-76007**	Western Maryland Flatcar "2622" with 48' trailer	70

Retail

Item	Description	Retail	
35-76008	Illinois Central Flatcar "62810" with 48' trailer	70	____
35-76009	Illinois Central Flatcar "62013" with 48' trailer	70	____
35-76010	New York Central Flatcar "506053" with 48' trailer	70	____
35-76011	New York Central Flatcar "506059" with 48' trailer	70	____
35-76012	Pennsylvania Flatcar "475260" with 48' trailer	70	____
35-76013	Pennsylvania Flatcar with 48' trailer	70	____
35-76014	PFE Flatcar "475200" with 48' trailer	70	____
35-76015	PFE Flatcar "475205" with 48' trailer	70	____
35-76016	Seaboard Flatcar "47128" with 48' trailer	70	____
35-76017	Seaboard Flatcar "47126" with 48' trailer	70	____
35-78001	Fairmont Creamery 40' Wood-sided Reefer "30210"	60	____
35-78002	Fairmont Creamery 40' Wood-sided Reefer "30219"	60	____
35-78003	Fulton Market 40' Wood-sided Reefer "10400"	60	____
35-78004	Fulton Market 40' Wood-sided Reefer "10402"	60	____
35-78005	Jelke Good Luck Margarine 40' Wood-sided Reefer "10803"	60	____
35-78006	Jelke Good Luck Margarine 40' Wood-sided Reefer "10805"	60	____
35-78007	Krey's Ham & Bacon 40' Wood-sided Reefer "873"	60	____
35-78008	Krey's Ham & Bacon 40' Wood-sided Reefer "875"	60	____
35-78009	M.K. Goetz Brewery 40' Wood-sided Reefer "14310"	60	____
35-78010	M.K. Goetz Brewery 40' Wood-sided Reefer "14313"	60	____
35-78011	Pacific Fruit Express 40' Wood-sided Reefer "74780"	60	____
35-78012	Pacific Fruit Express 40' Wood-sided Reefer "74781"	60	____
35-78013	Santa Fe 40' Wood-sided Reefer "25090"	60	____
35-78014	Santa Fe 40' Wood-sided Reefer "25094"	60	____
35-78015	Senate Beer 40' Wood-sided Reefer "100"	60	____
35-78016	Senate Beer 40' Wood-sided Reefer "105"	60	____
35-78027	Columbia Soups 40' Woodsided Reefer Car "7502"	60	____
35-78028	Baltimore American Bock Beer 40' Woodsided Reefer Car "21208"	60	____
35-78029	Baltimore American Bock Beer 40' Woodsided Reefer Car "21244"	60	____
35-78030	Schmidt's Beer 40' Woodsided Reefer Car "48219"	60	____
35-78031	Schmidt's Beer 40' Woodsided Reefer Car "48234"	60	____
35-78032	Sport Beer 40' Woodsided Reefer Car "48759"	60	____
35-78033	Sport Beer 40' Woodsided Reefer Car "48767"	60	____
35-78034	Sprecher 40' Woodsided Reefer Car (Hi-Rail Wheels, Yellow)	60	____
35-78035	Sprecher 40' Woodsided Reefer Car (Hi-Rail Wheels, Tan)	60	____
35-78036	Sprecher 40' Woodsided Reefer Car (Hi-Rail Wheels, Gray)	60	____
35-78037	Sprecher 40' Woodsided Reefer Car (Scale Wheels, Yellow)	60	____
35-78038	Sprecher 40' Woodsided Reefer Car (Scale Wheels, Gray)	60	____

Retail

____	**00001**	70-ton Truck, friction bearing, Code 110, pair	10
____	**00002**	70-ton Truck, friction bearing, hi-rail, pair	10
____	**00003**	70-ton Truck, roller bearing, Code 110, pair	10
____	**00004**	70-ton Truck, roller bearing, hi-rail, pair	10
____	**00005**	Freight Coupler, AF compatible, pair	3
____	**00006**	B&M PS-2 2-bay Covered Hopper	50
____	**00007**	NYC PS-2 2-bay Covered Hopper	50
____	**00008**	PRR PS-2 2-bay Covered Hopper, scheme I	50
____	**00009**	ATSF PS-2 2-bay Covered Hopper, scheme I #1	50
____	**00010**	Wabash PS-2 2-bay Covered Hopper	50
____	**00011**	WM PS-2 2-bay Covered Hopper	50
____	**00012**	BN PS-2 2-bay Covered Hopper, scheme I	50
____	**00013**	Chessie (WM) PS-2 2-bay Covered Hopper	50
____	**00014**	C&NW (M&StL) PS-2 2-bay Covered Hopper, scheme I	50
____	**00015**	Conrail PS-2 2-bay Covered Hopper, scheme I	50
____	**00016**	Soo Line PS-2 2-bay Covered Hopper #1	50
____	**00017**	SP PS-2 2-bay Covered Hopper, scheme I	50
____	**00018**	CNJ PS-2 2-bay Covered Hopper, scheme I	50
____	**00019**	MILW PS-2 2-bay Covered Hopper	50
____	**00020**	Trona PS-2 2-bay Covered Hopper	50
____	**00021**	PS-2 2-bay Covered Hopper, gray	50
____	**00022**	PRR PS-2 2-bay Covered Hopper, scheme I	50
____	**00023**	70-ton Truck, roller bearing, Code 110, 36" wheels, pair	7
____	**00024**	33" Scale Wheel Set, Code 10, 4-pack	4
____	**00025**	33" Wheel Set, hi-rail, 4-pack	4
____	**00026**	PRR PS-2 2-bay Covered Hopper, scheme II	50
____	**00027**	B&O PS-2 2-bay Covered Hopper	50
____	**00028**	D&RGW PS-2 2-bay Covered Hopper	50
____	**00029**	ATSF PS-2 2-bay Covered Hopper, scheme I #2	50
____	**00030**	MEC PS-2 2-bay Covered Hopper	50
____	**00031**	UP PS-2 2-bay Covered Hopper	50
____	**00032**	Wisconsin Central PS-2 2-bay Covered Hopper	50
____	**00033**	LV PS-2 2-bay Covered Hopper	50
____	**00034**	Rock Island PS-2 2-bay Covered Hopper #1	50
____	**00035**	Rock Island PS-2 2-bay Covered Hopper #2	50
____	**00036**	DT&I PS-2 2-bay Covered Hopper (NASG)	50
____	**00037**	CSX PS-2 2-bay Covered Hopper	50
____	**00038**	C&NW PS-2 2-bay Covered Hopper, scheme I	50
____	**00039**	C&NW (CGW) PS-2 2-bay Covered Hopper	50
____	**00040**	BN PS-2 2-bay Covered Hopper, scheme II	50
____	**00041**	DT&I PS-2 2-bay Covered Hopper #2 (NASG)	50
____	**00042**	IMCO PS-2 2-bay Covered Hopper	50
____	**00043**	PS-2 2-bay Covered Hopper, roller bearing, gray	50

00044	Chessie (B&O) PS-2 2-bay Covered Hopper	50 ____
00045	50-ton Truck, Code 110, pair	10 ____
00046	50-ton Truck, hi-rail, pair	10 ____
00047	50-ton Type Y Truck, Code 110, pair	10 ____
00048	50-ton Type Y Truck, hi-rail, pair	10 ____
00049	Stock Car, red	50 ____
00050	UP Stock Car #1	50 ____
00051	UP Stock Car #2	50 ____
00052	D&RGW Stock Car	50 ____
00053	C&NW Stock Car #1	50 ____
00054	C&NW Stock Car #2	50 ____
00055	ACL Stock Car	50 ____
00056	GN Stock Car #1	50 ____
00057	GN Stock Car #2	50 ____
00058	PRR Stock Car #1	50 ____
00059	PRR Stock Car #2	50 ____
00060	ATSF Stock Car, scheme I #1	50 ____
00061	ATSF Stock Car, scheme I #2	50 ____
00062	NP Stock Car (Leventon Hobby)	50 ____
00063	USRA Single-sheathed Boxcar, red	50 ____
00064	NYC Stock Car	50 ____
00065	WP Stock Car	50 ____
00066	PRR USRA Single-sheathed Boxcar, scheme I #1	50 ____
00067	PRR USRA Single-sheathed Boxcar, scheme I #2	50 ____
00068	CB&Q (C&S) USRA Single-sheathed Boxcar	50 ____
00069	CB&Q USRA Single-sheathed Boxcar	50 ____
00070	MEC (PTM) USRA Single-sheathed Boxcar	50 ____
00071	B&O USRA Single-sheathed Boxcar, scheme I	50 ____
00072	SP USRA Single-sheathed Boxcar	50 ____
00073	NYC USRA Single-sheathed Boxcar	50 ____
00074	Yakima Valley USRA Single-sheathed Boxcar (NMRA)	50 ____
00075	CP USRA Single-sheathed Boxcar	50 ____
00076	GN PS-2 2-bay Covered Hopper	50 ____
00077	NKP PS-2 2-bay Covered Hopper	50 ____
00078	NYC (PL&E) PS-2 2-bay Covered Hopper	50 ____
00079	Soo Line PS-2 2-bay Covered Hopper #2	50 ____
00080	NYNH&H PS-2 2-bay Covered Hopper	50 ____
00081	WP PS-2 2-bay Covered Hopper	50 ____
00082	MKT PS-2 2-bay Covered Hopper	50 ____
00083	BN PS-2 2-bay Covered Hopper, scheme II	50 ____
00084	PC PS-2 2-bay Covered Hopper	50 ____
00085	Chessie (CSXT) PS-2 2-bay Covered Hopper	50 ____
00086	C&NW PS-2 2-bay Covered Hopper, scheme II	50 ____
00087	Revere Sugar PS-2 2-bay Hopper (RSSVP Models)	75 ____
00088	Conrail PS-2 2-bay Covered Hopper, scheme II	50 ____
00089	GTW PS-2 2-bay Covered Hopper	50 ____

____	**00090**	Ready Mix Concrete PS-2 2-bay Covered Hopper	50
____	**00091**	SP PS-2 2-bay Covered Hopper, scheme II	50
____	**00092**	SW9 Diesel, black	200
____	**00093**	ACL SW9 Diesel #1	200
____	**00094**	ACL SW9 Diesel #2	200
____	**00097**	B&O SW9 Diesel #1	200
____	**00098**	B&O SW9 Diesel #2	200
____	**00099**	B&M SW9 Diesel #1	200
____	**00100**	B&M SW9 Diesel #2	200
____	**00101**	BN SW9 Diesel #1	200
____	**00102**	BN SW9 Diesel #2	200
____	**00103**	CP SW9 Diesel #1	200
____	**00104**	CP SW9 Diesel #2	200
____	**00105**	CB&Q SW9 Diesel #1	200
____	**00106**	CB&Q SW9 Diesel #2	200
____	**00107**	Chessie (C&O) SW9 Diesel	200
____	**00108**	Chessie (B&O) SW9 Diesel #1	200
____	**00109**	C&NW SW9 Diesel #1	200
____	**00110**	C&NW SW9 Diesel #2	200
____	**00111**	Conrail SW9 Diesel, scheme I #1	200
____	**00112**	Conrail SW9 Diesel, scheme I #2	200
____	**00113**	Erie-Lackawanna SW9 Diesel #1	200
____	**00114**	Erie-Lackawanna SW9 Diesel #2	200
____	**00115**	NYC SW9 Diesel #1	200
____	**00116**	NYC SW9 Diesel #2	200
____	**00117**	PRR SW9 Diesel #1	200
____	**00118**	PRR SW9 Diesel #2	200
____	**00119**	ATSF SW9 Diesel #1	200
____	**00120**	ATSF SW9 Diesel #2	200
____	**00121**	UP SW9 Diesel, scheme I #1	200
____	**00122**	UP SW9 Diesel, scheme I #2	200
____	**00123**	UP Stock Car #3	50
____	**00124**	40' Steel Rebuilt Boxcar, red	50
____	**00125**	C&O 40' Steel Rebuilt Boxcar #1	50
____	**00126**	C&NW 40' Steel Rebuilt Boxcar, scheme I	50
____	**00127**	DL&W 40' Steel Rebuilt Boxcar	50
____	**00128**	Frisco 40' Steel Rebuilt Boxcar, scheme I	50
____	**00129**	NYC (PMKY) 40' Steel Rebuilt Boxcar #1	50
____	**00130**	NYC (PMKY) 40' Steel Rebuilt Boxcar #2	50
____	**00131**	PRR 40' Steel Rebuilt Boxcar, scheme I #1	50
____	**00132**	PRR 40' Steel Rebuilt Boxcar, scheme I #2	50
____	**00133**	ATSF "Scout" 40' Steel Rebuilt Boxcar	50
____	**00134**	ATSF "Grand Canyon" 40' Steel Rebuilt Boxcar	50
____	**00135**	Vermont Central 40' Steel Rebuilt Boxcar	50
____	**00136**	CN Stock Car #1	50
____	**00137**	CB&Q Stock Car #1	50

Retail

Item	Description	Retail	
00138	MP Stock Car	50	____
00139	MKT Stock Car	50	____
00140	UP (Oregon Short Line) Stock Car, scheme I #1	40	____
00141	Rutland USRA Single-sheathed Boxcar	50	____
00142	Clinchfield USRA Single-sheathed Boxcar	50	____
00143	Erie USRA Single-sheathed Boxcar	50	____
00144	CMStP&P USRA Single-sheathed Boxcar	50	____
00145	PRR USRA Single-sheathed Boxcar	50	____
00146	Pacific Electric USRA Single-sheathed Boxcar	50	____
00147	Wabash USRA Single-sheathed Boxcar	50	____
00148	Chessie (B&O) SW9 Switcher #2	200	____
00149	CN 40' Stock Car #2	50	____
00150	CB&Q 40' Stock Car #2	50	____
00151	MKT 40' Stock Car #2	50	____
00152	UP (Oregon Short Line) 40' Stock Car, scheme I #2	40	____
00153	C&O 40' Steel Rebuilt Boxcar #2	50	____
00154	SLSF 40' Steel Rebuilt Boxcar, scheme I #2	50	____
00155	Bulkhead Flatcar	56	____
00156	BN Bulkhead Flatcar #1	56	____
00157	BN Bulkhead Flatcar #2	56	____
00158	CB&Q Bulkhead Flatcar #1	56	____
00159	CB&Q Bulkhead Flatcar #2	56	____
00160	D&RGW Bulkhead Flatcar	56	____
00161	IC Bulkhead Flatcar #1	56	____
00162	IC Bulkhead Flatcar #2	56	____
00163	Southern Bulkhead Flatcar	56	____
00164	UP Bulkhead Flatcar #1	56	____
00165	UP Bulkhead Flatcar #2	56	____
00166	Wabash Bulkhead Flatcar	56	____
00167	Standard Flatcar, red	50	____
00168	Standard Flatcar, black	50	____
00169	BN Standard Flatcar	50	____
00170	CB&Q Standard Flatcar	50	____
00171	D&RGW Standard Flatcar	50	____
00172	IC Standard Flatcar	50	____
00173	Southern Standard Flatcar	50	____
00174	UP Standard Flatcar, scheme I #1	50	____
00175	Wabash Standard Flatcar	50	____
00176	PRR Standard Flatcar #1	50	____
00177	Flatcar with trailer	63	____
00178	BAR Flatcar with trailer	63	____
00179	NKP Flatcar with trailer	63	____
00180	Rock Island Flatcar with trailer	63	____
00181	PRR Flatcar #1 with trailer	63	____
00182	PRR Flatcar #2 with trailer	63	____
00183	Seaboard Flatcar with trailer	63	____

_____ **00184**	UP Flatcar #1 with trailer	63
_____ **00185**	UP Flatcar #2 with trailer	63
_____ **00186**	Flatcar with trailer	63
_____ **00187**	C&NW Flatcar with trailer	63
_____ **00188**	C&NW Flatcar with trailer	63
_____ **00189**	NH Flatcar #1 with trailer	63
_____ **00190**	NH Flatcar #2 with trailer	63
_____ **00191**	NYC Flatcar #1 with trailer	63
_____ **00192**	NYC Flatcar #2 with trailer	63
_____ **00193**	TTX Flatcar with REA trailer, scheme I	63
_____ **00194**	TTX Flatcar with REA trailer, scheme II	63
_____ **00195**	35' Trailer, horizontal corrugations	16
_____ **00196**	35' Trailer, vertical ribs	16
_____ **00197**	B&A 35' Trailer, horizontal corrugations	16
_____ **00198**	NKP 35' Trailer, horizontal corrugations	16
_____ **00199**	Rock Island 35' Trailer, horizontal corrugations	16
_____ **00200**	PRR 35' Trailer, horizontal corrugations, scheme I	16
_____ **00201**	Seaboard 35' Trailer, horizontal corrugations	16
_____ **00202**	UP 35' Trailer, horizontal corrugations	16
_____ **00203**	C&NW 35' Trailer, vertical ribs	16
_____ **00204**	NYNH&H 35' Trailer, vertical ribs	16
_____ **00205**	NYC 35' Trailer, vertical ribs	16
_____ **00206**	REA 35' Trailer, vertical ribs, scheme I	16
_____ **00207**	REA 35' Trailer, vertical ribs, scheme II #1	16
_____ **00208**	B&A Standard Flatcar	50
_____ **00209**	C&NW Standard Flatcar	50
_____ **00210**	NH Standard Flatcar	50
_____ **00211**	NYC Standard Flatcar	50
_____ **00212**	NKP Standard Flatcar	50
_____ **00213**	PRR Standard Flatcar #1	50
_____ **00214**	Rock Island Standard Flatcar	50
_____ **00215**	Seaboard Standard Flatcar	50
_____ **00216**	UP Standard Flatcar, scheme II #1	50
_____ **00217**	Extended Vision Caboose	70
_____ **00218**	BN Extended Vision Caboose #1	70
_____ **00219**	BN Extended Vision Caboose #2	70
_____ **00220**	C&O Extended Vision Caboose #1	70
_____ **00221**	C&O Extended Vision Caboose #2	70
_____ **00222**	CB&Q Extended Vision Caboose, scheme I #1	70
_____ **00223**	CB&Q Extended Vision Caboose, scheme I #2	70
_____ **00224**	Chessie (B&O) Extended Vision Caboose #1	70
_____ **00225**	Chessie (B&O) Extended Vision Caboose #2	70
_____ **00226**	C&NW Extended Vision Caboose #1	70
_____ **00227**	C&NW Extended Vision Caboose #2	70
_____ **00228**	Conrail Extended Vision Caboose #1	70
_____ **00229**	Conrail Extended Vision Caboose #2	70

Retail

00230	D&RGW Extended Vision Caboose #1	70 ____
00231	D&RGW Extended Vision Caboose #2	70 ____
00232	GN Extended Vision Caboose #1	70 ____
00233	GN Extended Vision Caboose #2	70 ____
00234	ICG Extended Vision Caboose #1	70 ____
00235	ICG Extended Vision Caboose #2	70 ____
00236	MP Extended Vision Caboose #1	70 ____
00237	MP Extended Vision Caboose #2	70 ____
00238	NP Extended Vision Caboose #1	70 ____
00239	NP Extended Vision Caboose #2	70 ____
00240	ATSF Extended Vision Caboose, scheme I #1	70 ____
00241	ATSF Extended Vision Caboose, scheme I #2	70 ____
00242	Seaboard Extended Vision Caboose #1	70 ____
00243	Seaboard Extended Vision Caboose #2	70 ____
00244	Soo Line Extended Vision Caboose #1	70 ____
00245	Soo Line Extended Vision Caboose #2	70 ____
00246	Evans Product Load for flatcar	10 ____
00247	Gold Bond Product Load for flatcar, white	10 ____
00248	Gold Bond Product Load for flatcar, red	10 ____
00249	Johns Manville Product Load for flatcar	10 ____
00250	Masonite Product Load for flatcar	10 ____
00251	Plumb Creek Product Load for flatcar	10 ____
00252	United States Gypsum Product Load for flatcar	10 ____
00253	Rail Joiners, 12 pieces	5 ____
00254	Insulated Rail Joiners, 12 pieces	3 ____
00255	Rail Joiners with feeder wire, 12 pieces	8 ____
00256	Track Starter Set, 16 pieces	75 ____
00257	15" Straight Track, 6 pieces	40 ____
00258	10" Straight Track, 6 pieces	33 ____
00259	Curved Track, 20" radius, 30 degree, 6 pieces	33 ____
00260	BN Standard Flatcar #2	50 ____
00261	UP Standard Flatcar, scheme I #2	50 ____
00262	B&M Flatcar with trailer (NASG)	63 ____
00263	B&M Standard Flatcar (NASG)	50 ____
00264	B&M 35' Trailer, vertical ribs (NASG)	16 ____
00265	36" Scale Wheel Set, Code 110, 4-pack–99	4 ____
00266	CMStP&P Extended Vision Caboose #1	70 ____
00267	CMStP&P Extended Vision Caboose #2	70 ____
00268	MEC Extended Vision Caboose, scheme I	78 ____
00271	3-bay Covered Hopper	50 ____
00272	ATSF PS-2 3-bay Covered Hopper #1	50 ____
00273	BN PS-2 3-bay Covered Hopper #1	50 ____
00274	Chessie (B&O) PS-2 3-bay Covered Hopper #1	50 ____
00275	CB&Q PS-2 3-bay Covered Hopper, scheme I #1	50 ____
00276	C&NW PS-2 3-bay Covered Hopper, scheme I #2	50 ____
00277	Conrail PS-2 3-bay Covered Hopper #1	50 ____

____	**00278**	GN PS-2 3-bay Covered Hopper #1	50
____	**00279**	Erie-Lackawanna PS-2 3-bay Covered Hopper #1	50
____	**00280**	NYC PS-2 3-bay Covered Hopper #1	50
____	**00281**	UP PS-2 3-bay Covered Hopper #1	50
____	**00282**	C&NW (MStL) PS-2 2-bay Covered Hopper, scheme II #1	50
____	**00283**	Jack Frost PS-2 2-bay Hopper #1 (RSSVP Models)	68
____	**00284**	LNE PS-2 2-bay Covered Hopper #1	50
____	**00285**	MStL PS-2 2-bay Covered Hopper #2	50
____	**00286**	Central Soya PS-2 2-bay Covered Hopper #1	50
____	**00287**	NAHX PS-2 2-bay Covered Hopper #1	50
____	**00288**	NAHX PS-2 2-bay Covered Hopper #2	50
____	**00289**	Diesel Engineer and Fireman Figure Set	6
____	**00290**	AC/DC Reverse Unit with DCC socket	40
____	**00291**	Curved Track, 20" radius, 15 degree, 6 pieces	27
____	**00292**	Curved Track, 25" radius, 30 degree, 6 pieces	38
____	**00293**	Curved Track, 25" radius, 15 degree, 6 pieces	28
____	**00294**	Curved Track, 30" radius, 30 degree, 6 pieces	40
____	**00295**	Locomotive Coupler, AF compatible, pair	4
____	**00297**	5" Straight Track, 6 pieces	25
____	**00298**	No. 3 Switch, right hand, remote control	55
____	**00299**	No. 3 Switch, left hand, remote control	55
____	**00300**	ATSF Flatcar with trailer, scheme I	70
____	**00301**	B&O Flatcar with trailer	70
____	**00302**	Maine Central Bulkhead Flatcar	56
____	**00303**	CP Flatcar with Speedway trailer	70
____	**00304**	GN Flatcar with trailer	70
____	**00305**	NH Flatcar with Yale trailer	70
____	**00306**	PRR Flatcar with trailer #3	70
____	**00307**	TTX Flatcar with Carolina trailer	70
____	**00308**	D&RGW Flatcar with trailer	70
____	**00309**	UP Standard Flatcar #2	50
____	**00310**	WM Flatcar with trailer	70
____	**00311**	ATSF Standard Flatcar, scheme I	50
____	**00312**	B&O Standard Flatcar	50
____	**00313**	Maine Central Standard Flatcar	50
____	**00314**	CP Standard Flatcar	50
____	**00315**	GN Standard Flatcar, scheme I #1	50
____	**00316**	NYNH&H Standard Flatcar #3	50
____	**00317**	PRR Standard Flatcar #3	50
____	**00318**	D&RGW Standard Flatcar	50
____	**00319**	UP Standard Flatcar, scheme II #2	50
____	**00320**	WM Standard Flatcar	50
____	**00321**	ATSF 35' Trailer, horizontal corrugations, scheme I	16
____	**00322**	B&O 35' Trailer, horizontal corrugations	16
____	**00323**	Speedway 35' Trailer, horizontal corrugations	16
____	**00324**	GN 35' Trailer "G322," horizontal corrugations	16

Retail

00325	Yale 35' Trailer, vertical ribs	16	____
00326	PRR 35' Trailer, vertical ribs, scheme II	16	____
00327	Carolina 35' Trailer, vertical ribs	16	____
00328	D&RGW 35' Trailer, horizontal corrugations	16	____
00329	UP 35' Trailer #2, horizontal corrugations (NMRA)	16	____
00330	WM 35' Trailer, vertical ribs	16	____
00331	ATSF Bulkhead Flatcar #1	56	____
00332	ATSF Bulkhead Flatcar #2	56	____
00333	GN Bulkhead Flatcar #1	56	____
00334	GN Bulkhead Flatcar #2	56	____
00335	Soo Line Bulkhead Flatcar #1	56	____
00336	Soo Line Bulkhead Flatcar #2	56	____
00337	D&H Bulkhead Flatcar	56	____
00338	Chessie (WM) Bulkhead Flatcar	56	____
00339	ATSF Standard Flatcar, scheme II	50	____
00340	GN Standard Flatcar, scheme I #2	50	____
00341	Soo Line Standard Flatcar #2	50	____
00342	Delaware & Hudson Standard Flatcar	50	____
00343	Chessie (WM) Standard Flatcar	50	____
00344	ATSF Set, 3 cars	100	____
00345	C&NW Set, 3 cars	100	____
00346	GN 40' Steel Rebuilt Boxcar, scheme 1 #1	50	____
00347	GN 40' Steel Rebuilt Boxcar, scheme I #2	50	____
00348	MP (IGN) "Eagle" 40' Steel Rebuilt Boxcar #1	50	____
00349	MP (IGN) "Eagle" 40' Steel Rebuilt Boxcar #2	50	____
00350	NYC Set, 3 cars	100	____
00351	RS&P 40' Steel Rebuilt Boxcar	50	____
00352	UP Set, 3 cars	100	____
00353	Muncie & Western Ball Lines 40' Steel Rebuilt Boxcar #1	50	____
00354	Truck with gear box, hi-rail wheels	10	____
00355	Truck with gear box, Code 110 wheels	10	____
00356	AC PCB/DCC Socket Harness Set, DC plug	40	____
00357	Locomotive Coupler, AF compatible, pair	4	____
00358	Caboose Conductor and Brakeman Figure Set	6	____
00359	Caboose Coupler, AF compatible, pair	3	____
00362	B&O F3 Diesel AB Set #1, phase II, sound	500	____
00363	B&O F3 Diesel AB Set #2, phase II, sound	500	____
00364	CB&Q F3 Diesel AB Set #1, phase II, sound	500	____
00365	CB&Q F3 Diesel AB Set #2, phase II, sound	500	____
00366	C&NW F3 Diesel AB Set #1, phase II, sound	500	____
00367	C&NW F3 Diesel AB Set #2, phase II, sound	500	____
00368	DL&W F3 Diesel AB Set #1, phase II, sound	500	____
00369	DL&W F3 Diesel AB Set #2, phase II, sound	500	____
00370	Maine Central F3 Diesel AB Set #1, phase II, sound	500	____
00371	Maine Central F3 Diesel AB Set #2, phase II, sound	500	____
00372	NYC F3 Diesel AB Set #1, phase II, sound	500	____

			Retail
____	**00373**	NYC F3 Diesel A&B Set #2, phase II, sound	500
____	**00374**	Southern F3 Diesel AB Set #1, phase II, sound	500
____	**00375**	Southern F3 Diesel AB Set #2, phase II, sound	500
____	**00376**	SP F3 Diesel AB Set #1, phase II, sound	500
____	**00377**	SP F3 Diesel AB Set #2, phase II, sound	500
____	**00378**	UP F3 Diesel AB Set #1, phase II, sound	500
____	**00379**	UP F3 Diesel AB Set #2, phase II, sound	500
____	**00380**	WP F3 Diesel AB Set #1, phase II, sound	500
____	**00381**	WP F3 Diesel AB Set #2, phase II, sound	500
____	**00382**	F3 Diesel AB Set, phase II, sound	500
____	**00383**	Caboose Truck, roller bearing, Code 110, pair	10
____	**00384**	Caboose Truck, roller bearing, hi-rail, pair	10
____	**00385**	NYC F3 Diesel AB Freight Set #1, phase II, sound	500
____	**00386**	NYC F3 Diesel AB Freight Set #2, phase II, sound	500
____	**00387**	UP Flatcar with trailer (NMRA)	63
____	**00388**	Boise Cascade Wrapped Lumber Load	10
____	**00389**	Finlay Premium Wrapped Lumber Load	10
____	**00390**	Western Carrier Wrapped Lumber Load	10
____	**00391**	Weyerhauser Wrapped Lumber Load	10
____	**00392**	Pulpwood Load	13
____	**00393**	AF Track Adaptor, 8 pieces	5
____	**00394**	Bulb, 2.5-volt, 2 pieces	2
____	**00395**	Rail Joiner, insulated, yellow, 12 pieces	3
____	**00396**	ATSF PS-2 3-bay Covered Hopper #2	50
____	**00397**	BN PS-2 3-bay Covered Hopper #2	50
____	**00398**	Chessie (B&O) PS-2 3-bay Covered Hopper #2	50
____	**00399**	CB&Q PS-2 3-bay Covered Hopper, scheme I #2	50
____	**00400**	C&NW PS-2 3-bay Covered Hopper, scheme I #2	50
____	**00401**	Conrail PS-2 3-bay Covered Hopper #2	50
____	**00402**	GN PS-2 3-bay Covered Hopper #2	50
____	**00403**	Erie-Lackawanna PS-2 3-bay Covered Hopper #2	50
____	**00404**	NYC PS-2 3-bay Covered Hopper #2	50
____	**00405**	UP PS-2 3-bay Covered Hopper #2	50
____	**00407**	C&NW (M&StL) PS-2 2-bay Hopper, scheme II #2	50
____	**00408**	LNE PS-2 2-bay Covered Hopper #2	50
____	**00409**	Central Soya PS-2 2-bay Covered Hopper #2	50
____	**00410**	Roscoe, Snyder & Pacific 40' Steel Rebuilt Boxcar #2	50
____	**00411**	Muncie & Western Ball Lines 40' Steel Rebuilt Boxcar #2	50
____	**00412**	CB&Q PS-2 3-bay Covered Hopper, scheme II #1	50
____	**00413**	Jack Frost PS-2 2-bay Hopper #2 (RSSVP Models)	50
____	**00414**	Cedar Heights Clay PS-2 3-bay Covered Hopper	55
____	**00415**	Ann Arbor PS-2 2-bay Covered Hopper #1 (TCA)	50
____	**00416**	Ann Arbor PS-2 2-bay Covered Hopper #2 (TCA)	50
____	**00417**	M&StL PS-2 3-bay Covered Hopper #1	50
____	**00418**	M&StL PS-2 3-bay Covered Hopper #2	50
____	**00419**	M&StL PS-2 2-bay Covered Hopper #2	50

00420	CB&Q PS-2 3-bay Covered Hopper, scheme II #2	50	___
00421	Conrail SW9 Diesel Set, 4 cars	300	___
00422	BN SW9 Diesel Set, 5 cars	370	___
00423	ATSF SW9 Diesel Set, 6 cars	430	___
00425	Glencoe Skokie Valley Single-sheathed Boxcar (NMRA)	63	___
00426	Chesapeake & Ohio SW9 Diesel #1	200	___
00427	Chesapeake & Ohio SW9 Diesel #2	200	___
00428	Great Northern SW9 Diesel #1	200	___
00429	Great Northern SW9 Diesel #2	200	___
00430	D&RGW SW9 Diesel #1	200	___
00431	D&RGW SW9 Diesel #2	200	___
00432	ICG SW9 Diesel #1	200	___
00433	ICG SW9 Diesel #2	200	___
00434	Northern Pacific SW9 Diesel #1	200	___
00435	Northern Pacific SW9 Diesel #2	200	___
00436	UP SW9 Diesel, scheme II #1	200	___
00437	UP SW9 Diesel, scheme II #2	200	___
00438	SW1 Diesel	200	___
00439	Boston & Maine SW1 Diesel #1	200	___
00440	Boston & Maine SW1 Diesel #2	200	___
00441	Chessie (B&O) SW1 Diesel #1	200	___
00442	Chessie (B&O) SW1 Diesel #2	200	___
00443	C&NW SW1 Diesel #1	200	___
00444	C&NW SW1 Diesel #2	200	___
00445	WP SW1 Diesel #1	200	___
00446	WP SW1 Diesel #2	200	___
00447	CMStP&P SW1 Diesel #1	200	___
00448	CMStP&P SW1 Diesel #2	200	___
00449	PRR SW1 Diesel #1	200	___
00450	PRR SW1 Diesel #2	200	___
00451	Seaboard SW1 Diesel	200	___
00452	Soo Line SW1 Diesel	200	___
00453	Lehigh Valley SW1 Diesel #1	200	___
00454	Lehigh Valley SW1 Diesel #2	200	___
00455	SP SW1 Diesel #1	200	___
00456	SP SW1 Diesel #2	200	___
00457	C&O SW9 Diesel Set, 6 cars	370	___
00458	Conrail SW9 Diesel Set, 4 cars	300	___
00459	D&RGW SW9 Diesel Set, 6 cars	430	___
00460	GN SW9 Diesel Set, 6 cars	430	___
00461	ICG SW9 Diesel Set, 5 cars	370	___
00462	NP SW9 Diesel Set, 5 cars	370	___
00463	No. 3 Manual Switch, right hand	40	___
00464	No. 3 Manual Switch, left hand	40	___
00465	40" Flextrack, 6 pieces	51	___
00466	40" Flextrack, 24 pieces	186	___

____ **00468**	5" Straight Track with lighted bumper	22
____ **00469**	Flatcar with John Deere combine	55
____ **00470**	Flatcar with IH Harvestor combine	55
____ **00471**	Flatcar with John Deere log skidder	50
____ **00472**	Flatcar with John Deere backhoe and front-end loader	60
____ **00473**	Flatcar with 2 John Deere bulldozers	60
____ **00474**	PRR PS-2 2-bay Covered Hopper, scheme II #1	50
____ **00475**	PRR PS-2 2-bay Covered Hopper, scheme II #2	50
____ **00476**	Wooden Billboard Reefer	53
____ **00477**	Wooden Billboard Reefer, yellow	53
____ **00478**	Wooden Billboard Reefer, orange	53
____ **00479**	ART Wooden Billboard Reefer #1	53
____ **00480**	ART Wooden Billboard Reefer #2	53
____ **00481**	ATSF "Grand Canyon" Wooden Billboard Reefer	53
____ **00482**	ATSF "El Capitan" Wooden Billboard Reefer	53
____ **00483**	Burlington Wooden Billboard Reefer #1	53
____ **00484**	Burlington Wooden Billboard Reefer #2	53
____ **00485**	Robin Hood Beer Wooden Billboard Reefer #1	53
____ **00486**	Robin Hood Beer Wooden Billboard Reefer #2	53
____ **00487**	Gerber Wooden Billboard Reefer #1	53
____ **00489**	LV Wooden Billboard Reefer #1	53
____ **00490**	LV Wooden Billboard Reefer #2	53
____ **00491**	North Western Wooden Billboard Reefer, scheme I #1	53
____ **00492**	North Western Wooden Billboard Reefer, scheme I #2	53
____ **00493**	North Western Wooden Billboard Reefer, scheme II #1	53
____ **00494**	North Western Wooden Billboard Reefer, scheme II #2	53
____ **00495**	Merchants Despatch Wooden Billboard Reefer #1	53
____ **00496**	Merchants Despatch Wooden Billboard Reefer #2	53
____ **00497**	Pacific Great Eastern Wooden Billboard Reefer	74
____ **00498**	PFE Wooden Billboard Reefer #1	53
____ **00499**	PFE Wooden Billboard Reefer #2	53
____ **00500**	Tivoli Beer Wooden Billboard Reefer #1	53
____ **00501**	Tivoli Beer Wooden Billboard Reefer #2	53
____ **00502**	A&P Wooden Billboard Reefer #1	53
____ **00503**	A&P Wooden Billboard Reefer #2	53
____ **00504**	Old Heidelberg Beer Wooden Billboard Reefer #1	53
____ **00505**	Old Heidelberg Beer Wooden Billboard Reefer #2	53
____ **00506**	Chateau Martin Wooden Billboard Reefer #1 (NASG)	53
____ **00507**	Chateau Martin Wooden Billboard Reefer #2 (NASG)	53
____ **00508**	Chateau Martin Wooden Billboard Reefer #3 (NASG)	53
____ **00509**	CUVA PS-2 2-bay Covered Hopper #1 (CVSG)	50
____ **00510**	CUVA PS-2 2-bay Covered Hopper #2 (CVSG)	50
____ **00511**	Flatcar with John Deere excavator	50
____ **00512**	Flatcar with 3 Bobcats	55
____ **00513**	Berghoff Beer Billboard Reefer (Scenery Unlimited)	53
____ **00514**	Wilson Car Lines Billboard Reefer (Scenery Unlimited)	53

S-HELPER SERVICE 1994-2012

Retail

00515	Zion Figs Wooden Billboard Reefer	53 ____
00516	Ballantine Beer Wooden Billboard Reefer #1	53 ____
00517	Ballantine Beer Wooden Billboard Reefer #2	53 ____
00518	Parrot Potatoes Wooden Billboard Reefer	53 ____
00519	40' Steel Rebuilt Boxcar, S Gaugian 40th Anniversary	50 ____
00520	B&O 40' Steel Rebuilt Boxcar #1 (Boys RR Club)	50 ____
00521	PRR Merchandise Service Rebuilt Boxcar, scheme I	50 ____
00522	GN 40' Steel Rebuilt Boxcar, scheme II #1	50 ____
00523	GN 40' Steel Rebuilt Boxcar, scheme II #2	50 ____
00524	B&O 40' Steel Rebuilt Boxcar #2 (Boys RR Club)	50 ____
00525	IGA Wooden Billboard Reefer #1 (RSSVP Models)	53 ____
00526	IGA Wooden Billboard Reefer #2 (RSSVP Models)	53 ____
00527	Narragansett Billboard Reefer #1 (RSSVP Models)	53 ____
00528	Narragansett Billboard Reefer #2 (RSSVP Models)	53 ____
00529	Flatcar with 3 New Holland grinder mixers	55 ____
00530	Flatcar with Terra Gator dry fertilizer spreader	55 ____
00531	Flatcar with Terra Gator liquid fertilizer spreader	55 ____
00532	Flatcar with 4 John Deere skid loaders	60 ____
00533	Switch Controller with 42" wire and extension	10 ____
00534	Switch Controller with extension wire, 3 pieces	8 ____
00535	IC Bulkhead Flatcar with pipe load	56 ____
00536	ICG Switcher Set, 4 cars	300 ____
00537	Soo Switcher Set, 5 cars	370 ____
00538	CMStP&P Switcher Set, 5 cars	370 ____
00539	GN Switcher Set, 6 cars	400 ____
00540	Seaboard Switcher Set, 6 cars	400 ____
00541	CB&Q F3 Diesel Freight Set, 6 cars	430 ____
00542	USRA Double-sheathed Boxcar	50 ____
00543	ACL USRA Double-sheathed Boxcar	50 ____
00544	B&M USRA Double-sheathed Boxcar	50 ____
00545	C&NW USRA Double-sheathed Boxcar	50 ____
00546	D&LW USRA Double-sheathed Boxcar	50 ____
00547	GN USRA Double-sheathed Boxcar	50 ____
00548	NYC USRA Double-sheathed Boxcar	50 ____
00549	Toronto, Hamilton & Buffalo Double-sheathed Boxcar #1	50 ____
00550	Union Pacific USRA Double-sheathed Boxcar	50 ____
00551	Flatcar with IH Harvestor and corn load	55 ____
00552	LocoMatic 10-button Controller	70 ____
00554	C&NW MOW Flatcar	50 ____
00555	C&NW (M&StL) MOW Flatcar	50 ____
00556	Conrail Standard Flatcar #1	50 ____
00557	Conrail Standard Flatcar #2	50 ____
00558	Grand Truck Western Standard Flatcar #1	50 ____
00559	Grand Truck Western Standard Flatcar #2	50 ____
00560	Reading Standard Flatcar #1	50 ____
00561	Reading Standard Flatcar #2	50 ____

			Retail
____	**00562**	Union Pacific Standard Flatcar, scheme II #1	50
____	**00563**	Union Pacific Standard Flatcar, scheme II #2	50
____	**00564**	NP USRA Double-sheathed Boxcar	70
____	**00565**	Bulb 12-volt, 2 pieces	2
____	**00566**	PFE Wooden Billboard Reefer, scheme II #1	53
____	**00567**	PFE Wooden Billboard Reefer, scheme II #2	53
____	**00568**	Lackawanna Wooden Billboard Reefer #1 (NASG)	53
____	**00569**	Lackawanna Wooden Billboard Reefer #2 (NASG)	53
____	**00570**	Baby Ruth Wooden Billboard Reefer #1	53
____	**00571**	Baby Ruth Wooden Billboard Reefer #2	56
____	**00572**	Ralston Purina Wooden Billboard Reefer	53
____	**00573**	BAR Wooden Billboard Reefer #1	53
____	**00574**	BAR Wooden Billboard Reefer #2	53
____	**00575**	MP (NOT&M) "Eagle" 40' Steel Rebuilt Boxcar #1	50
____	**00576**	MP (NOT&M) "Eagle" 40' Steel Rebuilt Boxcar #2	50
____	**00577**	CStP&O 40' Steel Rebuilt Boxcar #1	50
____	**00578**	CStP&O 40' Steel Rebuilt Boxcar #2	50
____	**00579**	CGW "C" 40' Steel Rebuilt Boxcar	50
____	**00580**	CGW "SL" 40' Steel Rebuilt Boxcar	50
____	**00581**	CGW "DF" 40' Steel Rebuilt Boxcar	50
____	**00582**	CGW "DFb" 40' Steel Rebuilt Boxcar	50
____	**00583**	Dutch Cleanser Wooden Billboard Reefer #1	53
____	**00584**	Land O' Lakes Wooden Billboard Reefer #1	53
____	**00585**	Land O' Lakes Billboard Reefer #2 (Scenery Unlimited)	53
____	**00586**	Flatcar with 4 John Deere 430 Crawlers	60
____	**00587**	Switch Stand with marker light	6
____	**00588**	Coupler, F3 mount, Kadee style, pair	3
____	**00589**	Flatcar with 4 New Holland skid steers	60
____	**00590**	Flatcar with John Deere wheel loader	50
____	**00591**	Flatcar with John Deere grader	50
____	**00592**	Dutch Cleanser Wooden Billboard Reefer #2	53
____	**00593**	Chessie Extended Vision Caboose #1	70
____	**00594**	Chessie Extended Vision Caboose #2	70
____	**00595**	Chessie Safety Special Extended Vision Caboose	70
____	**00596**	C&NW Extended Vision Caboose #3	70
____	**00597**	C&NW Extended Vision Caboose #4	70
____	**00598**	MEC Extended Vision Caboose, scheme II	70
____	**00599**	Reading Extended Vision Caboose #1	70
____	**00600**	Reading Extended Vision Caboose #2	70
____	**00601**	Rock Island Extended Vision Caboose #1	70
____	**00602**	Rock Island Extended Vision Caboose #2	70
____	**00603**	ATSF Extended Vision Caboose, scheme II #1	70
____	**00604**	ATSF Extended Vision Caboose, scheme II #2	70
____	**00605**	CGW "C" 40' Steel Boxcar, scheme II (State Line)	50
____	**00606**	CGW "SL" 40' Steel Boxcar, scheme II (State Line)	50
____	**00607**	CGW "DF" 40' Steel Boxcar, scheme II (State Line)	50

Retail

00608	CGW "DFb" 40' Steel Boxcar, scheme II (State Line)	50 ____
00609	Flatcar with Caterpillar 609 Scraper	50 ____
00610	Kahn's Wooden Billboard Reefer #1 (Scenery Unlimited)	53 ____
00611	Kahn's Wooden Billboard Reefer #2 (Scenery Unlimited)	53 ____
00612	B&O F3 Diesel A Unit #1, phase II, sound	300 ____
00613	B&O F3 Diesel A Unit #2, phase II, sound	300 ____
00614	CB&Q F3 Diesel A Unit #1, phase II, sound	300 ____
00615	CB&Q F3 Diesel A Unit #2, phase II, sound	300 ____
00616	C&NW F3 Diesel A Unit #1, phase II, sound	300 ____
00617	C&NW F3 Diesel #2, phase II, sound	300 ____
00618	DL&W F3 Diesel A Unit #1, phase II, sound	300 ____
00619	DL&W F3 Diesel A Unit #2, phase II, sound	300 ____
00620	MEC F3 Diesel A Unit #1, phase II, sound	300 ____
00621	MEC F3 Diesel A Unit #2, phase II, sound	300 ____
00622	NYC Passenger F3 Diesel A Unit #1, phase II, sound	300 ____
00623	NYC Passenger F3 Diesel A Unit #2, phase II, sound	300 ____
00624	Southern F3 Diesel A Unit #1, phase II, sound	300 ____
00625	Southern F3 Diesel A Unit #2, phase II, sound	300 ____
00626	SP F3 Diesel A Unit #1, phase II, sound	300 ____
00627	SP F3 Diesel A Unit #2, phase II, sound	300 ____
00628	UP F3 Diesel A Unit #1, phase II, sound	300 ____
00629	UP F3 Diesel A Unit #2, phase II, sound	300 ____
00630	WP F3 Diesel A Unit #1, phase II, sound	300 ____
00631	WP F3 Diesel A Unit #2, phase II, sound	300 ____
00632	F3 Diesel A Unit, phase II, sound	300 ____
00633	NYC Freight F3 Diesel A Unit #1, phase II, sound	300 ____
00634	NYC Freight F3 Diesel A Unit #2, phase II, sound	300 ____
00635	B&O F3 Diesel B Unit #1, phase II, sound	290 ____
00636	B&O F3 Diesel B Unit #2, phase II, sound	290 ____
00637	CB&Q F3 Diesel B Unit #1, phase II, sound	290 ____
00638	CB&Q F3 Diesel B Unit #2, phase II, sound	290 ____
00639	C&NW F3 Diesel B Unit #1, phase II, sound	290 ____
00640	C&NW F3 Diesel B Unit #2, phase II, sound	290 ____
00641	D&LW F3 Diesel B Unit #1, phase II, sound	290 ____
00642	D&LW F3 Diesel B Unit #2, phase II, sound	290 ____
00643	MEC F3 Diesel B Unit #1, phase II, sound	290 ____
00644	MEC F3 Diesel B Unit #2, phase II, sound	290 ____
00645	NYC Passenger F3 Diesel B Unit #1, phase II, sound	290 ____
00646	NYC Passenger F3 Diesel B Unit #2, phase II, sound	290 ____
00647	Southern F3 Diesel B Unit #1, phase II, sound	290 ____
00648	Southern F3 Diesel B Unit #2, phase II, sound	290 ____
00649	SP F3 Diesel B Unit #1, phase II, sound	290 ____
00650	SP F3 Diesel B Unit #2, phase II, sound	290 ____
00651	UP F3 Diesel B Unit #1, phase II, sound	290 ____
00652	UP F3 Diesel B Unit #2, phase II, sound	290 ____
00653	WP F3 Diesel B Unit #1, phase II, sound	290 ____

____	**00654**	WP F3 Diesel B Unit #2, phase II, sound	290
____	**00655**	F3 Diesel B Unit, phase II, sound	290
____	**00656**	NYC F3 Diesel B Unit #1, phase II, sound	290
____	**00657**	NYC F3 Diesel B Unit #2, phase II, sound	290
____	**00658**	Brookside Milk Wooden Billboard Reefer (Port Lines)	53
____	**00659**	Saval Foods Wooden Billboard Reefer #1 (Port Lines)	53
____	**00660**	Metal Rail Joiners for flex track, 36 pieces	4
____	**00661**	PRR 40' Steel Rebuilt Boxcar, scheme II	50
____	**00662**	GN 40' Steel Rebuilt Boxcar, scheme III #1	50
____	**00663**	GN 40' Steel Rebuilt Boxcar, scheme III #2	50
____	**00664**	33" Scale Caboose Wheel Set, Code 110, 4-pack	4
____	**00665**	Speaker, 36mm diameter	3
____	**00666**	Chessie SW1 Diesel Freight Set, 6 cars	370
____	**00667**	MU Cables, pair	2
____	**00670**	5" Uncoupler Track	22
____	**00671**	5" Accessory Track	22
____	**00672**	Flatcar with 2 Caterpillar D6R XL Bulldozers	60
____	**00673**	Flatcar with Caterpillar D25D Articulated Truck	55
____	**00674**	Flatcar with Caterpillar 950F Wheel Loader	50
____	**00675**	Flatcar with Caterpillar 12G Grader	50
____	**00676**	Flatcar with 2 Caterpillar Challenger Tractors	60
____	**00677**	Flatcar with Caterpillar tractor and boom sprayer	55
____	**00678**	Flatcar with Caterpillar tractor and spreader	55
____	**00679**	Flatcar with Caterpillar tractor and Knight Slinger	55
____	**00680**	Flatcar with 2 Caterpillar D6R Bulldozers	60
____	**00681**	Flatcar with Caterpillar 611 Scraper	55
____	**00682**	PFE Wooden Billboard Reefer Set, 3 cars	110
____	**00683**	Burlington Wooden Billboard Reefer Set, 3 cars	110
____	**00684**	North Western Wooden Billboard Reefer Set, 3 cars	110
____	**00685**	FGE Wooden Billboard Reefer Set #1, 3 cars	110
____	**00686**	NP Wooden Billboard Reefer #1	53
____	**00687**	NP Wooden Billboard Reefer #2	53
____	**00688**	Knickerbocker Billboard Reefer #1 (Port Lines)	53
____	**00689**	Knickerbocker Billboard Reefer #2 (Port Lines)	53
____	**00690**	Carling Black Label Billboard Reefer #1 (Port Lines)	53
____	**00691**	Carling Black Label Billboard Reefer #2 (Port Lines)	53
____	**00692**	C&NW SW9 Diesel Set, 5 cars	370
____	**00693**	C&NW Diesel F Unit Set, 6 cars	430
____	**00694**	MEC Diesel F Unit Set, 5 cars	370
____	**00697**	Edelweiss Beer Wooden Billboard Reefer	53
____	**00698**	Kraft Cheese Wooden Billboard Reefer	53
____	**00699**	CN Wooden Billboard Reefer #1	53
____	**00700**	CN Wooden Billboard Reefer #2	53
____	**00701**	B&M 40' Steel Rebuilt Boxcar #1 (Boys RR Club)	50
____	**00702**	B&M 40' Steel Rebuilt Boxcar #2 (Boys RR Club)	50
____	**00703**	ATSF 40' Steel Rebuilt Boxcar #1 (Boys RR Club)	50

Retail

Code	Description	Retail	
00704	ATSF 40' Steel Rebuilt Boxcar #2 (Boys RR Club)	50	____
00705	D&RGW 40' Steel Boxcar #1, white (Boys RR Club)	50	____
00706	D&RGW 40' Steel Boxcar #2, white (Boys RR Club)	50	____
00707	D&RGW 40' Steel Boxcar #1, silver (Boys RR Club)	50	____
00708	D&RGW 40' Steel Boxcar #2, silver (Boys RR Club)	50	____
00709	Central of Georgia Boxcar, black #1 (Boys RR Club)	50	____
00710	Central of Georgia Boxcar, maroon (Boys RR Club)	50	____
00711	Central of Georgia Boxcar, black #2 (Boys RR Club)	50	____
00712	Central of Georgia Boxcar, black #3 (Boys RR Club)	50	____
00713	NP SW9 Diesel Freight Set, 4 cars	300	____
00714	CMStP&P SW1 Diesel Freight Set, 5 cars	370	____
00715	CB&Q F3 Diesel Freight Set, 6 cars	430	____
00716	Santa Fe "The Scout" Wooden Billboard Reefer	53	____
00717	Wooden Billboard Reefer, red	53	____
00720	Saval Foods Billboard Reefer #2 (Port Lines)	53	____
00721	B&O 40' Steel Rebuilt Boxcar #3 (Boys RR Club)	50	____
00722	B&O 40' Steel Rebuilt Boxcar #4 (Boys RR Club)	50	____
00723	Ore Car, black	40	____
00724	Ore Car, red	40	____
00725	DM&IR Ore Car	40	____
00726	DM&IR Ore Car 5-pack Set A	180	____
00727	B&LE Ore Car	40	____
00728	B&LE Ore Car 5-pack Set A	180	____
00729	CN Ore Car	40	____
00730	CN Ore Car 5-pack	180	____
00731	CP Ore Car	40	____
00732	CP Ore Car 5-pack	180	____
00735	GN Ore Car, scheme I	40	____
00736	GN Ore Car 5-pack Set A, scheme I	180	____
00737	CMStP&P Ore Car, scheme I	40	____
00738	CMStP&P Ore Car 5-pack Set A, scheme I	180	____
00741	SP Ore Car	40	____
00742	SP Ore Car 5-pack	180	____
00743	UP Ore Car	40	____
00744	UP Ore Car 5-pack	180	____
00745	DCC Sound Decoder, F Unit	160	____
00746	ATSF 40' Steel Rebuilt Boxcar	50	____
00747	C&NW 40' Steel Rebuilt Boxcar	50	____
00748	NYC (P&LE) 40' Steel Rebuilt Boxcar #1	50	____
00749	UP 40' Steel Rebuilt Boxcar	50	____
00750	ATSF USRA Single-sheathed Boxcar	50	____
00751	C&NW USRA Single-sheathed Boxcar	50	____
00752	NYC USRA Single-sheathed Boxcar	50	____
00753	UP USRA Single-sheathed Boxcar	50	____
00754	ATSF Stock Car, scheme II	50	____
00755	C&NW Stock Car #3	50	____

Retail

_____ **00756**	NYC Stock Car	50
_____ **00757**	UP (OSL) Stock Car, scheme II #3	50
_____ **00758**	Composite Side Hopper, black	50
_____ **00759**	Composite Side Hopper, red	50
_____ **00760**	Ann Arbor Composite Side Hopper 3-pack	100
_____ **00761**	Ann Arbor Composite Side Hopper	50
_____ **00762**	ATSF Composite Side Hopper 3-pack	100
_____ **00763**	ATSF Composite Side Hopper	50
_____ **00764**	B&O Composite Side Hopper 3-pack	100
_____ **00765**	B&O Composite Side Hopper	50
_____ **00766**	C&O Composite Side Hopper 3-pack	100
_____ **00767**	C&O Composite Side Hopper	50
_____ **00768**	CB&Q Composite Side Hopper 3-pack	100
_____ **00769**	CB&Q Composite Side Hopper	50
_____ **00770**	Clinchfield Composite Side Hopper 3-pack	100
_____ **00771**	Clinchfield Composite Side Hopper	50
_____ **00772**	LV Composite Side Hopper 3-pack	100
_____ **00773**	LV Composite Side Hopper	50
_____ **00774**	L&N Composite Side Hopper 3-pack	100
_____ **00775**	L&N Composite Side Hopper	50
_____ **00776**	NKP Composite Side Hopper 3-pack	100
_____ **00777**	NKP Composite Side Hopper	50
_____ **00778**	PRR Composite Side Hopper 3-pack	100
_____ **00779**	PRR Composite Side Hopper #4	50
_____ **00780**	Virginian Composite Side Hopper 3-pack	100
_____ **00781**	Virginian Composite Side Hopper	50
_____ **00782**	Wabash Composite Side Hopper 3-pack	100
_____ **00783**	Wabash Composite Side Hopper	50
_____ **00788**	Feeder Wire Terminal, 12 pieces	4
_____ **00796**	NKP Wooden Billboard Reefer (CVSG)	53
_____ **00797**	NKP Wooden Billboard Reefer (CVSG)	53
_____ **00798**	NYNH&H Wooden Billboard Reefer #1 (Port Lines)	53
_____ **00799**	NYNH&H Wooden Billboard Reefer #2 (Port Lines)	53
_____ **00800**	Grand Union Wooden Billboard Reefer	53
_____ **00801**	Borden's Cheese Wooden Billboard Reefer	53
_____ **00802**	Pabst Blue Ribbon Wooden Billboard Reefer	53
_____ **00803**	Mexene Chili Powder Wooden Billboard Reefer	53
_____ **00804**	Swift Wooden Billboard Reefer 3-pack	110
_____ **00805**	B&O 40' Steel Rebuilt Boxcar #5 (Boys RR Club)	50
_____ **00806**	North Stratford 40' Steel Boxcar (Bristol S Gauge)	50
_____ **00807**	North Stratford 40' Steel Boxcar (Bristol S Gauge)	50
_____ **00808**	Frisco 40' Steel Rebuilt Boxcar 3-pack	100
_____ **00809**	F7 Diesel A Unit, phase I, AC/DC LocoMatic sound	300
_____ **00810**	ATSF Passenger F7 Diesel A Unit #1, phase I	300
_____ **00811**	ATSF Passenger F7 Diesel A Unit #2, phase I	300
_____ **00812**	ATSF Freight F7 Diesel A Unit #1, phase I	300

00813	ATSF Freight F7 Diesel A Unit #2, phase I	300 ____
00814	B&M F7 Diesel A Unit #1, phase I	300 ____
00815	B&M F7 Diesel A Unit #2, phase I	300 ____
00816	D&RGW F7 Diesel A Unit #1, phase I	300 ____
00817	D&RGW F7 Diesel A Unit #2, phase I	300 ____
00818	GN F7 Diesel A Unit #1, phase I	300 ____
00819	GN F7 Diesel A Unit #2, phase I	300 ____
00820	MP F7 Diesel A Unit #1, phase I	300 ____
00821	MP F7 Diesel A Unit #2, phase I	300 ____
00822	PRR F7 Diesel A Unit #1, phase I	300 ____
00823	PRR F7 Diesel A Unit #2, phase I	300 ____
00824	F7 Diesel B Unit, phase I, AC/DC LocoMatic sound	290 ____
00825	ATSF Passenger F7 Diesel B Unit #1, phase I	290 ____
00826	ATSF Passenger F7 Diesel B Unit #2, phase I	290 ____
00827	ATSF Freight F7 Diesel B Unit #1, phase I	290 ____
00828	ATSF Freight F7 Diesel B Unit #2, phase I	290 ____
00829	B&M F7 Diesel B Unit #1, phase I	290 ____
00830	B&M F7 Diesel B Unit #2, phase I	290 ____
00831	D&RGW F7 Diesel B Unit #1, phase I	290 ____
00832	D&RGW F7 Diesel B Unit #2, phase I	290 ____
00833	GN F7 Diesel B Unit #1, phase I	290 ____
00834	GN F7 Diesel B Unit #2, phase I	290 ____
00835	MP F7 Diesel B Unit #1, phase I	290 ____
00836	MP F7 Diesel B Unit #2, phase II	290 ____
00837	PRR F7 Diesel B Unit #1, phase I	290 ____
00838	PRR F7 Diesel B Unit #2, phase I	290 ____
00839	F7 Diesel A Unit, phase I, DCC sound	300 ____
00840	ATSF Passenger F7 Diesel A Unit #1, phase I	300 ____
00841	ATSF Passenger F7 Diesel A Unit #2, phase I	300 ____
00842	ATSF Freight F7 Diesel A Unit #1, phase I	300 ____
00843	SF Freight F7 Diesel A Unit #2, phase I	300 ____
00844	B&M F7 Diesel A Unit #1, phase I	300 ____
00845	B&M F7 Diesel A Unit #2, phase I	300 ____
00846	D&RGW F7 Diesel A Unit #1, phase I	300 ____
00847	D&RGW F7 Diesel A Unit #2, phase I	300 ____
00848	GN F7 Diesel A Unit #1, phase I	300 ____
00849	GN F7 Diesel A Unit #2, phase I	300 ____
00850	MP F7 Diesel A Unit #1, phase I	300 ____
00851	MP F7 Diesel A Unit #2, phase I	300 ____
00852	PRR F7 Diesel A Unit #1, phase I	300 ____
00853	PRR F7 Diesel A Unit #2, phase I	300 ____
00854	F7 Diesel B Unit, phase I, DCC sound	290 ____
00855	ATSF Passenger F7 Diesel B Unit #1, phase I	290 ____
00856	ATSF Passenger F7 Diesel B Unit #2, phase I	290 ____
00857	ATSF Freight F7 Diesel B Unit #1, phase I	290 ____
00858	SF Freight F7 Diesel B Unit #2, phase I	290 ____

____	**00859**	B&M F7 Diesel B Unit #1, phase I	290
____	**00860**	B&M F7 Diesel B Unit #2, phase I	290
____	**00861**	D&RGW F7 Diesel B Unit #1, phase I	290
____	**00862**	D&RGW F7 Diesel B Unit #2, phase I	290
____	**00863**	GN F7 Diesel B Unit #1, phase I	290
____	**00864**	D&RGW F7 Diesel B Unit #2, phase I	290
____	**00865**	MP F7 Diesel B Unit #1, phase I	290
____	**00866**	MP F7 Diesel B Unit #2, phase I	290
____	**00867**	PRR F7 Diesel B Unit #1, phase I	290
____	**00868**	PRR F7 Diesel B Unit #2, phase I	290
____	**00869**	F7 Diesel A Unit, phase I, DC no sound	200
____	**00870**	ATSF Passenger F7 Diesel A Unit #1, phase I	200
____	**00871**	ATSF Passenger F7 Diesel A Unit #2, phase I	200
____	**00872**	ATSF Freight F7 Diesel A Unit #1, phase I	200
____	**00873**	SF Freight F7 Diesel A Unit #2, phase I	200
____	**00874**	B&M F7 Diesel A Unit #1, phase I	200
____	**00875**	B&M F7 Diesel A Unit #2, phase I	200
____	**00876**	D&RGW F7 Diesel A Unit #1, phase I	200
____	**00877**	D&RGW F7 Diesel A Unit #2, phase I	200
____	**00878**	GN F7 Diesel A Unit #1, phase I	200
____	**00879**	GN F7 Diesel A Unit #1, phase I	200
____	**00880**	MP F7 Diesel A Unit #1, phase I	200
____	**00881**	MP F7 Diesel A Unit #2, phase I	200
____	**00882**	PRR F7 Diesel A Unit #1, phase I	200
____	**00883**	PRR F7 Diesel A Unit #2, phase I	200
____	**00884**	F7 Diesel B Unit, phase I, DC no sound	190
____	**00885**	ATSF Passenger F7 Diesel B Unit #1, phase I	190
____	**00886**	ATSF Passenger F7 Diesel B Unit #2, phase I	190
____	**00887**	ATSF Freight F7 Diesel B Unit #1, phase I	190
____	**00888**	ATSF Freight F7 Diesel B Unit #2, phase I	190
____	**00889**	B&M F7 Diesel B Unit #1, phase I	190
____	**00890**	B&M F7 Diesel B Unit #2, phase I	190
____	**00891**	D&RGW F7 Diesel B Unit #1, phase I	190
____	**00892**	D&RGW F7 Diesel B Unit #2, phase I	190
____	**00893**	GN F7 Diesel B Unit #1, phase I	190
____	**00894**	GN F7 Diesel B Unit #2, phase I	190
____	**00895**	MP F7 Diesel B Unit #1, phase I	190
____	**00896**	MP F7 Diesel B Unit #2, phase I	190
____	**00897**	PRR F7 Diesel B Unit #1, phase I	190
____	**00898**	PRR F7 Diesel B Unit #2, phase I	190
____	**00899**	F7 Diesel ABA Set, phase I, DC LocoMatic sound	680
____	**00900**	ATSF Passenger F7 Diesel ABA, phase I	680
____	**00901**	ATSF Freight F7 Diesel ABA Set, phase I	680
____	**00902**	B&M F7 Diesel ABA Set, phase I	680
____	**00903**	D&RGW F7 Diesel ABA Set, phase I	680
____	**00904**	GN F7 Diesel ABA Set, phase I	680

00905	MP F7 Diesel ABA Set, phase I	680 ____
00906	PRR F7 Diesel ABA Set, phase I	680 ____
00907	F7 Diesel ABA Set, phase I, DCC sound	680 ____
00908	ATSF Passenger F7 Diesel ABA Set, phase I	680 ____
00909	ATSF Freight F7 Diesel ABA Set, phase I	680 ____
00910	B&M F7 Diesel ABA Set, phase I	680 ____
00911	D&RGW F7 Diesel ABA Set, phase I	680 ____
00912	GN F7 Diesel ABA Set, phase I	680 ____
00913	MP F7 Diesel ABA Set, phase I	680 ____
00914	PRR F7 Diesel ABA Set, phase I	680 ____
00915	F7 Diesel ABA Set, phase I, DC no sound	680 ____
00916	ATSF Passenger F7 Diesel ABA Set, phase I	680 ____
00917	ATSF Freight F7 Diesel ABA Set, phase I	680 ____
00918	B&M F7 Diesel ABA Set, phase I	680 ____
00919	D&RGW F7 Diesel ABA Set, phase I	680 ____
00920	GN F7 Diesel ABA Set, phase I	680 ____
00921	MP F7 Diesel ABA Set, phase I	680 ____
00922	PRR F7 Diesel ABA Set, phase I	680 ____
00923	Kahn's Wooden Billboard Reefer, scheme II #1	53 ____
00924	Kahn's Wooden Billboard Reefer, scheme II #2	53 ____
00925	Accessory Control Button	10 ____
00926	5" Straight Track with unlighted bumper	15 ____
00927	F7 Diesel AB Set, phase I, DC LocoMatic sound	490 ____
00928	ATSF Passenger F7 Diesel AB Set #1, phase I	490 ____
00929	ATSF Passenger F7 Diesel AB Set #2, phase I	490 ____
00930	ATSF Freight F7 Diesel AB Set #1, phase I	490 ____
00931	ATSF Freight F7 Diesel AB Set #2, phase I	490 ____
00932	B&M F7 Diesel AB Set #1, phase I	490 ____
00933	B&M F7 Diesel AB Set #2, phase I	490 ____
00934	D&RGW F7 Diesel AB Set #1, phase I	490 ____
00935	D&RGW F7 Diesel AB Set #2, phase I	490 ____
00936	GN F7 Diesel AB Set #1, phase I	490 ____
00937	GN F7 Diesel AB Set #2, phase I	490 ____
00938	MP F7 Diesel AB Set #1, phase I	490 ____
00939	MP F7 Diesel AB Set #2, phase I	490 ____
00940	PRR F7 Diesel AB Set #1, phase I	490 ____
00941	PRR F7 Diesel AB Set #2, phase I	490 ____
00942	F7 Diesel AA Set, phase I, AC/DC LocoMatic sound	490 ____
00943	ATSF Passenger F7 Diesel AA Set, phase I	490 ____
00944	ATSF Freight F7 Diesel AA Set, phase I	490 ____
00945	B&M F7 Diesel AA Set, phase I	490 ____
00946	D&RGW F7 Diesel AA Set, phase I	490 ____
00947	GN F7 Diesel AA Set, phase I	490 ____
00948	MP F7 Diesel AA Set, phase I	490 ____
00949	PRR F7 Diesel AA Set, phase I	490 ____
00950	F7 Diesel ABB Set, phase I, AC/DC LocoMatic sound	680 ____

___	**00951** ATSF Passenger F7 Diesel ABB Set, phase I	680
___	**00952** ATSF Freight F7 Diesel ABB Set, phase I	680
___	**00953** B&M F7 Diesel ABB Set, phase I	680
___	**00954** D&RGW F7 Diesel ABB Set, phase I	680
___	**00955** GN F7 Diesel ABB Set, phase I	680
___	**00956** MP F7 Diesel ABB Set, phase I	680
___	**00957** PRR F7 Diesel ABB Set, phase I	680
___	**00958** F7 Diesel ABBA Set, phase I, AC/DC LocoMatic sound	880
___	**00959** ATSF Passenger F7 Diesel ABBA Set, phase I	880
___	**00960** ATSF Freight F7 Diesel ABBA Set, phase I	880
___	**00961** B&M F7 Diesel ABBA Set, phase I	880
___	**00962** D&RGW F7 Diesel ABBA Set, phase I	880
___	**00963** GN F7 Diesel ABBA Set, phase I	880
___	**00964** MP F7 Diesel ABBA Set, phase I	880
___	**00965** PRR F7 Diesel ABBA Set, phase I	880
___	**00966** CNJ PS-2 2-bay Covered Hopper, scheme II	50
___	**00967** 33" Wheel Set, AF, single insulated, 4-pack	5
___	**00968** Brachs PS-2 2-bay Hopper, scheme I #1 (RSSVP Models)	50
___	**00969** Brachs PS-2 2-bay Hopper, scheme I #2 (RSSVP Models)	50
___	**00970** Brachs PS-2 2-bay Hopper, scheme II #1 (RSSVP Models)	50
___	**00971** Brachs PS-2 2-bay Hopper, scheme II #2 (RSSVP Models)	50
___	**00972** Jack Frost PS-2 2-bay Hopper #2 (RSSVP Models)	58
___	**00973** G&W PS-2 3-bay Covered Hopper #1	50
___	**00974** G&W PS-2 3-bay Covered Hopper #2	50
___	**00975** Reading PS-2 3-bay Covered Hopper #1	50
___	**00976** Reading PS-2 3-bay Covered Hopper #2	50
___	**00977** Wabash PS-2 3-bay Covered Hopper #1	50
___	**00978** Wabash PS-2 3-bay Covered Hopper #2	50
___	**00979** 33" Wheel Set, AF, double insulated, 4-pack	5
___	**00980** Panel Side Hopper, black	50
___	**00981** Panel Side Hopper, red	50
___	**00982** Anderson Panel Side Hopper 3-pack Set A	100
___	**00983** Anderson Panel Side Hopper #4	50
___	**00984** Ann Arbor Panel Side Hopper 3-pack	100
___	**00985** Ann Arbor Panel Side Hopper	50
___	**00986** C&O Panel Side Hopper 3-pack	100
___	**00987** C&O Panel Side Hopper	50
___	**00988** SLSF Panel Side Hopper 3-pack	100
___	**00989** SLSF Panel Side Hopper	50
___	**00990** D&H Panel Side Hopper 3-pack	100
___	**00991** D&H Panel Side Hopper	50
___	**00992** NYC Panel Side Hopper Car 3-pack, scheme I	100
___	**00993** NYC Panel Side Hopper Car, scheme I	50
___	**00994** NYC Panel Side Hopper 3-pack, scheme II	100
___	**00995** NYC Panel Side Hopper, scheme I	50
___	**00996** NYNH&H Panel Side Hopper	50

Retail

00997	PRR Panel Side Hopper	50 ____
00998	Wabash Panel Side Hopper 3-pack	100 ____
00999	Wabash Panel Side Hopper	50 ____
01000	PFE Wooden Billboard Reefer, scheme I #1	53 ____
01001	PFE Wooden Billboard Reefer, scheme I #2	53 ____
01002	ART Wooden Billboard Reefer #3	53 ____
01003	ART Wooden Billboard Reefer #4	53 ____
01004	CNW Wooden Billboard Reefer #1 (Chicagoland)	53 ____
01005	CNW Wooden Billboard Reefer #2 (Chicagoland)	59 ____
01006	Northern "Bananas" Wooden Billboard Reefer	53 ____
01007	Schlitz Beer Wooden Billboard Reefer	53 ____
01008	MP "Eagle" 40' Steel Rebuilt Boxcar #1	50 ____
01009	MP "Eagle" 40' Steel Rebuilt Boxcar #2	50 ____
01010	CN 40' Steel Rebuilt Boxcar #1	50 ____
01011	CN 40' Steel Rebuilt Boxcar #2	50 ____
01012	Seaboard "Orange Blossom Special" Rebuilt Boxcar	50 ____
01013	Seaboard "Silver Meteor" 40' Steel Rebuilt Boxcar	50 ____
01014	ATSF "Super Chief" 40' Steel Rebuilt Boxcar	50 ____
01015	FGE Wooden Billboard Reefer #1	53 ____
01016	FGE Wooden Billboard Reefer #2	53 ____
01017	Century Beer Wooden Billboard Reefer	53 ____
01018	Burlington Route 40' Steel Boxcar #1 (Boys RR Club)	53 ____
01019	Burlington Route 40' Steel Boxcar #2 (Boys RR Club)	53 ____
01020	State of Maine BAR 40' Steel Boxcar (Boys RR Club)	53 ____
01021	State of Maine NYNH&H 40' Steel Boxcar (Boys RR Club)	53 ____
01022	L&N "Dixie" 40' Steel Rebuilt Boxcar #1 (Boys RR Club)	53 ____
01023	L&N "Dixie" 40' Steel Rebuilt Boxcar #2 (Boys RR Club)	53 ____
01024	WP 40' Steel Rebuilt Boxcar #1 (Boys RR Club)	53 ____
01025	WP 40' Steel Rebuilt Boxcar #2 (Boys RR Club)	53 ____
01026	PRR 40' Steel Rebuilt Boxcar #1 (Boys RR Club)	53 ____
01027	PRR 40' Steel Rebuilt Boxcar #2 (Boys RR Club)	53 ____
01028	NYC 40' Steel Rebuilt Boxcar #1 (Boys RR Club)	53 ____
01029	NYC 40' Steel Rebuilt Boxcar #2 (Boys RR Club)	53 ____
01030	NYC 40' Steel Rebuilt Boxcar #3 (Boys RR Club)	53 ____
01031	40' Steel Rebuilt Boxcar (CVSG)	53 ____
01032	Tipo Wine Billboard Reefer #1 (Scenery Unlimited)	53 ____
01033	Tipo Wine Billboard Reefer #2 (Scenery Unlimited)	53 ____
01034	ATSF F7 Diesel Freight Set, 6 cars	430 ____
01036	MP F7 Diesel Freight Set, 6 cars	430 ____
01037	S-Trax Bumper, yellow, 2-pack	6 ____
01038	S-Trax Bumper, red, 2-pack	6 ____
01043	ICG SW9 Diesel Freight Set, 4 cars	300 ____
01044	D&RGW SW9 Diesel Freight Set, 5 cars	370 ____
01045	Seaboard SW1 Diesel Freight Set, 5 cars	370 ____
01046	MEC F3 Diesel Freight Set, 5 cars	400 ____
01047	D&RGW Extended Vision Caboose #3	70 ____

____ **01048**	D&RGW Extended Vision Caboose #4	70
____ **01049**	GTW Panel Side Hopper 3-pack	100
____ **01050**	GTW Panel Side Hopper	50
____ **01051**	2-8-0 Locomotive, hi-rail wheels, AC/DC LocoMatic sound	600
____ **01052**	B&O 2-8-0 Locomotive #1	600
____ **01053**	B&O 2-8-0 Locomotive #2	600
____ **01054**	ATSF 2-8-0 Locomotive #1	600
____ **01055**	ATSF 2-8-0 Locomotive #2	600
____ **01056**	C&NW 2-8-0 Locomotive #1	600
____ **01057**	C&NW 2-8-0 Locomotive #2	600
____ **01058**	Erie 2-8-0 Locomotive #1	600
____ **01059**	Erie 2-8-0 Locomotive #2	600
____ **01060**	MEC 2-8-0 Locomotive #1	600
____ **01061**	MEC 2-8-0 Locomotive #2	600
____ **01062**	NYC 2-8-0 Locomotive #1	600
____ **01063**	NYC 2-8-0 Locomotive #2	600
____ **01064**	Southern 2-8-0 Locomotive #1	600
____ **01066**	UP 2-8-0 Locomotive #1	600
____ **01067**	UP 2-8-0 Locomotive #2	600
____ **01068**	WM 2-8-0 Locomotive #1	600
____ **01069**	WM 2-8-0 Locomotive #2	600
____ **01070**	Flatcar with Oliver corn picker	55
____ **01071**	2-8-0 Locomotive, hi-rail wheels, DCC sound	600
____ **01072**	B&O 2-8-0 Locomotive #1	600
____ **01073**	B&O 2-8-0 Locomotive #2	600
____ **01074**	ATSF 2-8-0 Locomotive #1	600
____ **01075**	ATSF 2-8-0 Locomotive #2	600
____ **01076**	C&NW 2-8-0 Locomotive #1	600
____ **01077**	C&NW 2-8-0 Locomotive #2	600
____ **01078**	Erie 2-8-0 Locomotive #1	600
____ **01079**	Erie 2-8-0 Locomotive #2	600
____ **01080**	MEC 2-8-0 Locomotive #1	600
____ **01081**	MEC 2-8-0 Locomotive #2	600
____ **01082**	NYC 2-8-0 Locomotive #1	600
____ **01083**	NYC 2-8-0 Locomotive #2	600
____ **01084**	Southern 2-8-0 Locomotive #1	600
____ **01086**	UP 2-8-0 Locomotive #1	600
____ **01087**	UP 2-8-0 Locomotive #2	600
____ **01088**	WM 2-8-0 Locomotive #1	600
____ **01089**	WM 2-8-0 Locomotive #2	600
____ **01090**	Flatcar with IH Farmall corn picker	55
____ **01091**	2-8-0 Locomotive, hi-rail wheels, DC no sound	450
____ **01092**	B&O 2-8-0 Locomotive #1	450
____ **01093**	B&O 2-8-0 Locomotive #2	450
____ **01094**	ATSF 2-8-0 Locomotive #1	450
____ **01095**	ATSF 2-8-0 Locomotive #2	450

Retail

Item	Description	Price	
01096	C&NW 2-8-0 Locomotive #1	450	____
01097	C&NW 2-8-0 Locomotive #2	450	____
01098	Erie 2-8-0 Locomotive #1	450	____
01099	Erie 2-8-0 Locomotive #2	450	____
01100	MEC 2-8-0 Locomotive #1	450	____
01101	MEC 2-8-0 Locomotive #2	450	____
01102	NYC 2-8-0 Locomotive #1	450	____
01103	NYC 2-8-0 Locomotive #2	450	____
01104	Southern 2-8-0 Locomotive #1	450	____
01106	UP 2-8-0 Locomotive #1	450	____
01107	UP 2-8-0 Locomotive #2	450	____
01108	WM 2-8-0 Locomotive #1	450	____
01109	WM 2-8-0 Locomotive #2	450	____
01110	GN Offset Hopper	50	____
01111	Green Bay & Western Offset Hopper 3-pack	100	____
01112	Green Bay & Western Offset Hopper	50	____
01113	IC Offset Hopper 3-pack	100	____
01114	IC Offset Hopper	50	____
01115	LNE Offset Hopper 3-pack	100	____
01116	LNE Offset Hopper	50	____
01117	NYC Offset Hopper 3-pack	100	____
01118	NYC Offset Hopper	50	____
01119	Peabody Offset Hopper 3-pack	100	____
01120	Peabody Offset Hopper	50	____
01121	Detroit & Mackinac Offset Hopper 3-pack	100	____
01122	S-Trax Track Planning Guide	8	____
01123	Detroit & Mackinac Offset Hopper	50	____
01124	TP&W Offset Hopper 3-pack	100	____
01125	TP&W Offset Hopper	50	____
01126	DT&I 40' Steel Rebuilt Boxcar #1	50	____
01127	DT&I 40' Steel Rebuilt Boxcar #2	50	____
01128	GN 40' Steel Rebuilt Boxcar, scheme IV #1	50	____
01129	GN 40' Steel Rebuilt Boxcar, scheme IV #2	50	____
01130	Swift Wooden Billboard Reefer, scheme I	53	____
01131	Swift Wooden Billboard Reefer, scheme II	53	____
01132	Swift Wooden Billboard Reefer, scheme III	53	____
01133	SLSF 40' Steel Rebuilt Boxcar, scheme II	50	____
01134	SLSF 40' Steel Rebuilt Boxcar, scheme III	50	____
01135	SLSF 40' Steel Rebuilt Boxcar, scheme I #2	50	____
01136	Armour Stock Express 40' Stock Car #1	50	____
01137	Armour Stock Express 40' Stock Car #2	50	____
01138	GN 40' Stock Car	73	____
01139	Nickel Plate Road 40' Stock Car #1	50	____
01140	Nickel Plate Road 40' Stock Car #2	50	____
01141	UP 40' Stock Car, scheme II #1	50	____
01142	UP 40' Stock Car, scheme II #2	50	____

		Retail
____ **01143**	BN PS-2 2-bay Covered Hopper, scheme III #1	50
____ **01144**	BN PS-2 2-bay Covered Hopper, scheme III #2	50
____ **01145**	Chessie (C&O) PS-2 2-bay Covered Hopper #1	50
____ **01146**	Chessie (C&O) PS-2 2-bay Covered Hopper #2	50
____ **01147**	D&H PS-2 2-bay Covered Hopper #1	50
____ **01148**	D&H PS-2 2-bay Covered Hopper #2	50
____ **01149**	Boraxo PS-2 2-bay Covered Hopper	50
____ **01150**	Susquehanna 40' Steel Rebuilt Boxcar #1	50
____ **01151**	Susquehanna 40' Steel Rebuilt Boxcar #2	50
____ **01152**	PRR 40' Steel Rebuilt Boxcar, scheme II #1	50
____ **01153**	Offset Hopper, black	50
____ **01154**	Offset Hopper, red	50
____ **01155**	CNJ Offset Hopper 3-pack	100
____ **01156**	CNJ Offset Hopper	50
____ **01157**	DL&W Offset Hopper 3-pack	100
____ **01158**	DL&W Offset Hopper	50
____ **01159**	GN Offset Hopper 3-pack	100
____ **01160**	PRR 40' Steel Rebuilt Boxcar, scheme II #2	50
____ **01161**	GN Standard Flatcar, scheme II #1	50
____ **01162**	GN Standard Flatcar, scheme II #2	50
____ **01163**	NP Standard Flatcar #1	50
____ **01164**	NP Standard Flatcar #2	50
____ **01165**	SLSF Standard Flatcar #1	50
____ **01166**	SLSF Standard Flatcar #2	50
____ **01167**	SP Standard Flatcar, scheme I #1	50
____ **01168**	SP Standard Flatcar, scheme I #2	50
____ **01170**	Anderson Panel Side Hopper 3-pack Set B	100
____ **01171**	Anderson Panel Side Hopper Car #8	50
____ **01172**	CN Panel Side Hopper 3-pack	100
____ **01173**	CN Panel Side Hopper Car	50
____ **01174**	Rock Island Panel Side Hopper 3-pack	100
____ **01175**	Rock Island Panel Side Hopper Car	50
____ **01176**	USRA Rib Side Hopper, black	50
____ **01177**	USRA Rib Side Hopper, red	50
____ **01178**	B&O USRA Rib Side Hopper 3-pack	100
____ **01179**	B&O USRA Rib Side Hopper	50
____ **01180**	CNJ USRA Rib Side Hopper 3-pack	100
____ **01181**	CNJ USRA Rib Side Hopper	50
____ **01182**	CB&Q USRA Rib Side Hopper 3-pack	100
____ **01183**	CB&Q USRA Rib Side Hopper	50
____ **01184**	IH USRA Rib Side Hopper 3-pack	100
____ **01185**	IH USRA Rib Side Hopper	50
____ **01186**	L&N USRA Rib Side Hopper 3-pack	100
____ **01187**	L&N USRA Rib Side Hopper	50
____ **01188**	NYNH&H USRA Rib Side Hopper 3-pack	100
____ **01189**	NYNH&H USRA Rib Side Hopper	50

S-HELPER SERVICE 1994-2012

Retail

01190	NYC USRA Rib Side Hopper 3-pack	100 ____
01191	NYC USRA Rib Side Hopper	50 ____
01192	NYO&W USRA Rib Side Hopper 3-pack	100 ____
01193	NYO&W USRA Rib Side Hopper	50 ____
01194	PRR USRA Rib Side Hopper 3-pack	100 ____
01195	PRR USRA Rib Side Hopper	50 ____
01196	Reading USRA Rib Side Hopper 3-pack	100 ____
01197	Reading USRA Rib Side Hopper	50 ____
01198	32" Pipe Load	13 ____
01199	F7 DCC Sound Decoder	180 ____
01200	F3 AC/DC LocoMatic Sound Unit	160 ____
01201	F7 AC/DC LocoMatic Sound Unit	160 ____
01202	N&W USRA Rib Side Hopper 3-pack	100 ____
01203	N&W USRA Rib Side Hopper #4	50 ____
01204	N&W USRA Rib Side Hopper #5	50 ____
01205	Control Button, slide switch	8 ____
01206	Peabody USRA Rib Side Hopper 3-pack	100 ____
01207	Peabody USRA Rib Side Hopper	50 ____
01208	Andrews Tender Truck, 33" Code 110 wheels	11 ____
01209	Andrews Tender Truck, 33" hi-rail wheels	11 ____
01210	Flatcar with Case IH grinder mixers	60 ____
01211	Track-cleaning USRA Double-sheathed Boxcar	150 ____
01212	Track-cleaning Standard Flatcar	150 ____
01214	Custom Trax No. 6 Switch, right hand	48 ____
01215	Custom Trax No. 6 Switch, left hand	48 ____
01216	Custom Trax No. 8 Switch, right hand	50 ____
01217	Custom Trax No. 8 Switch, left hand	50 ____
01218	Flextrack, 36" roadbed	15 ____
01219	HomaBed 48' Straight	69 ____
01220	HomaBed 48' Curved	74 ____
01221	HomaBed 48' Straight/Curved	81 ____
01222	Monon Composite Side Hopper Car 3-pack	100 ____
01223	Monon Composite Side Hopper Car	50 ____
01224	LV Composite Side Hopper Car 3-pack Set B	100 ____
01225	LV Composite Side Hopper Car #8	50 ____
01226	PRR Composite Side Hopper Car 3-pack Set B	100 ____
01227	PRR Composite Side Hopper Car #8	50 ____
01228	36" Weathered Rail, Code 131, 33 pieces	70 ____
01229	CB&Q SW1 Diesel #1	200 ____
01230	CB&Q SW1 Diesel #2	200 ____
01231	CNJ SW1 Diesel #1	200 ____
01232	CNJ SW1 Diesel #2	200 ____
01233	Erie-Lackawanna SW1 Diesel #1	200 ____
01234	Erie-Lackawanna SW1 Diesel #2	200 ____
01235	GN SW1 Diesel #1	200 ____
01236	GN SW1 Diesel #2	200 ____

___ **01237**	B&M SW8 Diesel #1	200
___ **01238**	B&M SW8 Diesel #2	200
___ **01239**	BN SW8 Diesel #1	200
___ **01240**	BN SW8 Diesel #2	200
___ **01241**	C&NW SW8 Diesel #1	200
___ **01242**	C&NW SW8 Diesel #2	200
___ **01243**	CRI&P SW8 Diesel #1	200
___ **01244**	CRI&P SW8 Diesel #2	200
___ **01245**	Conrail SW9 Diesel, scheme II #1	200
___ **01246**	Conrail SW9 Diesel, scheme II #2	200
___ **01247**	FEC SW9 Diesel #1	200
___ **01248**	FEC SW9 Diesel #2	200
___ **01249**	SLSF SW9 Diesel #1	200
___ **01250**	SLSF SW9 Diesel #2	200
___ **01251**	Lehigh Valley SW9 Diesel #1	200
___ **01252**	Lehigh Valley SW9 Diesel #2	200
___ **01253**	ATSF NW2 Diesel #1	200
___ **01254**	ATSF NW2 Diesel #2	200
___ **01255**	Chessie (C&O) NW2 Diesel #1	200
___ **01256**	Chessie (C&O) NW2 Diesel #2	200
___ **01259**	PRR NW2 Diesel, scheme I	200
___ **01260**	PRR NW2 Diesel, scheme II	200
___ **01261**	NW2 Diesel	200
___ **01262**	SLSF Extended Vision Caboose #1	70
___ **01263**	SLSF Extended Vision Caboose #2	70
___ **01264**	CB&Q Extended Vision Caboose, scheme II #1	70
___ **01265**	CB&Q Extended Vision Caboose, scheme II #2	70
___ **01266**	D&RGW Extended Vision Caboose #5	70
___ **01267**	D&RGW Extended Vision Caboose #6	70
___ **01268**	GN Extended Vision Caboose #3	70
___ **01269**	GN Extended Vision Caboose #4	70
___ **01270**	MEC Extended Vision Caboose, scheme III	78
___ **01271**	Silver Edge Beer Wooden Billboard Reefer	53
___ **01272**	Columbia Soups Wooden Billboard Reefer	53
___ **01273**	Niblets Corn Wooden Billboard Reefer	53
___ **01274**	Monarch Foods Wooden Billboard Reefer	53
___ **01275**	Wilson Milk Wooden Billboard Reefer #1 (Port Lines)	53
___ **01276**	Wilson Milk Wooden Billboard Reefer #2 (Port Lines)	53
___ **01277**	URTX MILW Wooden Billboard Reefer #1	53
___ **01278**	URTX MILW Wooden Billboard Reefer #2	53
___ **01279**	WFE GN Wooden Billboard Reefer #1	53
___ **01280**	WFE GN Wooden Billboard Reefer #2	53
___ **01281**	CNJ USRA Single-sheathed Boxcar #1	50
___ **01282**	CNJ USRA Single-sheathed Boxcar #2	50
___ **01283**	CMStP&P USRA Single-sheathed Boxcar #1	50
___ **01284**	CMStP&P USRA Single-sheathed Boxcar #2	50

S-HELPER SERVICE 1994-2012

Retail

01285	MKT USRA Single-sheathed Boxcar #1	50 ____
01286	MKT USRA Single-sheathed Boxcar #2	50 ____
01287	Wellsville, Addison & Galeton Single-sheathed Boxcar	50 ____
01288	CB&Q F3 Diesel ABA Set, phase II, DC no sound	590 ____
01290	BN Ore Car 5-pack	180 ____
01291	BN Ore Car	40 ____
01292	GN Ore Car 5-pack, scheme II	180 ____
01293	GN Ore Car, scheme II	40 ____
01294	DM&IR Ore Car 5-pack	180 ____
01295	Coupler, Kadee style, 2 pair	6 ____
01296	CNJ Composite Side Hopper 3-pack, scheme II (Hoquat)	100 ____
01297	CNJ Composite Side Hopper, scheme II (Hoquat)	50 ____
01298	DL&W Composite Side Hopper 3-pack, scheme II (Hoquat)	100 ____
01299	DL&W Composite Side Hopper, scheme II (Hoquat)	50 ____
01300	Public Service Composite Side Hopper 3-pack (Hoquat)	100 ____
01301	Public Service Composite Side Hopper (Hoquat)	50 ____
01302	AC/DC LocoMatic Sound Switcher Board	150 ____
01303	Conrail SW9 Diesel Freight Set, 4 cars	300 ____
01304	C&NW F3 Diesel Freight Set, 4 cars	330 ____
01305	Chessie (C&O) NW2 Diesel Freight Set, 5 cars	370 ____
01306	D&RGW F7 Diesel Freight Set, 6 cars	430 ____
01307	CB&Q SW1 Diesel Freight Set, 6 cars	400 ____
01308	GN F7 Diesel Freight Set, 6 cars	430 ____
01310	Freight Coupler, short shank, AF compatible, pair	3 ____
01333	CMStP&P Wooden Billboard Reefer #1 (Badgerland)	53 ____
01363	CMStP&P Wooden Billboard Reefer #2 (Badgerland)	53 ____
01393	CMStP&P Wooden Billboard Reefer #3 (Badgerland)	53 ____
01402	DM&IR Ore Car 5-pack Set B	180 ____
01403	CMStP&P Wooden Billboard Reefer #4 (Badgerland)	53 ____
01413	CMStP&P Wooden Billboard Reefer #5 (Badgerland)	53 ____
01422	GN Ore Car 5-pack Set B, scheme I	180 ____
01423	Control Button, passing siding	8 ____
01432	CMStP&P Ore Car 5-pack Set B	180 ____
01433	Ore Car Sampler 10-pack	360 ____
01442	Flatcar with 4 Farmall tractors	60 ____
01443	D&RGW 40' Steel Rebuilt Boxcar (Boys RR Club)	50 ____
01452	D&RGW 40' Steel Rebuilt Boxcar (Boys RR Club)	50 ____
01453	Central of Georgia 40' Steel Boxcar (Boys RR Club)	50 ____
01501	MEC SW9 Diesel	200 ____
01502	MEC SW9 Diesel, holiday	200 ____
01503	MEC SW9 Diesel, AC/DC LocoMatic sound	290 ____
01504	MEC SW9 Diesel, holiday, AC/DC LocoMatic sound	290 ____
01505	MEC SW9 Diesel, DCC sound	290 ____
01506	MEC SW9 Diesel, holiday, DCC sound	290 ____
01507	MEC Locomotive and Caboose, holiday	270 ____
01508	MEC Locomotive and Caboose, holiday, AC/DC sound	360 ____

____ **01509**	MEC Locomotive and Caboose, holiday, DCC sound	360
____ **01510**	Hood Milk Wooden Billboard Reefer #1 (Port Lines)	53
____ **01511**	Hood Milk Wooden Billboard Reefer #2 (Port Lines)	53
____ **01512**	Merchants Biscuit Wooden Billboard Reefer	53
____ **01513**	E&A Opler Wooden Billboard Reefer	53
____ **01514**	Carnation Milk Wooden Billboard Reefer	53
____ **01515**	Great Falls Beer Wooden Billboard Reefer	53
____ **01516**	Curve Beer Wooden Billboard Reefer #1 (NASG)	53
____ **01517**	Curve Beer Wooden Billboard Reefer #2 (NASG)	53
____ **01518**	B&M SW8 Diesel #1, AC/DC LocoMatic sound	290
____ **01519**	B&M SW8 Diesel #2, AC/DC LocoMatic sound	290
____ **01520**	BN SW8 Diesel #1, AC/DC LocoMatic sound	290
____ **01521**	BN SW8 Diesel #2, AC/DC LocoMatic sound	290
____ **01522**	C&NW SW8 Diesel #1, AC/DC LocoMatic sound	290
____ **01523**	C&NW SW8 Diesel #2, AC/DC LocoMatic sound	290
____ **01524**	CRI&P SW8 Diesel #1, AC/DC LocoMatic sound	290
____ **01525**	CRI&P SW8 Diesel #2, AC/DC LocoMatic sound	290
____ **01526**	Conrail SW9 Diesel, scheme II #1, AC/DC LocoMatic sound	290
____ **01527**	FEC SW9 Diesel #1, AC/DC LocoMatic sound	290
____ **01528**	FEC SW9 Diesel #2, AC/DC LocoMatic sound	290
____ **01529**	SLSF SW9 Diesel #1, AC/DC LocoMatic sound	290
____ **01530**	SLSF SW9 Diesel #2, AC/DC LocoMatic sound	290
____ **01531**	Lehigh Valley SW9 Diesel #1, AC/DC LocoMatic sound	290
____ **01532**	Lehigh Valley SW9 Diesel #2, AC/DC LocoMatic sound	290
____ **01535**	Chessie (C&O) NW2 Diesel #1, AC/DC LocoMatic sound	290
____ **01536**	Chessie (C&O) NW2 Diesel #2, AC/DC LocoMatic sound	290
____ **01539**	PRR NW2 Diesel, scheme I, AC/DC LocoMatic sound	290
____ **01540**	PRR NW2 Diesel, scheme II, AC/DC LocoMatic sound	290
____ **01541**	NW2 Diesel, AC/DC LocoMatic sound	290
____ **01550**	Conrail Quality SW9 Diesel #1, DCC sound	290
____ **01551**	Florida East Coast SW9 Diesel #1, DCC sound	290
____ **01552**	Florida East Coast SW9 Diesel #2, DCC sound	290
____ **01553**	SLSF SW9 Diesel #1, DCC sound	290
____ **01554**	SLSF SW9 Diesel #2, DCC sound	290
____ **01555**	Lehigh Valley SW9 Diesel #1, DCC sound	290
____ **01556**	Lehigh Valley SW9 Diesel #2, DCC sound	290
____ **01557**	ATSF NW2 Diesel #1, DCC sound	290
____ **01558**	ATSF NW2 Diesel #2, DCC sound	290
____ **01559**	Chessie NW2 Diesel #1, DCC sound	290
____ **01560**	Chessie NW2 Diesel #2, DCC sound	290
____ **01563**	PRR NW2 Diesel, scheme I, DCC sound	290
____ **01564**	PRR NW2 Diesel, scheme II, DCC sound	290
____ **01565**	NW2 Diesel, DCC sound, DCC sound	290
____ **01566**	ATSF USRA Double-sheathed Boxcar, scheme I	50
____ **01568**	Duluth, South Shore & Atlantic Double-sheathed Boxcar	50
____ **01569**	Ivory USRA Double-sheathed Boxcar #1 (Miami Valley)	50

01570	Ivory USRA Double-sheathed Boxcar #2 (Miami Valley)	50 ____
01571	NWP USRA Double-sheathed Boxcar #1	50 ____
01572	D&RGW 40' Steel Rebuilt Boxcar #1 (Boys RR Club)	50 ____
01573	D&RGW 40' Steel Rebuilt Boxcar #2 (Boys RR Club)	50 ____
01574	D&RGW 40' Steel Rebuilt Boxcar #3 (Boys RR Club)	50 ____
01575	Central of Georgia 40' Steel Boxcar #1 (Boys RR Club)	50 ____
01576	Central of Georgia 40' Steel Boxcar #2 (Boys RR Club)	50 ____
01577	Central of Georgia 40' Steel Boxcar #3 (Boys RR Club)	50 ____
01578	Ann Arbor 40' Steel Rebuilt Boxcar	50 ____
01579	Lancaster & Chester 40' Steel Rebuilt Boxcar #1	50 ____
01580	Lancaster & Chester 40' Steel Rebuilt Boxcar #2	50 ____
01581	Soo Line 40' Steel Rebuilt Boxcar #1	50 ____
01582	Soo Line 40' Steel Rebuilt Boxcar #2	50 ____
01583	B&O 2-8-0 Locomotive #3, hi-rail wheels, AC/DC sound	600 ____
01584	B&O 2-8-0 Locomotive #3, hi-rail wheels, DCC sound	600 ____
01585	B&O 2-8-0 Locomotive #3, hi-rail wheels	450 ____
01586	B&O 2-8-0 Locomotive #3, Code 110 wheels, AC/DC sound	600 ____
01587	B&O 2-8-0 Locomotive #3, Code 110 wheels, DCC sound	600 ____
01588	B&O 2-8-0 Locomotive #3, Code 110 wheels	450 ____
01589	Christmas Figure and Wreath Set	15 ____
01590	Santa and Mrs. Claus Figure Set	9 ____
01591	Matawan Junction Track Layout	430 ____
01592	Maybrook Bridge Line Track Layout	416 ____
01593	Tacoma Transfer Track Layout	410 ____
01594	Norwalk Crossing Track Layout	340 ____
01595	Macoon Yard Track Layout	630 ____
01596	Utica Terminal Track Layout	840 ____
01597	Decatur Exchange Track Layout	600 ____
01598	Gome & Dapgetid Track Layout	760 ____
01599	S-Helper Service Track Layout	620 ____
01601	B&M Double-sheathed Boxcar, scheme II #1 (Hoquat)	53 ____
01602	B&M Double-sheathed Boxcar, scheme II #2 (Hoquat)	53 ____
01603	DL&W Double-sheathed Boxcar, scheme II #1 (Hoquat)	53 ____
01604	DL&W Double-sheathed Boxcar, scheme II #2 (Hoquat)	53 ____
01605	Erie Wooden Billboard Reefer #1 (Hoquat)	53 ____
01606	Erie Wooden Billboard Reefer #2 (Hoquat)	53 ____
01607	NWX Wooden Billboard Reefer #6 (Hoquat)	53 ____
01608	NWX Wooden Billboard Reefer #7 (Hoquat)	53 ____
01609	PFE (WP) Wooden Billboard Reefer #1	53 ____
01610	PFE (WP) Wooden Billboard Reefer #2	53 ____
01611	SFRD "Super Chief" Wooden Billboard Reefer	53 ____
01612	Speaker/Switcher	40 ____
01613	NdeM 40' Steel Rebuilt Boxcar #1 (Mainstreeter)	50 ____
01614	NdeM 40' Steel Rebuilt Boxcar #2 (Mainstreeter)	50 ____

____	**01615** Conrail SW9 Diesel Freight Set, 4 cars	300
____	**01616** SLSF SW9 Diesel Freight Set, 4 cars	300
____	**01617** Chessie (C&O) NW2 Diesel Freight Set, 5 cars	375
____	**01618** GN SW1 Diesel Freight Set, 5 cars	370
____	**01619** ATSF F7 Diesel Freight Set, 6 cars	430
____	**01620** Conrail SW9 Diesel Freight Set, 4 cars, sound	390
____	**01621** SLSF SW9 Diesel Freight Set, 4 cars, sound	390
____	**01622** Chessie (C&O) NW2 Diesel Freight Set, 5 cars, sound	460
____	**01623** NWP USRA Double-sheathed Boxcar, scheme I #2	50
____	**01624** Ann Arbor 40' Steel Rebuilt Boxcar #2	50
____	**01625** Domino Sugar PS-2 3-bay Covered Hopper	50
____	**01626** Jack Frost PS-2 3-bay Covered Hopper	50
____	**01627** B&O PS-2 3-bay Covered Hopper #1	50
____	**01628** B&O PS-2 3-bay Covered Hopper #2	50
____	**01629** C&NW PS-2 3-bay Covered Hopper, scheme II #1	50
____	**01630** C&NW PS-2 3-bay Covered Hopper, scheme II #2	50
____	**01631** SP PS-2 3-bay Covered Hopper #1	50
____	**01632** SP PS-2 3-bay Covered Hopper #2	50
____	**01633** AC/DC LocoMatic Sound Unit	180
____	**01634** DCC Socket Set for Switchers #2	25
____	**01636** MTC Brookside Wooden Billboard Reefer #3 (Port Lines)	53
____	**01637** Sunrise Onions Wooden Billboard Reefer	53
____	**01638** OTOE Food Products Wooden Billboard Reefer	53
____	**01639** PFE Wooden Billboard Reefer, scheme III #1	53
____	**01640** PFE Wooden Billboard Reefer, scheme III #2	53
____	**01641** PFE Wooden Billboard Reefer, scheme III #3	53
____	**01642** Heileman's Old Style Lager Wooden Billboard Reefer	53
____	**01643** Domino Sugar Double-sheathed Boxcar #1 (Port Lines)	50
____	**01644** Domino Sugar Double-sheathed Boxcar #2 (Port Lines)	50
____	**01645** MEC Offset Hopper	50
____	**01646** C&O USRA Rib Side Hopper #1	50
____	**01647** C&O USRA Rib Side Hopper #2	50
____	**01648** C&O USRA Rib Side Hopper #3	50
____	**01649** C&O USRA Rib Side Hopper #4	50
____	**01650** Waddell Coal USRA Rib Side Hopper #1	53
____	**01651** Waddell Coal USRA Rib Side Hopper #2	53
____	**01652** Waddell Coal USRA Rib Side Hopper #3	53
____	**01653** Waddell Coal USRA Rib Side Hopper #4	53
____	**01654** PRR Composite Side Hopper, scheme II #1	50
____	**01655** PRR Composite Side Hopper, scheme II #2	50
____	**01656** PRR Composite Side Hopper, scheme II #3	50
____	**01657** PRR Composite Side Hopper, scheme II #4	50
____	**01658** Spiral Hill USRA Rib Side Hopper #1 (Lehigh Valley)	50
____	**01659** Spiral Hill USRA Rib Side Hopper #2 (Lehigh Valley)	50
____	**01660** MKT 40' Steel Rebuilt Boxcar (TCA)	50
____	**01661** Smoke Unit Funnels, 3 pieces	3

Retail

01664	Spiral Hill USRA Rib Side Hopper #3 (Lehigh Valley)	50 ____
01666	Flatcar with 2 Humvees	60 ____
01667	Flatcar with 2 Humvee ambulances	60 ____
01668	ATSF F7 Diesel Freight Set, 6 cars, sound	490 ____
01669	Locomotive Figure Set	6 ____
01670	Tender Coupler, AF compatible, pair	3 ____
01671	Speaker, 1-watt, 8-ohm	9 ____
01672	Tender LED Light Set, golden white, pair	6 ____
01673	Smoke Unit, pair	10 ____
01674	Infrared Sensor, pair	10 ____
01675	1.6mm Wrench	4 ____
01676	Motor with flywheel, pair	15 ____
01677	Flatcar with Bradley Fighting Vehicle	63 ____
01678	Headlight LED Accessory, golden white, pair	10 ____
01679	Headlight Top LED Accessory, golden white, pair	10 ____
01680	Coal Load with snow	6 ____
01681	Mine Run Coal Load	6 ____
01682	Classification Lights, brass, pair	5 ____
01683	C&NW Stock Car #1 (Hoquat)	50 ____
01684	C&NW Stock Car #2 (Hoquat)	50 ____
01685	Grand Trunk Western Stock Car #1 (Hoquat)	50 ____
01686	Grand Trunk Western Stock Car #2 (Hoquat)	50 ____
01687	N&W Stock Car #1	50 ____
01688	N&W Stock Car #2	50 ____
01689	SLSF Stock Car #1	50 ____
01690	SLSF Stock Car #2	50 ____
01691	Santa Fe "Chief" Wooden Billboard Reefer (Hoquat)	53 ____
01692	Berkshire Wooden Billboard Reefer (Hoquat)	53 ____
01693	Peerless Beer Wooden Billboard Reefer	53 ____
01694	Skyland Eggs Wooden Billboard Reefer	53 ____
01695	Priebe Wooden Billboard Reefer	53 ____
01696	Central of Georgia 40' Steel Boxcar, red (Boys RR Club)	50 ____
01697	Central of Georgia 40' Steel Boxcar, black (Boys RR Club)	50 ____
01698	Central of Georgia 40' Steel Boxcar, maroon (Boys RR Club)	50 ____
01699	Central of Georgia 40' Steel Boxcar, blue (Boys RR Club)	50 ____
01700	MEC 2-8-0 Locomotive #1, Code 110 wheels	450 ____
01701	MEC 2-8-0 Locomotive #2, Code 110 wheels	450 ____
01702	NYC 2-8-0 Locomotive #1, Code 110 wheels	450 ____
01703	NYC 2-8-0 Locomotive #2, Code 110 wheels	450 ____
01704	Southern 2-8-0 Locomotive, Code 110 wheels	450 ____
01706	UP 2-8-0 Locomotive #1, Code 110 wheels	450 ____
01707	UP 2-8-0 Locomotive #2, Code 110 wheels	450 ____
01708	WM 2-8-0 Locomotive #1, Code 110 wheels	450 ____
01709	WM 2-8-0 Locomotive #2, Code 110 wheels	450 ____
01710	B&O 40' Steel Rebuilt Boxcar, blue roof (Boys RR Club)	50 ____

____ 01711	B&O 40' Steel Rebuilt Boxcar, silver roof (Boys RR Club)	50
____ 01712	B&O 40' Steel Rebuilt Boxcar, blue roof (Boys RR Club)	50
____ 01713	B&O 40' Steel Rebuilt Boxcar, silver roof (Boys RR Club)	50
____ 01714	Great American Circus Steel Boxcar (Scenery Unlimited)	50
____ 01715	Great American Circus Steel Boxcar (Scenery Unlimited)	50
____ 01716	Great American Circus Steel Boxcar (Scenery Unlimited)	50
____ 01717	Great American Circus Stock Car (Scenery Unlimited)	50
____ 01718	Great American Circus Stock Car (Scenery Unlimited)	50
____ 01719	Great American Circus Stock Car (Scenery Unlimited)	50
____ 01720	MNS 40' Steel Rebuilt Boxcar #1 (Pines & Prairies)	50
____ 01721	MNS 40' Steel Rebuilt Boxcar #2 (Pines & Prairies)	50
____ 01722	Great American Circus Flatcar (Scenery Unlimited)	50
____ 01723	Great American Circus Flatcar (Scenery Unlimited)	50
____ 01724	Great American Circus Flatcar (Scenery Unlimited)	50
____ 01725	Great American Circus Flatcar (Scenery Unlimited)	50
____ 01726	Great American Circus Flatcar (Scenery Unlimited)	50
____ 01727	Great American Circus Flatcar (Scenery Unlimited)	50
____ 01728	BN Christmas Bulkhead Flatcar #3 with presents	56
____ 01729	GM&O Bulkhead Flatcar #1 with pipe load	56
____ 01730	GM&O Bulkhead Flatcar #2 with pipe load	56
____ 01731	BAAFC Wooden Billboard Reefer (NASG)	53
____ 01732	BAAFC Wooden Billboard Reefer (NASG)	53
____ 01734	40" Unweathered Rail, Code 131, 33 pieces	70
____ 01735	33" Scale Wheel Set/Pickup, Code 110, 4-pack	5
____ 01736	CB&Q (FWD) NW2 Diesel	200
____ 01737	CB&Q NW2 Diesel	200
____ 01738	CB&Q (FWD) NW2 Diesel, AC/DC LocoMatic sound	290
____ 01739	CB&Q NW2 Diesel, AC/DC LocoMatic sound	290
____ 01740	CB&Q (FWD) NW2 Diesel, DCC sound	290
____ 01741	CB&Q NW2 Diesel, DCC sound	290
____ 01742	ICG PS-2 2-bay Covered Hopper #1	50
____ 01743	ICG PS-2 2-bay Covered Hopper #2	50
____ 01744	SP PS-2 2-bay Covered Hopper, scheme III #1	50
____ 01745	SP PS-2 2-bay Covered Hopper, scheme III #2	50
____ 01746	Lancaster & Chester PS-2 2-bay Covered Hopper #1	50
____ 01747	Lancaster & Chester PS-2 2-bay Covered Hopper #2	50
____ 01748	Maryland Midland PS-2 2-bay Covered Hopper (NASG)	50
____ 01749	Maryland Midland PS-2 2-bay Covered Hopper (NASG)	50
____ 01750	Kerr-McGee PS-2 2-bay Covered Hopper	50
____ 01751	2-8-0 Locomotive, AC/DC LocoMatic sound	600
____ 01752	B&O 2-8-0 Locomotive #1	600
____ 01753	B&O 2-8-0 Locomotive #2	600
____ 01754	ATSF 2-8-0 Locomotive #1	600
____ 01755	ATSF 2-8-0 Locomotive #2	600
____ 01756	C&NW 2-8-0 Locomotive #1	600
____ 01757	C&NW 2-8-0 Locomotive #2	600

S-HELPER SERVICE 1994-2012

		Retail	
01758	Erie 2-8-0 Locomotive #1	600	____
01759	Erie 2-8-0 Locomotive #2	600	____
01760	MEC 2-8-0 Locomotive #1	600	____
01761	MEC 2-8-0 Locomotive #2	600	____
01762	NYC 2-8-0 Locomotive #1	600	____
01763	NYC 2-8-0 Locomotive #2	600	____
01764	Southern 2-8-0 Locomotive #1	600	____
01766	UP 2-8-0 Locomotive #1	600	____
01767	UP 2-8-0 Locomotive #2	600	____
01768	WM 2-8-0 Locomotive #1	600	____
01769	WM 2-8-0 Locomotive #2	600	____
01771	2-8-0 Locomotive, DCC sound	600	____
01772	B&O 2-8-0 Locomotive #1	600	____
01773	B&O 2-8-0 Locomotive #2	600	____
01774	ATSF 2-8-0 Locomotive #1	600	____
01775	ATSF 2-8-0 Locomotive #2	600	____
01776	C&NW 2-8-0 Locomotive #1	600	____
01777	C&NW 2-8-0 Locomotive #2	600	____
01778	Erie 2-8-0 Locomotive #1	600	____
01779	Erie 2-8-0 Locomotive #2	600	____
01780	MEC 2-8-0 Locomotive #1	600	____
01781	MEC 2-8-0 Locomotive #2	600	____
01782	NYC 2-8-0 Locomotive #1	600	____
01783	NYC 2-8-0 Locomotive #2	600	____
01784	Southern 2-8-0 Locomotive #1	600	____
01786	UP 2-8-0 Locomotive #1	600	____
01787	UP 2-8-0 Locomotive #2	600	____
01788	WM 2-8-0 Locomotive #1	600	____
01789	WM 2-8-0 Locomotive #2	600	____
01790	GTW USRA Rebuilt Covered Hopper #1	50	____
01791	2-8-0 Locomotive, DC, no sound	450	____
01792	B&O 2-8-0 Locomotive #1	450	____
01793	B&O 2-8-0 Locomotive #2	450	____
01794	ATSF 2-8-0 Locomotive #1	450	____
01795	ATSF 2-8-0 Locomotive #2	450	____
01796	C&NW 2-8-0 Locomotive #1	450	____
01797	C&NW 2-8-0 Locomotive #2	450	____
01798	Erie 2-8-0 Locomotive #1	450	____
01799	Erie 2-8-0 Locomotive #2	450	____
01800	Chicago Macaroni Wooden Billboard Reefer	53	____
01801	Hamm Brewing Wooden Billboard Reefer	53	____
01802	Westcott & Winks Wooden Billboard Reefer	53	____
01803	Marhoefer Wooden Billboard Reefer #1	53	____
01804	Flatcar with 2 Stuart tanks	60	____
01807	Santa Fe Flatcar with trailer, scheme II #1	63	____
01808	Santa Fe Flatcar with trailer, scheme II #2	63	____

_____ **01809**	Reading Flatcar #1 with trailer	63
_____ **01810**	Reading Flatcar #2 with trailer	63
_____ **01811**	Flatcar with REA trailer, 2007 Christmas Car	63
_____ **01812**	SP Flatcar #1 with trailer	63
_____ **01813**	SP Flatcar #2 with trailer	63
_____ **01814**	CGW Bulkhead Flatcar with pipes #1	56
_____ **01815**	CGW Bulkhead Flatcar with pipes #2	56
_____ **01816**	ACL Bulkhead Flatcar #1 with pipes	56
_____ **01817**	ACL Bulkhead Flatcar #2 with pulpwood	56
_____ **01818**	ATSF Standard Flatcar #2, red	50
_____ **01819**	ATSF Standard Flatcar #3, red	50
_____ **01820**	Reading Standard Flatcar #1	50
_____ **01821**	Reading Standard Flatcar #2	50
_____ **01822**	ACL Standard Flatcar #1	50
_____ **01823**	ACL Standard Flatcar #2	50
_____ **01824**	PRR Standard Flatcar #4	50
_____ **01825**	PRR Standard Flatcar #5	50
_____ **01826**	SP Standard Flatcar, scheme II #1	50
_____ **01827**	SP Standard Flatcar, scheme II #2	50
_____ **01828**	Santa Fe Wooden Billboard Reefer #1	53
_____ **01829**	Santa Fe Wooden Billboard Reefer #2	53
_____ **01830**	Carling Black Label Billboard Reefer #3 (Port Lines)	53
_____ **01831**	B&O USRA Single-sheathed Boxcar, scheme II #1	50
_____ **01832**	B&O USRA Single-sheathed Boxcar, scheme II #2	50
_____ **01833**	CNJ USRA Single-sheathed Boxcar #1	50
_____ **01834**	CNJ USRA Single-sheathed Boxcar #2	50
_____ **01835**	MEC USRA Single-sheathed Boxcar #1	50
_____ **01836**	MEC USRA Single-sheathed Boxcar #2	50
_____ **01839**	PRR USRA Single-sheathed Boxcar #3	50
_____ **01840**	PRR USRA Single-sheathed Boxcar #4	50
_____ **01842**	Canada Southern USRA Rebuilt Covered Hopper #1	50
_____ **01843**	Canada Southern USRA Rebuilt Covered Hopper #2	50
_____ **01845**	RFP Express USRA Double-sheathed Boxcar #1	50
_____ **01846**	RFP Express USRA Double-sheathed Boxcar #2	50
_____ **01847**	DCC Interface PCB for Switchers	25
_____ **01848**	B&O USRA Rebuilt Covered Hopper #1	50
_____ **01849**	B&O USRA Rebuilt Covered Hopper #2	50
_____ **01850**	CNJ USRA Rebuilt Covered Hopper #1	50
_____ **01851**	CNJ USRA Rebuilt Covered Hopper #2	50
_____ **01852**	C&O USRA Rebuilt Covered Hopper #1	50
_____ **01853**	C&O USRA Rebuilt Covered Hopper #2	50
_____ **01854**	D&H USRA Rebuilt Covered Hopper #1	50
_____ **01855**	D&H USRA Rebuilt Covered Hopper #2	50
_____ **01856**	LNE USRA Rebuilt Covered Hopper #1	50
_____ **01857**	LNE USRA Rebuilt Covered Hopper #2	50
_____ **01858**	LV USRA Rebuilt Covered Hopper #1	50

01859	LV USRA Rebuilt Covered Hopper #2	50 ____
01861	MEC USRA Rebuilt Covered Hopper #2	55 ____
01862	NYC USRA Rebuilt Covered Hopper #1	50 ____
01863	NYC USRA Rebuilt Covered Hopper #2	50 ____
01864	NKP USRA Rebuilt Covered Hopper #1	50 ____
01865	NKP USRA Rebuilt Covered Hopper #2	50 ____
01866	Reading USRA Rebuilt Covered Hopper #1	50 ____
01867	Reading USRA Rebuilt Covered Hopper #2	50 ____
01868	Cambria & Indiana Offset Hopper #1	50 ____
01869	Cambria & Indiana Offset Hopper #2	50 ____
01870	USRA Rebuilt Covered Hopper, gray	50 ____
01871	PRR Standard Flatcar #4	50 ____
01872	S-Helper Service 35' Trailer, horizontal corrugations	20 ____
01874	ATSF 35' Trailer, horizontal corrugations, scheme II	20 ____
01875	Reading 35' Trailer, vertical ribs	20 ____
01876	Moxie Wooden Billboard Reefer #1 (NASG)	53 ____
01877	Moxie Wooden Billboard Reefer #2 (NASG)	53 ____
01878	REA 35' Trailer, vertical ribs	20 ____
01879	SP 35' Trailer, horizontal corrugations	20 ____
01880	ATSF 35' Trailer, vertical ribs, scheme II	20 ____
01881	Weber Wooden Billboard Reefer #1 (Badgerland)	53 ____
01882	Weber Wooden Billboard Reefer #2 (Badgerland)	53 ____
01883	Weber Wooden Billboard Reefer #3 (Badgerland)	53 ____
01884	Sampson Canning Wooden Billboard Reefer	53 ____
01885	ATSF USRA Double-sheathed Boxcar #1	50 ____
01886	ATSF USRA Double-sheathed Boxcar #2	50 ____
01887	CB&Q USRA Double-sheathed Boxcar #1	50 ____
01888	CB&Q USRA Double-sheathed Boxcar #2	50 ____
01889	CH&D USRA Double-sheathed Boxcar #1	50 ____
01890	CH&D USRA Double-sheathed Boxcar #2 (Miami Valley)	50 ____
01891	NKP USRA Double-sheathed Boxcar #1 (Hoosier)	50 ____
01892	NKP USRA Double-sheathed Boxcar #2 (Hoosier)	50 ____
01893	NKP USRA Double-sheathed Boxcar #3	50 ____
01894	NKP USRA Double-sheathed Boxcar #4	50 ____
01895	NWP Double-sheathed Boxcar, scheme II #1 (O West)	50 ____
01896	NWP Double-sheathed Boxcar, scheme II #2 (O West)	50 ____
01897	NWP USRA Double-sheathed Boxcar, scheme II #3	50 ____
01898	NWP USRA Double-sheathed Boxcar, scheme II #4	50 ____
01899	Frank Fehr Brewery Wooden Billboard Reefer	53 ____
01900	Buffalo Creek & Gauley USRA Rib Side Hopper #1	50 ____
01901	Buffalo Creek & Gauley USRA Rib Side Hopper #2	50 ____
01902	Buffalo Creek & Gauley USRA Rib Side Hopper #3	50 ____
01903	Buffalo Creek & Gauley USRA Rib Side Hopper #4	50 ____
01904	C&O USRA Rib Side Hopper #5	50 ____
01905	C&O USRA Rib Side Hopper #6	50 ____
01906	PRR USRA Rib Side Hopper, scheme II #1	50 ____

____ **01907**	PRR USRA Rib Side Hopper, scheme II #2	50
____ **01908**	GTW USRA Rebuilt Covered Hopper #2	50
____ **01909**	CB&Q NW2 Diesel Freight Set, 5 cars	350
____ **01910**	SLSF SW9 Diesel Freight Set, 5 cars	350
____ **01911**	MP F7A Diesel Freight Set, 6 cars	430
____ **01912**	GN SW1 Diesel Freight Set, 4 cars	315
____ **01913**	CRI&P 40' Steel Rebuilt Boxcar #1 (State Line)	50
____ **01914**	CRI&P 40' Steel Rebuilt Boxcar #2 (State Line)	50
____ **01915**	CRI&P 40' Steel Rebuilt Boxcar #3 (State Line)	50
____ **01916**	ATSF "Chief" 40' Steel Rebuilt Boxcar #1	50
____ **01917**	ATSF "Chief" 40' Steel Rebuilt Boxcar #2	50
____ **01918**	C&O 40' Steel Rebuilt Boxcar #3	50
____ **01919**	C&O 40' Steel Rebuilt Boxcar #4	50
____ **01920**	P&LE (NYC) 40' Steel Rebuilt Boxcar #2	50
____ **01921**	P&LE (NYC) 40' Steel Rebuilt Boxcar #3	50
____ **01922**	MP "Eagle" 40' Steel Rebuilt Boxcar #3	50
____ **01923**	MP "Eagle" 40' Steel Rebuilt Boxcar #4	50
____ **01941**	CNJ USRA Rebuilt Covered Hopper #3	50
____ **01942**	CNJ USRA Rebuilt Covered Hopper #4	50
____ **01943**	Moxie Wooden Billboard Reefer #3	53
____ **01944**	Moxie Wooden Billboard Reefer #4	53
____ **01946**	Santa Fe Wooden Billboard Reefer #3	53
____ **01947**	Santa Fe Wooden Billboard Reefer #4	53
____ **01951**	PFE Wooden Billboard Reefer, scheme IV #1	53
____ **01952**	PFE Wooden Billboard Reefer, scheme IV #2	53
____ **01957**	PFE Wooden Billboard Reefer, scheme IV #3	53
____ **01958**	B&A 40' Steel Rebuilt Boxcar #1 (Daniel Lundy)	50
____ **01959**	B&A 40' Steel Rebuilt Boxcar #2 (Daniel Lundy)	50
____ **01960**	B&A 40' Steel Rebuilt Boxcar #3 (Daniel Lundy)	50
____ **01961**	B&A 40' Steel Rebuilt Boxcar #4 (Daniel Lundy)	50
____ **01962**	Sherman Williams PS-2 2-bay Hopper #1 (CVSG)	50
____ **01963**	Sherman Williams PS-2 2-bay Hopper #2 (CVSG)	50
____ **01964**	Sherman Williams PS-2 2-bay Hopper #3 (CVSG)	50
____ **01965**	Sherman Williams PS-2 2-bay Hopper #4 (CVSG)	50
____ **01966**	Sherman Williams PS-2 2-bay Hopper #5 (CVSG)	50
____ **01967**	Union Carbide "Bakelite" PS-2 3-bay Covered Hopper	50
____ **01968**	ATSF PS-2 3-bay Covered Hopper #1	50
____ **01969**	ATSF PS-2 3-bay Covered Hopper #2	50
____ **01970**	Erie PS-2 3-bay Covered Hopper #1	50
____ **01971**	Erie PS-2 3-bay Covered Hopper #2	50
____ **01972**	Erie PS-2 3-bay Covered Hopper #3	50
____ **01973**	CRI&P 40' Steel Boxcar, scheme II #2 (State Line)	50
____ **01976**	GN PS-2 3-bay Covered Hopper #3	50
____ **01977**	GN PS-2 3-bay Covered Hopper #4	50
____ **01978**	SW8/9 Diesel, DCC sound	290
____ **01979**	C&NW (CGW) PS-2 3-bay Covered Hopper #1	50

Retail

01980	C&NW (CGW) PS-2 3-bay Covered Hopper #2	50 ____
01981	Marhoefer Wooden Billboard Reefer #2	50 ____
01982	Marhoefer Wooden Billboard Reefer #3	50 ____
01983	CP Stock Car #1	50 ____
01984	CP Stock Car #2	50 ____
01985	CB&Q Stock Car #3	50 ____
01986	CB&Q Stock Car #4	50 ____
01987	UP Stock Car #7	50 ____
01988	UP Stock Car #8	50 ____
01989	B&O Composite Side Hopper #5	53 ____
01990	B&O Composite Side Hopper #6	53 ____
01991	PRR Composite Side Hopper, scheme II #5	53 ____
01992	PRR Composite Side Hopper, scheme II #6	53 ____
01993	Black Fishbelly Hopper	53 ____
01994	Red Fishbelly Hopper	53 ____
01995	Akron, Canton & Youngstown Fishbelly Hopper #1	53 ____
01996	Akron, Canton & Youngstown Fishbelly Hopper #2	53 ____
01997	Akron, Canton & Youngstown Fishbelly Hopper #3	53 ____
01998	Akron, Canton & Youngstown Fishbelly Hopper #4	53 ____
01999	ACL Fishbelly Hopper #1	53 ____
02000	ACL Fishbelly Hopper #2	53 ____
02001	ACL Fishbelly Hopper #3	53 ____
02002	ACL Fishbelly Hopper #4	53 ____
02003	B&O Fishbelly Hopper #1	53 ____
02004	B&O Fishbelly Hopper #2	53 ____
02005	B&O Fishbelly Hopper #3	53 ____
02006	B&O Fishbelly Hopper #4	53 ____
02007	CNJ Fishbelly Hopper #1	53 ____
02008	CNJ Fishbelly Hopper #2	53 ____
02009	CNJ Fishbelly Hopper #3	53 ____
02010	CNJ Fishbelly Hopper #4	53 ____
02011	C&O Fishbelly Hopper #1	53 ____
02012	C&O Fishbelly Hopper #2	53 ____
02013	C&O Fishbelly Hopper #3	53 ____
02014	C&O Fishbelly Hopper #4	53 ____
02015	D&H Fishbelly Hopper #1	53 ____
02016	D&H Fishbelly Hopper #2	53 ____
02017	D&H Fishbelly Hopper #3	53 ____
02018	D&H Fishbelly Hopper #4	53 ____
02019	LV Fishbelly Hopper #1	53 ____
02020	LV Fishbelly Hopper #2	53 ____
02021	LV Fishbelly Hopper #3	53 ____
02022	LV Fishbelly Hopper #4	53 ____
02023	N&W Fishbelly Hopper #1	53 ____
02024	N&W Fishbelly Hopper #2	53 ____
02025	N&W Fishbelly Hopper #3	53 ____

_____ **02026**	N&W Fishbelly Hopper #4	53
_____ **02027**	NS Fishbelly Hopper #1	53
_____ **02028**	NS Fishbelly Hopper #2	53
_____ **02029**	NS Fishbelly Hopper #3	53
_____ **02030**	NS Fishbelly Hopper #4	53
_____ **02031**	Reading Fishbelly Hopper #1	53
_____ **02032**	Reading Fishbelly Hopper #2	53
_____ **02033**	Reading Fishbelly Hopper #3	53
_____ **02034**	Reading Fishbelly Hopper #4	53
_____ **02035**	WM Fishbelly Hopper #1	53
_____ **02036**	WM Fishbelly Hopper #2	53
_____ **02037**	WM Fishbelly Hopper #3	53
_____ **02038**	WM Fishbelly Hopper #4	53
_____ **02039**	Ballantine Beer Wooden Billboard Reefer #3 (Hoquat)	53
_____ **02040**	Ballantine Beer Wooden Billboard Reefer #4 (Hoquat)	53
_____ **02043**	DL&W Reefer #1	53
_____ **02044**	DL&W Reefer #2	53
_____ **02045**	Eatmor Cranberries Wooden Billboard Reefer	53
_____ **02046**	Falstaff Wooden Billboard Reefer #1 (NASG)	53
_____ **02047**	Falstaff Wooden Billboard Reefer #2 (NASG)	53
_____ **02048**	Lemp Falstaff Wooden Billboard Reefer #1 (NASG)	53
_____ **02049**	Lemp Falstaff Wooden Billboard Reefer #2 (NASG)	53
_____ **02050**	Prima Special Wooden Billboard Reefer	53
_____ **02051**	CB&Q NW2 Diesel Freight Set, 6 cars	390
_____ **02052**	BN SW8 Diesel Freight Set, 4 cars	346
_____ **02053**	CRI&P SW8 Diesel Freight Set, 5 cars	360
_____ **02054**	GN 2009 Christmas Boxcar	63
_____ **02055**	Toronto, Hamilton & Buffalo Double-sheathed Boxcar #2	50
_____ **02056**	3M USRA Double-sheathed Boxcar #1	50
_____ **02057**	3M USRA Double-sheathed Boxcar #2	50
_____ **02058**	Flatcar with 4 wrapped steel coils	63
_____ **02059**	Mine Run Coal Load	7
_____ **02060**	Gluek Brewing Billboard Reefer, blue (Hoquat)	53
_____ **02061**	Gluek Brewing Billboard Reefer, red (Hoquat)	53
_____ **02065**	Gray Steel Coil Loads	63
_____ **02066**	Metal Rail Joiners, unweathered, 36 pieces	7
_____ **02070**	Laser Cut Reels with rack	75
_____ **02071**	PRR 2D-F1 Archbar Truck, code 110, pair	25
_____ **02072**	PRR 2D-F1 Archbar Truck, hi-rail, pair	25
_____ **02073**	B&O USRA Rib Side Hopper, scheme II #1	53
_____ **02074**	B&O USRA Rib Side Hopper, scheme II #2	53
_____ **02075**	B&O USRA Rib Side Hopper, scheme II #3	53
_____ **02076**	B&O USRA Rib Side Hopper, scheme II #4	53
_____ **02077**	Reading USRA Rib Side Hopper #5	53
_____ **02078**	Reading USRA Rib Side Hopper #6	53
_____ **02079**	ATSF Composite Side Hopper #5	53

S-HELPER SERVICE 1994-2012

Retail

02080	ATSF Composite Side Hopper #6	53 ____
02081	CB&Q Composite Side Hopper #5	53 ____
02082	CB&Q Composite Side Hopper #6	53 ____
02083	LV Composite Side Hopper #9	53 ____
02084	LV Composite Side Hopper #10	53 ____
02086	C&O Composite Side Hopper #5	53 ____
02087	C&O Composite Side Hopper #6	53 ____
02109	GN 40' Steel Rebuilt Boxcar, scheme III #3	53 ____
02110	GN 40' Steel Rebuilt Boxcar, scheme III #4	53 ____
02111	NKP Steel Rebuilt Boxcar #1	53 ____
02112	NKP Steel Rebuilt Boxcar #2	53 ____
02113	NKP Steel Rebuilt Boxcar #3	53 ____
02114	NKP Steel Rebuilt Boxcar #4	53 ____
02115	Seaboard "Orange Blossom Special" Rebuilt Boxcar #2	53 ____
02116	Seaboard "Orange Blossom Special" Rebuilt Boxcar #3	53 ____
02117	SP Steel Rebuilt Boxcar #1 (S Scale West)	53 ____
02118	SP Steel Rebuilt Boxcar #2 (S Scale West)	53 ____
02119	SP Steel Rebuilt Boxcar #3 (S Scale West)	53 ____
02120	SP Steel Rebuilt Boxcar #4 (S Scale West)	53 ____
02127	40" SW/NW Wheelset, Code 110	16 ____
02128	40" SW/NW Wheelset, AF compatible	16 ____
02129	40" F unit Wheelset, Code 110	16 ____
02130	40" F unit Wheelset, AF compatible	16 ____
02149	WM Fishbelly Hopper, scheme II #1	53 ____
02150	WM Fishbelly Hopper, scheme II #2	53 ____
ART-5400	DC Power Pack, 24VDC	50 ____
20064	Rock Island Boxcar, silver (State-Line S Gaugers)	45 ____
20070	Rock Island Boxcar, green (State-Line S Gaugers)	45 ____

Unnumbered Items

Train Pack Lube Set	15 ____

			Good (P-5)	Exc (P-7)
		1946		
____	**D1451**	Consumer Catalog	35	138
____		with red binder	75	450
____	**D1455**	Dealer Catalog	27	172
____	**D1457**	Gilbert Scientific Toys	10	26
____	**D1458**	Appointment Card	1	2
____	**M2499**	Instruction Sheet		1
____		Envelope for D1451	2	10
		1947		
____	**D1462**	Catalog Mailer	14	60
____	**D1472**	Catalog Mailer	14	50
____	**D1473**	Consumer Catalog	27	70
____	**D1482**	Dealer Catalog	20	75
____	**D1492**	Erector Fun and Action	4	13
____	**D1495**	What Retail Stores Should Know	4	13
____	**D1496**	Display Suggestions	45	270
____	**D1502**	Advance Catalog	13	46
____	**M2502**	Instruction Book	2	5
____		Envelope for D1473	2	4
		1948		
____	**D1505**	Advance Catalog	10	56
____	**D1507**	Consumer Catalog	15	50
____	**D1508**	Superman	17	100
____	**D1508**	Consumer Catalog	10	24
____		with prepaid postage	5	18
____	**D1517**	HO Catalog	9	23
		1949		
____	**D1524**	Gilbert Scientific Toys Catalog	5	9
____	**D1525**	Bang Bang Torpedo	45	115
____	**D1530**	Advance Catalog	18	55
____	**D1531**	Gilbert Scientific Toys Catalog	5	9
____	**D1536**	Consumer Catalog	9	25
____	**D1547**	Catalog Envelope	1	4
____	**D1552**	How to Sell American Flyer	5	18
	M2690	Instruction Booklet		
____		(A) Yellow cover	1	3
____		(B) White cover	2	4
		1950		
____	**D1578**	Dealer Catalog	13	45
____	**D1579**	Gilbert Toys	5	16
____	**D1581/A**	Red/Blue Ad		180
____	**D1604**	Consumer Catalog	16	35

GILBERT PAPER 1946–1967		Good (P-5)	Exc (P-7)	
D1610	Catalog Envelope	1	4	____
D1629	Dealer Action Displays Sheet		NRS	____
D1631	Dealer TV Ad	9	18	____
	Ready Again Booklet		300	____

1951

D1637	Dealer Catalog	13	50	____
D1637A	Advance Catalog	8	33	____
D1640	Consumer Catalog	15	30	____
D1641	Erector and Gilbert Toys Catalog	2	5	____
D1652	Facts About AF Trains		60	____
D1656	AF and Toys	5	9	____
D1660	Gilbert Electric Eye	5	9	____

1952

D1667	Advance Catalog	10	45	____
D1667A	Advance Catalog	11	45	____
D1668A	Consumer Catalog		35	____
D1670	Single Sheet 200 Series Buildings	2	9	____
D1677	Consumer Catalog	8	25	____
D1678	Facts About AF Trains	7	11	____
M2978	AF Model Railroad Handbook	5	9	____
M2984	Instruction Book	1	3	____
	Advance Catalog		NRS	____
	Consumer Catalog, Spanish		NRS	____

1953

D1699	Consumer Catalog		40	____
D1703	Erector and Other Toys	3	7	____
D1704	Dealer Catalog	9	37	____
D1714	Dealer Catalog, East	8	35	____
D1715	Consumer Catalog, West	11	27	____
D1727	Tips on Selling AF Trains	5	9	____
D1728	Tips on Erector	2	8	____

1954

D1734	Catalog Envelope	1	4	____
D1740	Erector and Gilbert Toys	1	4	____
D1744	AF and Erector Ad Program	4	16	____
D1746	Dealer Catalog			
	(A) Pulp	8	35	____
	(B) Glossy	8	47	____
D1748	Catalog, East			
	(A) Consumer	3	15	____
	(B) Dealer	4	20	____
D1749	Dealer Catalog, West	11	29	____
D1750	Dealer Displays		NRS	____
D1751	Microscope Flysheet	1	2	____
D1760	Consumer Catalog, East	10	44	____
D1761	Consumer Catalog, West	12	37	____
D1762	Boys Railroad Club Letter	1	5	____

GILBERT PAPER 1946–1967		Good (P-5)	Exc (P-7)
____ **D1769**	Read All About Ad Campaign		NRS
____ **D1774**	Erector and Other Gilbert Toys	2	5
____ **D1777**	Reply Postcard	1	2
____ **M3290**	Instruction Book	1	4

1955

____ **D1782**	Dealer Catalog	8	30
____ **D1783**	Certificate of Registry	5	9
____ **D1784**	Erector and Other Gilbert Toys		80
____ **D1801**	Consumer Catalog, East	7	15
____ **D1802**	Consumer Catalog, West	9	20
____ **D1814**	Choo Choo Sound Foldout	1	4
____ **D1816**	Dealer Catalog	9	29
____ **D1820**	HO Consumer Catalog	1	5
____ **D1835**	Tips for Selling Erector	1	2
____ **D1840**	Envelope	1	4
____ **M3450**	Instruction Book	1	5

1956

____ **D1866**	Consumer Catalog, East	7	10
____ **D1867**	Consumer Catalog, West	8	10
____ **D1874**	Dealer Catalog	14	39
____ **D1879**	Gilbert and Erector Toys	1	6
____ **D1882**	AF and Erector Displays	1	7
____ **D1892**	Store Banner (Dealer)		525
____ **D1893**	Store Banner		1250
____ **D1899**	Big Value AF Trestle System Special Set Brochure		100
____ **D1904**	Gilbert HO Catalog	2	6
____ **D1907**	Dealer Catalog	6	28
____ **D1920**	How to Build a Model Railroad	2	15
____ **D1922**	Miniature Catalog	6	25
____ **D1925**	Erector Folder	2	7
____ **D1926**	Envelope for D1922 Catalog	1	4

1957

____ **D1937**	Dealer Catalog	9	35
____ **D1966**	Consumer Catalog	2	10
____ **D1973**	Erector and Other Toys	1	2
____ **D1980**	Cardboard		35
____ **D1981**	Same as D1980		35
____ **D2006**	Consumer Catalog, East	5	15
____ **D2007**	Consumer Catalog, West	13	20
____ **D2008**	Erector and Toys	1	4
____ **D2022**	Dealer Flyer		55
____ **D2031**	Consumer Catalog		41
____ **D2037**	Erector and Gilbert Toys	1	5
____ **D2045**	Gilbert Promotion Kit		NRS
____ **M3817**	HO Instructions	2	7
____	Same as M3450 (1955) but without number		20

		Good (P-5)	Exc (P-7)	

1958

		Good (P-5)	Exc (P-7)	
D2047	Consumer Catalog	21	87	____
D2048	Catalog, West	25	70	____
D2058	Erector and Toys	1	5	____
D2060	Erector and Gilbert Toys	2	10	____
D2073	Advance Catalog	6	17	____
D2080	Smoking Caboose		125	____
D2086	Consumer Folder, East	2	8	____
D2087	Consumer Folder, West	1	10	____
D2088	Consumer Folder	2	11	____
D2101	Career Building Science Toys	1	2	____
D4106	HO Catalog	1	4	____
M4195	Accessory Folder	1	4	____
M4202	Color Billboards		10	____

1959

		Good (P-5)	Exc (P-7)	
D2115	Dealer Catalog	12	50	____
D2118	AF No. 20142, Willit		15	____
D2120	Career Building Science Toys	1	12	____
D2125	Overland Express Sheet	1	2	____
D2132	HO Catalog		30	____
D2146	Consumer Catalog	1	8	____
D2148	Consumer Catalog	1	7	____
D2171/-79	Dealer Promotional Set		NRS	____
D2179	Promotional Sheet, Franklin Set	1	5	____
D2180	Gilbert Science Toys	1	4	____
M4225	Train Assembly and Operating Instructions		NRS	____
M4326	Accessory Catalog	1	4	____
M4869	AF Maintenance Manual	1	2	____
	Canadian D2115 Catalog		NRS	____
	Catalog, Gilbert Toys		NRS	____

1960

		Good (P-5)	Exc (P-7)	
D2192	Catalog			
	(A) Dealer	5	28	____
	(B) Advance		33	____
D2193	Consumer Catalog	2	9	____
D2193REV	Revised Consumer Catalog	2	7	____
D2196	Dealer Catalog		120	____
D2197	Dealer Display Catalog		85	____
D2198	Action and Fun Catalog	2	6	____
D2205	Gilbert Toys	2	9	____
D2208	Dealer Advance Catalog		75	____
D2223	Gilbert Science Toys	1	4	____
D2224	Consumer Folder	1	5	____
D2225	Consumer Folder	3	6	____
D2226	Consumer Folder	1	4	____
D2230	Consumer Catalog	9	30	____
D2231	Consumer Catalog	2	7	____
	Truscott Set Promotional Sheet		50	____

			Good (P-5)	Exc (P-7)

1961

			Good (P-5)	Exc (P-7)
____	D2238	Career Building Science Toys	2	25
____	D2239	Consumer Catalog	4	8
____	D2242REV	Auto Rama Catalog	1	2
____	D2255	1961–62 Retail Display	1	2
____	D2266	Gilbert Science Toys	1	5
____	D2267	Consumer Catalog	4	8
____	D2268	Auto Rama Folder	1	2

1962

			Good (P-5)	Exc (P-7)
____	D2277REV	Career Building Science Toys	7	24
____	D2278	Dealer Catalog	2	22
____	D2278REV	Revised Dealer Catalog	2	13
____	D2282	Dealer Catalog		35
____	D2283	HO Trains and Accessories	2	8
____	D2307	Consumer Ad Mats		75
____	D2310	Consumer Catalog	4	10
____	D2329	HO Catalog		45
____	M6874	Instruction Booklet	1	4
____		The Big Ones Come From Gilbert		35

1963

			Good (P-5)	Exc (P-7)
____	D2321	Dealer Catalog	1	15
____	D2321REV	Revised Dealer Catalog	5	14
____	D2328	Consumer Catalog		13
____	X863-3	Consumer Catalog	4	31

1964

			Good (P-5)	Exc (P-7)
____	X264-6	Consumer Catalog	3	21
____	564-11	Dealer Catalog	2	7
____		Similar to X264-6, 8 pages		NRS
____		Similar to X264-6, black binding		NRS

1965

			Good (P-5)	Exc (P-7)
____	X165-12	Dealer Catalog	6	29
____	X165-12REV	Revised Dealer Catalog	6	13
____	X365-10	Consumer Folder	1	5
____	T465-5REV	Dealer Folder	1	2

1966

			Good (P-5)	Exc (P-7)
____	T166-6	Dealer Catalog	4	21
____	T166-7	Gilbert Action Toys	6	32
____	X466-1	Consumer Catalog	3	14
____	T1065-11	Dealer Sales Folder		200
____	M6788	All Aboard Instructions	3	8

1967*

			Good (P-5)	Exc (P-7)
____		Four-page Folder	1	4

*Gilbert train production ended in 1966; however, an American Flyer Industries Folder was released for 1967.

ABBREVIATIONS

Descriptions

AF	American Flyer
AFL	American Flyer Lines
ART	American Refrigerator Transit Co.
BAAFC	Baltimore Area American Flyer Club
CC	Command Control
CD	Center discharge
CVSG	Cuyahoga Valley S Gauge Association
EMD	Electro-Motive Division
FGE	Fruit Growers Express
FM	Fairbanks-Morse
GP	Diesel locomotive
GM	General Motors
MDT	Merchants Despatch Transportation
MOW	Maintenance-of-way
NASG	National Association of S-Gaugers
NETCA	New England Division, TCA
NMRA	National Model Railroad Association
PA	Alco diesel with cab
PB	Alco diesel without cab
PFE	Pacific Fruit Express
PM	Pike Master
REA	Railway Express Agency
s-i-b	Smoke in boiler
s-i-t	Smoke in tender
TCA	Train Collectors Association
TTOS	Toy Train Operating Society
UFGE	United Fruit Growers Express
USRA	United States Railroad Administration
WFE	Western Fruit Express
1-D	One dome
3-D	Three dome

ABBREVIATIONS
Railroad names

ACL	Atlantic Coast Line
ATSF	Atchison, Topeka & Santa Fe
B&A	Boston & Albany
BAR	Bangor & Aroostook
B&LE	Bessemer & Lake Erie
B&M	Boston & Maine
BN	Burlington Northern
BNSF	Burlington Northern Santa Fe
B&O	Baltimore & Ohio
CB&Q	Chicago, Burlington & Quincy
CMStP&P	Chicago, Milwaukee, St. Paul & Pacific
CN	Canadian National
CGW	Chicago Great Western
CNJ	Central of New Jersey
C&NW	Chicago & North Western
C&O	Chesapeake & Ohio
CP	Canadian Pacific
CRI&P	Chicago, Rock Island & Pacific
C&S	Colorado Southern
CUVA	Cuyahoga Valley Railway
D&H	Delaware & Hudson
D&RGW	Denver & Rio Grande Western
DT&I	Detroit, Toledo & Ironton
DM&IR	Duluth, Missabe & Iron Range
Erie-Lack.	Erie-Lackawanna
FEC	Florida East Coast
FWD	Fort Worth & Denver
GM&O	Gulf, Mobile & Ohio
GN	Great Northern
GN&W	Genesee & Wyoming
GTW	Grand Trunk Western
IC	Illinois Central
ICG	Illinois Central Gulf
IGN	International-Great Northern
KCS	Kansas City Southern

L&N	Louisville & Nashville
LNE	Lehigh New England
LV	Lehigh Valley
MEC	Maine Central
MILW	Milwaukee Road
MKT	Missouri-Kansas-Texas
MNS	Minnesota, Northfield & Southern
MP	Missouri Pacific
M&StL	Minneapolis & St. Louis
NdeM	Nacionales de Mexico Railway
NH	New Haven
NKP	Nickel Plate Road
NOT&M	New Orleans, Texas & Mexico
NP	Northern Pacific
NS	Norfolk Southern
N&W	Norfolk & Western
NWP	Northwestern Pacific
NYC	New York Central
NYO&W	New York, Ontario & Western
NYNH&H	New York, New Haven & Hartford
OSL	Oregon Short Line
P&LE	Pittsburgh & Lake Erie
PC	Penn Central
PRR	Pennsylvania Railroad
PMKY	Pittsburgh, McKeesport & Youghiogheny
PTM	ST Rail System
RFP	Richmond, Fredericksburg & Potomac
SF	Santa Fe
SLSF	St. Louis-San Francisco
SP	Southern Pacific
SSW	St. Louis Southwestern
T&P	Texas & Pacific
TP&W	Toledo, Peoria & Western
UP	Union Pacific
WM	Western Maryland
WP	Western Pacific

Build Your Toy Train Library

Scenery Techniques for Toy Trains

For toy train operators looking to add scenery and dimension to their layouts, this book offers simple solutions. It explains how to use foam as a scenery base and how to shape it into mountains and rivers. Step-by-step photographs and instructions illustrate techniques for adding streets, accessories, and even a working drive-in theater.

10-8400 • $17.95

Trackwork for Toy Trains

This essential guide addresses O gauge trackwork from nearly all of today's major manufacturers. Peter H. Riddle provides an overview of the various lines of sectional and flexible track, then demonstrates with step-by-step photography the basic techniques for cutting, bending, wiring, and layout installation. Also includes tips and tricks fo working with special trackwork, such as switches, crossings, and accessory-activation sections.

10-8365 • $19.95

Lionel Pocket Price Guide 1901–2019

A must-have resource for toy train collectors and operators, this pocket-size book features the latest market values for prewar, postwar, modern, and tinplate trains, as well as postwar boxes and sets. The 400+ page guide also features identification and evaluation tips.

#10-8719 • $21.99

Buy now from your local hobby shop! Shop at KalmbachHobbyStore.com

Kalmbach Media

P33108